북한 핵 문제

총괄 1

북한 핵 문제

총괄 1

• 외교문서 비밀해제 – 북한핵문제 1 •

한국학술정보

| 머리말

　1985년 북한은 소련의 요구로 핵확산금지조약(NPT)에 가입한다. 그러나 그로부터 4년 뒤, 60년대 소련이 영변에 조성한 북한의 비밀 핵 연구단지 사진이 공개된다. 냉전이 종속되어 가던 당시 북한은 이로 인한 여러 국제사회의 경고 및 외교 압력을 받았으며, 1990년 국제원자력기구(IAEA)는 북핵 문제에 대해 강력한 사찰을 추진한다. 북한은 영변 핵시설의 사찰 조건으로 남한 내 미군기지 사찰을 요구하는 등 여러 이유를 댔으나 결국 3차에 걸친 남북 핵협상과 남북핵통제공동위원회 합의 등을 통해 이를 수용하였고, 결국 1992년 안전조치협정에도 서명하겠다고 발표한다. 그러나 그로부터 1년 뒤 북한은 한미 합동훈련의 재개에 반대하며 IAEA의 특별사찰을 거부하고 NPT를 탈퇴한다. 이에 UN 안보리는 대북 제재를 실행하면서 1994년 제네바 합의 전까지 남북 관계는 극도로 경직되게 된다.

　본 총서는 외교부에서 작성하여 최근 공개한 1991~1992년 북한 핵 문제 관련 자료를 담고 있다. 북한의 핵안전조치협정의 체결 과정과 북한 핵시설 사찰 과정, 그와 관련된 미국의 동향과 일본, 러시아, 중국 등 우방국 협조와 관련한 자료까지 총 14권으로 구성되었다. 전체 분량은 약 7천여 쪽에 이른다.

2024년 3월
한국학술정보(주)

| 일러두기

· 본 총서에 실린 자료는 2022년 4월과 2023년 4월에 각각 공개한 외교문서 4,827권, 76만여 쪽 가운데 일부를 발췌한 것이다.

· 각 권의 제목과 순서는 공개된 원본을 최대한 반영하였으나, 주제에 따라 일부는 적절히 변경하였다.

· 원본 자료는 A4 판형에 맞게 축소하거나 원본 비율을 유지한 채 A4 페이지 안에 삽입하였다. 또한 현재 시점에선 공개되지 않아 '공란'이란 표기만 있는 페이지 역시 그대로 실었다.

· 외교부가 공개한 문서 각 권의 첫 페이지에는 '정리 보존 문서 목록'이란 이름으로 기록물 종류, 일자, 명칭, 간단한 내용 등의 정보가 수록되어 있으며, 이를 기준으로 0001번부터 번호가 매겨져 있다. 이는 삭제하지 않고 총서에 그대로 수록하였다.

· 보고서 내용에 관한 더 자세한 정보가 필요하다면, 외교부가 온라인상에 제공하는 『대한민국 외교사료요약집』 1991년과 1992년 자료를 참조할 수 있다.

| 차례

정 리 보 존 문 서 목 록

기록물종류	일반공문서철	등록번호	32692	등록일자	2009-02-26
분류번호	726.61	국가코드		보존기간	영구
명 칭	북한 핵문제, 1992. 전13권				
생 산 과	북미1과/북미2과	생산년도	1992~1992	담당그룹	
권 차 명	V.1 1월				
내용목차	* 구 소련 핵전문가 해외 유출 관련 문서 포함 * 북한 핵관련 대책, 한.미국간 협의, 미국의 사찰과정 참여 요구 등				

0001

공 란

공   란

공　　　　란

공   란

공   란

공   란

공 란

공　　란

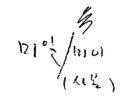

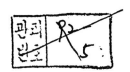

외 무 부

110-760 서울 종로구 세종로 77번지　　　/ (02)720-4503　　　/ (02)722-6803

문서번호　정특 2026- 5

시행일자　1992. 1. 3.

(경유)

수신　수신처 참조

참고

선결			지시		
접수	일자시간		결재·공람		
	번호				
처리과					
담당자					

제목　1992년도 김일성 신년사

1991(12.3)에 **외교문서** 의거 일반문서로 재분 됨

　　1992년도 김일성 신년사 요지 및 분석·평가를 별첨과 같이 송부하오니

참고하시기 바랍니다.

　　첨　부 : 1. 1992년도 김일성 신년사 요지 및 분석·평가 1부.

　　　　　　2. '91년, '92년 김일성 신년사 주요내용 비교표 1부.　　끝.

　　수신처 : 외교안보연구원장, 각실·국장

외 교 정 책 기 획 실 장

0010

1992 년도 김일성 신년사

1992. 1. 3.

펄(1992. 6. 30.) 83

외 교 정 책 기 획 실

1. 예년과 같이 3개분야에 관해 언급
   o 대내분야
   o 대남 및 통일분야
   o 대외정책 분야

2. 대내분야
   o 사상, 기술, 문화의 3대혁명 강화로 격변하는 정세에 주동적으로 대처
   o 기본과업은 자립적 민족경제 건설노선을 철저히 관철하고 인민들의 의식주 문제를 원만히 해결하는 것
   o 가장 긴요하고 절실한 과업은 전력과 석탄의 생산증대와 철도운수를 발전시키는 것
   o 인민생활 향상을 위해 농업과 경공업발전에 주력해야하며, 올해는 대농의 해로 정해 농업생산의 획기적 증대를 도모

3. 대남 및 통일분야
   o 남북합의서는 7.4 공동성명과 더불어 가장 정당한 통일강령
     - 합의서를 성실히 이행함으로써 통일을 하루빨리 앞당겨야 할 것
   o 조선의 통일문제는 역사적으로 국제관계와 관련되어 있는 것인 만큼 남북합의서를 이행하는데서 유관국들의 협조 필요
     - 유관국들은 남북합의서 정신을 존중해야하며 자주적·평화적 통일문제를 해결하도록 적극 도와주어야 함

- 1 -

o 조선반도의 비핵지대.평화지대화는 일관된 입장

  - 부당한 핵사찰 압력은 불용납

  - 핵무기 개발의사도 능력도 없고 공정성 보장 조건에서 핵사찰 수용 용의

o 남.북, 해외동포의 대단결은 통일의 근본

  - 당국자들은 민족내부의 오해.불신해소 및 대화.교류 발전을 위해 적극
    노력 필요

4. 대외분야

o 반제.자주에 입각한 사회주의 노선 견지

  - 일부 사회주의 나라들의 좌절을 사회주의의 종말이라고 말하는 것은 무지
    를 들어낸 것

  - 사회주의 국가들의 몰락은 사회주의원칙을 옳게 구현하지 못한 결과

- 2 -

공   란

1992. 1. 3.
특수정책과

구분	'91 년 도	'92 년 도

대
내
분
야
	(정 치)
	
	o 당의 주체적 혁명노선 계속 견지
	 - 사회주의의 불패성과 승리의 비결
	  은 주체의 사회주의 건설
	
	(경 제)
	
	o '91년도 경제정책 방향
	 - 제3차 7개년 계획 주요 대상 건설
	  우선적 추진
	  · 석탄·전력·수송·금속공업을 선행
	   부문으로 설정
	  · 알곡·천·인민 소비품 증산으로
	   인민 물질생활 향상
		(정 치)
		
		o 우리식 사회주의 건설에 총력
		 - 3대 혁명 강화로 주체를 더욱 튼
		  튼히 세우고, 격변하는 정세에
		  주동적으로 대처
		
		(경 제)
		
		o '92년도 과업
		 - 기본과업은 자립적 민족경제 건설
		  노선을 철저히 관철하고 인민들의
		  의식주 문제를 원만히 해결하는
		  것
		  * "모든 사람이 다같이 흰쌀밥에
		   고기국을 먹으며, 비단옷을 입
		   고 기와집에 살려는 우리 인민
		   의 세기적 염원을 실현하는 것
		   이 당면한 중요목표임"
		 - 가장 긴요하고 절실한 과업은 전
		  력과 석탄의 생산증대와 철도운
		  수를 발전시키는 것
		 - 인민생활 향상을 위해 농업과 경
		  공업 발전에 주력해야 하며, 올
		  해를 「대농의 해」로 정해 농업
		  생산을 결정적으로 증대시킴
		 - 「과학기술발전 3개년 계획」수
		  행을 위한 투쟁을 벌여 인민경제
		  의 주체화, 현대화, 과학화를 적
		  극 실현

대
남
및
통
일
분·야
	(군사문제)
	
	o 군사문제 선차적 해결
	 - 왕래나 교류의 필요성은 인정하나
	  군사문제 해결을 뒤로 미루는데는
	  타협할 수 없음.
	
	o 불가침 선언에 대한 우리측 입장
	  비난
	 - 신뢰조성 우선은 불가침 선언 회
	  피의 구실
	 - 불가침선언을 휴지장이라고 한 말
	  은 남북이 합의할 것이란 아무것
	  도 없다는 것으로 회담자체가 무
	  의미
		(군사문제)
		
		o 북남합의서 정신에 맞게 군축실현,
		  긴장상태 완화노력 경주 강조
		 - 조선반도를 비핵지대·평화지대화
		  실현 노력 경주
		
		o 조선반도의 비핵지대·평화지대화는
		  일관된 입장
		 - 핵무기개발의 능력도 의사도 없음
		 - 공정성 보장조건에서 핵사찰 수용
		  용의
		
		o 부당한 핵사찰 압력은 불용납

0015

구분	'91 년도	'92 년도
대남 및 통일 분야	(통일문제) 0 대미평화협정 촉구(3자회담 논리) - 미국과 평화협정을 체결하고 주한 미군이 핵무기를 철수 0 조국통일방도 확정 필요(연방제) - 조국통일은 하나의 민족, 하나의 국가, 두개제도, 두개정부에 기초한 연방제 0 제도의 단일화·통일(제도적 통일) 반대 - 제도의 통일은 먹는것을 전제로 한 것으로 접수될 수 없으며 강요시는 충돌과 민족재난 야기 - 지역적 자치정부에 더많은 권한 잠정 부여후 중앙정부 기능을 더욱 높여가는 방향으로 연방제의 완성문제 협의 용의 - 통일방도에 대한 전민주적 합의를 위한 당국·정당·단체대표 참가 민족통일협상회의 소집 제의	(통일문제) 0 합의서는 통일실현의 새로운 이정표 - 7.4 공동성명과 더불어 가장 정당한 조국통일 강령 - 합의서의 성실한 이행으로 통일 실현 0 유관국의 협조 강조 - 조선의 통일문제는 역사적으로 국제관계와 관련되어있는 것인만큼 북남합의서를 이행하는데에 유관국들의 협조가 필요 - 유관국들은 북남합의서의 정신을 존중하여야 하며 우리민족의 조국통일문제를 자주적으로 평화적으로 해결하도록 적극 도와주어야 함 0 남.북, 해외동포의 대단결이 통일의 근본 0 당국자들은 폭넓은 대화 및 다방면적 협력.교류의 발전을 위해 적극 노력 필요
대외 분야	0 반제.자주적 대외정책 견지 - 우리당이 일관하게 견지하고 있는 반제.자주적 대외정책의 정당성을 뚜렷이 실증 - 국제정세에 있어 사회주의와 제국주의, 진보와 반동사이의 첨예한 대립과 투쟁이 계속 0 자주.평화.친선의 정책기조 유지 - 사회주의.불럭 불가담 나라들을 비롯한 세계 여러나라들 인민들과 친선.협조관계 발전 0 아시아 인민의 단결.협조 - 아시안들이 자주성과 단결.협조로 아세아의 안정과 공동번영 이룩, 세계평화 위업에 이바지	0 반제.자주적 대외정책 견지 - 제국주의자들의 침략책동 분쇄 투쟁 강화 - 사회주의 는 반드시 승리 . 일부 사회주의 나라들의 좌절을 사회주의의 종말이라고 말하는 것은 무지를 들어낸 것 . 사회주의 건설에서 사회주의적 원칙을 옳게 구현하지 못하면 좌절을 면치 못하게 됨. 0 자주.평화.친선의 정책기조 유지 - 사회주의 나라들과의 단결과 연대성 강화 - 불럭 불가담 나라들과의 친선. 협조 강화 0 아시아와 세계의 평화.안전 수호에 노력 - 핵무기.대량 살육무기 폐기

외 무 부

종 별 :

번 호 : USW-0030

일 시 : 92 0103 1900

수 신 : 장 관(미일,미이,정뷰,정안)사본:주미대사

발 신 : 주 미 대사대리

제 목 : 국무부 브리핑(한국관계)

1. 금 1.3 국무부 브리핑시 하기와 같이 아국 관련 질의응답이 있었는바, 동 내용 하기 보고함.

(질문) 북한과의 북경 주재 정무 참사관급 접촉을 격상한다는 결정이 있었는지 ? 결정이 있었다면 그것이 지난 수주 북한이 취한 조치에 대한 반응인지 ?

(답) 확인해 봐야 될 사항임.

질문 : KAL 007 폭파 사건과 관련, 소련 군당국이 동기의 블랙박스 를 발견 하였다는 이즈배치아지 보도가 있었는데 블랙박스내 수록된 정보를 얻고자 하는 요청을 한적이 있는지 ?

답 : 모르는 사항임.

질문 : 한반도 정세 진전 사항에 대해 알려줄것이 있는지 ?

답 : 금일 알려줄 새로운 사항은 없음. 미국은 노대통령이 취한 조치와 이룩한 발전을 환영한바있음.

질문 : 남.북한간에 한반도 비핵화에 대해 합의가 있었는바, 미.북한 관계 진전이있게 되는지 ?

답 : 그점에 대해 새로이 언급할 사항이 없음. 최근 취해진 조치나 합의된 것들은 한반도 정세를 개선시키는데 있어 남.북한간 대화의 일차적 중요성을 부각시키고 있다는점을 강조하고져함. 현 시점에서 미측으로부터의 어떠한 조치에 대해아는바 없음.

질문 : 작일 주 유엔 북한 대사는 소련으로부터 의위협이 소멸되었으므로 주한 미군은 철수되어야 한다는 주장을 했는데 이에 대한 미국의 반응은 어떤지 ?

답 : 국방성에서 주한 미군에 대한 계획에 대해 말해야할것임. 잘 알다시피 미국이 취하는 조치는 한국과 주의깊은 협의를 통해 이루어지고 있으며, 현재 주한 미군 철수

미주국   1차보   미주국 ㉢ 외정실   외정실   분석관   정와대   안기부

관련 어떠한 계획에 대해서도 알고 있지 않음.
2.동 관려부분은 별전 (USWF- 0051) FAX송부함.
(대사 대리 김봉규-국장)

0018

주 미 대 사 관

USW(F) : 5/   년월일 :91.1.3   시간 : 19:00

수 신 : 장 관 (미일. 미이. 정특. 정란)

발 신 : 주 미 대 사

제 목 : 국무부 브리핑

보 안
통 제   6

(출처 :   )

STATE DEPARTMENT REGULAR BRIEFING
BRIEFER: RICHARD BOUCHER
12:49 PM EST   FRIDAY, JANUARY 3, 1992

Q   Has there been a decision made to upgrade the level of
talks with North Korea in Beijing above the political counsellor
level? And if so, is that a response to actions by North Korea in
the past few weeks?

MR. BOUCHER: That's something I'll have to check on for you.

Q   Shortly. One other question, then, on a related matter.
Izvestia has also reported several times the recovery by the USSR
military of the black box off of KAL-007. Is there any request
outstanding for access to this black box information?

MR. BOUCHER: I don't know that.

Q   Do you have anything to say about the developments on the
Korean Peninsula?

MR. BOUCHER: I have nothing new to say today. I think we've
welcomed the steps that President Roh has taken and the progress
that he's achieved, and --

Q   A North --

MR. BOUCHER: I don't have anything -- I'm not aware of
anything brand new today.

Q   A North Korean nuclear threat has been a primary concern
of the United States, and now that North Korea has agreed with the
South Korea -- the nuclear-free Korean peninsula, can we expect the
improvement of relations between North Korea and the United States?

(5| - 2-|)   외신 1과
                     동   제

0019

MR. BOUCHER: I have nothing really new to say on that at this point. We've -- we stress that the steps that were taken and agreed to recently emphasize primary importance of the North-South dialogue in improving the situation on the peninsula, so -- I don't have anything from the US side at this point.

Q   Yes. Yesterday, the ambassador of North Korea to the United Nations said the United States should pull out the military from the South Korea now that the threat of the Soviet Union has disappeared. What is the reaction of the United States on that?

MR. BOUCHER: I think I'll let the Pentagon update you on their plans for the military in Korea. As you know, what we do is done in careful consultation with our Korean ally. At this point, I'm not aware of any plans to pull out the US military from Korea.

51-2-2

0020

공   란

공   란

공   란

공   란

공   란

공   란

주 미 대 사 관

USW(F) : 0083
~~0060~~   년월일 : 92.1.6   시간 : 11:10AM

수 신 : 장 관 (머1, 정12, 저1속)

발 신 : 주미대사

제 목 : 북한에 정보 U-2 출동,   (출처 : 7 N3)

ABC "THIS WEEK" HOSTED BY DAVID BRINKLEY JOINED BY SAM DONALDSON AND
GEORGE WILL. INTERVIEW WITH: BRENT SCOWCROFT, NATIONAL SECURITY ASSISTANT
SUNDAY, JANUARY 5, 1992

    MR. DONALDSON: All right. Let me ask you about a political
question, General. North Korea is complaining today that we have
flown a U-2 flight over North Korea sometime in the last two or
three days, and this was very provocative, particularly in light of
the President's trip. What can you tell us about that?

    GEN. SCOWCROFT: Nothing.

    MR. DONALDSON: In other words, that's the kind of thing that
you don't want to discuss in public?

    GEN. SCOWCROFT: We will continue our intelligence
surveillance of North Korea, pending their fulfillment of their
claim to go toward -- toward denuclearization of their part of the
peninsula, and when they -- when they agree to an inspection system
which -- which will clearly demonstrate that they are avoiding or
denuclearizing their part of the peninsula, then we can change our
intelligence surveillance.

배부처	장관실	차관실	一	二	기					구주국	중아국	국기국	경제국	통상국	문협국	영교국	총무과	감사관	공보관	외연원	청와대	안	경	상공부

(0060 - (-1)

외신 1과	
통 제	

0027

SBD PD1   WOI   '92-01-07 01:46

27-4

외 무 부

종 별 :

번 호 : USW-0116   일 시 : 92 0109 1854

수 신 : 장 관(미일,미이,정특)

발 신 : 주 미 대사

제 목 : 북한 핵관련 미.북 접촉

1. 금 1.9 국무부 정례 브리핑시 북한 핵 문제에 관한 질의.응답이 있었는바, 동
내용 하기 보고함.

질문: 미국과 북한이 핵문제에 대한 협의 일정을 재조정했다는 보도에 대해 의견이
있는지 ?

답: 없음. 그러한 보도를 본적이 없음.

질문: 일정이 확정되지 않았는지 ?

답: 일정이 확정되었는지 안되었는지 알지 못함.

그것에 대한 기사를 본적이 없음.

질문: SCOWCROFT 안보 보좌관은 동경에서 대화가 이달 말경 개최될 것이라고
말한것으로 인용 되었음. (

답: 미국과의 대화와 관련 질문 사항이 무엇인지 ?

질문: 중국 및 북한과의 대화임.

답: 질문중 처음 부분을 오해 했었음. 유일하게 답변할수 있는것은 SCOWCROFT
보좌관이 말한것을 알고 있다는 것임.

SCOWCROFT 보좌관은 지금 대화가 언제 개최하는지에 대해 협의가 진행중에 있으나,
현재로서 확정된바는 없다고 말했음. SCOWCROFT보좌관이 언급한것 이상 알고 있지
않음.

2. 상기 관련 부분은 별전(USWF-0146) FAX송부함.

(대사 현홍주-국장)

미주국   1차보   미주국   외정실   분석관   정와대   안기부

34   북한 핵 문제 총괄 1

주 미 대 사 관

USW(F) : 0146   년월일 : 92.1.9. 시간 : 19:46PM

수 신 : 장 관 (미완. 미이. 허특)

발 신 : 주 미 대 사

제 목 : 북한핵 관련 미·북한접촉   (출처 : FNS)

보 안
통 제

STATE DEPARTMENT REGULAR BRIEFING   BRIEFER: MARGARET TUTWILER
12:29 P.M., EST   THURSDAY, JANUARY 9, 1992

    Q   Do you have any comment on a news report this morning
that the United States and North Korea rescheduled the nuclear talks?

    MS. TUTWILER: Have rescheduled nuclear talks?

    Q   Yes.

    MS. TUTWILER: No, I haven't seen that.

    Q   The schedule has not been set?

    MS. TUTWILER: I don't know whether the schedule has or hasn't
been set. I just haven't seen that particular report.

    Q   Well, Scowcroft in Tokyo said that -- he was quoted that
the talks will be held later in the month.

    MS. TUTWILER: On the United States talks, is what you're
asking me?

    Q   With China -- with North Korea.

    MS. TUTWILER: I misunderstood your first part of your
question. The only thing I have for you is, yes, I am aware of what
General Scowcroft said. He said that there are now discussions
about when that meeting would be held, but there's nothing set at
this time. I have nothing further than what the General said.

(0146 - / - /)

외신 1과
통   제

0029

공   란

공   란

공   란

공   란

분류번호	보존기간

발 신 전 보

번 호 : WUS-0137   920113 1515 WG   종별 : 지 급

수 신 : 주 미   대사, 총영사

발 신 : 장 관   (미이)

제 목 : 구 소련 핵 전문가 해외유출

1. 소연방 해체에 따른 구 소연방내 핵통제 기능 약화우려와 관련, 일부
   외신들은 구 소연방내 핵무기 제조 기술자들(약 5천여명)중 약 5백명이
   이미 리비아, 시리아, 남아공, 파키스탄 등에 고용되어 나갔으며, 북한도
   이들의 유치를 위해 노력하고 있어 미국이 이를 심각하게 받아들이고 있다고
   Magaret Tutwiler 국무부 대변인의 말을 인용, 보도하고 있음.

2. 본부는 현재 91. 12. 31. 합의된 한반도 비핵화에 관한 공동선언의
   구체적 이행을 위한 작업을 준비중에 있는바, 만일 상기보도가 사실일
   경우 남.북 핵협상에 중대한 영향을 미칠 것으로 우려되는 바, 귀관은
   1. 14-22간 독립국가연합 4개국을 순방 예정인 Bartholomew 귀 주재국
   국무차관측에 이와같은 우리의 우려를 전달하고 이와 관련된 사항들을
   동 방문시 파악해 줄 것을 요청해 주기 바람. 또한 상기 보도에 대한
   현재까지의 국무부 평가를 파악보고 바람.   끝.

예 고 : 92. 12. 31 일반

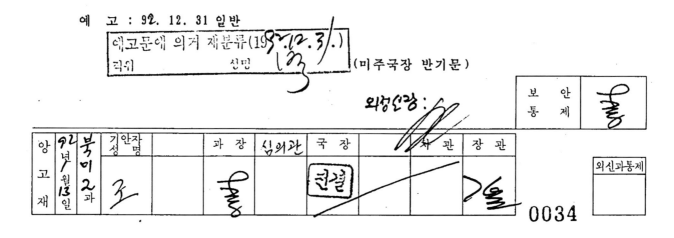

예고문에 의거 재분류(1992.12.31.)
각의   신민 (미주국장 반기문)

외정신강 :

보안통제

앙 고 재	92 년 1 월 13 일	북 미 2 과	기안자 성명 조	과 장	심의관	국 장 전결	차 관	장 관

외신과통제

0034

공   란

공　　란

공   란

공   란

공   란

공   란

공　　　란

공 란

공   란

공   란

공   란

공   란

공   란

공 란

공　　　란

공   란

공   란

공　　　란

공   란

공 란

공   란

공   란

공   란

공   란

공   란

공　　란

공　　　란

공 란

공   란

공   란

공   란

공   란

공   란

공   란

공　　　란

공   란

공   란

공   란

공　　　란

공 란

공   란

공   란

분류번호	보존기간

발 신 전 보

번   호 : WUS-0205   920116 1816 DW 종별 : _____

수   신 : 주 미   대사. 총영사

발   신 : 장 (尙이)

제   목 : 북한 핵문제에 대한 미측 입장

연 : WUS-0204

연호, 미측 non-paper 별첨 타전함.

첨 부 : 상기 non-paper.   끝.

(미주국장 반기문)
예고: 1992.12.31 일반

검토필(19○. 12.31.)

외교문서 의거 재분류(19○.12.3)
직위   성명

| 앙고재 | 92년 1월 16일 | 북미2과 | 기안자 성명 | 조 | 과장 선의라 | 국장 전결 | 차관 | 장관 | 보안통제 | | 외신과통제 |

0077

공   란

공   란

공   란

공 란

공   란

원 본

외 무 부

종 별 : 긴 급

번 호 : USW-0283

일 시 : 92 0117 1651

수 신 : 장 관 (미이,미일,정북)

발 신 : 주 미 대사

제 목 : 북한 핵문제

연: USW-0208

국무부 한국과 SCHMIEL 부과장은 금 1.17. 당관 안호영 서기관에게 연호 3 항 군축처가 준비한 핵사찰 문제에 대한 의견서를 아측에 전달하도록 작 1.16. 주한 미국대사관에 타전하였다고 알려왔으니 참고바람. 끝.

(대사 현홍주-국장)

예고: 92.12.31. 일반문서로 재분류

검토필(19 92. 6. 30.)

외 무 부

종 별 :

번 호 : USW-0284

일 시 : 92 0117 1652

수 신 : 장 관(미일,미이,정특,기정)

발 신 : 주 미 대사

제 목 : 미.북한 고위접촉(국무부 브리핑)

1. 금 1.17 국무부 정례브리핑시 BOUCHER부대변인은 KANTER 국무부 정무차관과 북한 김용순 노동당 국제부장이 관심사항 협의를위해 1.22 뉴욕에서 접촉을 가질 예정임을 발표하였는 바, 동 관련 주요 질의응답 내용을 하기 보고함.

(질문) 핵문제에 국한해서 협의가 이루어질것인지?

(답) 현재 의제 전반에 대해서는 알고 있지못하나, 핵문제를 협의하게 되며 기타 관심사항에 대해서도 협의를 할 예정임.

과거 미국이 계속 말해왔듯이, 한반도 문제의 일차적 해결 방안으로서 남북한의 관계개선 및 핵문제등 매우 시급한 문제를 북한으로 하여금 해결케 한다는 점에서 미국은 북한과의 관계개선 용의가 있음.

(질문) 핵문제를 제외한 기타 사안에 대해 말해줄 수 있는지?

(답) 현재로서는 말해줄 수 없음. 과거에 여러문제 및 사안이 무엇인지에 대해 말한 바 있으며, 아직도 그런 문제 및 사안이 그대로 있음.

(질문) 금번 북한과의 접촉으로 인해 미.북관계가 긴밀해 질 것으로 보는지?

(답) 반드시 그런 측면으로 볼 수 없음. 현재로서는 후속접촉에 대한 어떠한 계획도 없음.

(질문) 금번 접촉이 북경 참사관급 접촉을 대체하게 되는지, 별도로 열리는 것인지?

(답) 88.10이후 북경 참사관급 접촉이 18회열렸으며, 앞으로도 계속되리라고 봄. 그러나 현재로서 어떤 특정계획이 있는지에 대해서는 알고 있지 못함.

(질문) 금번 접촉이 현재까지 열린 미.북한 접촉중 가장 고위급인지?

(답) 그렇다고 알고 있음.

(질문) 금번 접촉은 일회에 한해 열리는지?

미주국   1차보   미주국   외정실   분석관   정와대   안기부

92.01.18   08:55 WG

외신 1과 통제관

0084

(답) 말한바 있듯이 현재로서 추후 접촉이 계획된 바 없음.

(질문) 금번 접촉에 대해 한국정부와 협의가 있었는지?

(답) 한국정부와는 모든 문제에 대해 긴밀히 협의해 오고 있으며, 동건도 협의하였음.

2. 관련 부분은 별전(USWF-0320) FAX 송부함.

(대사 현홍주 - 국장

주 미 대 사 관

USW(F) : **0320**   년월일 :**92. 1. 17** 시간 : **16:52PM**

수 신 : 장 관 (미밋·미이·점특·기정)

발 신 : 주 미 대 사

제 목 : 미·북한 고위 접촉   (출처 : **FNS**)

보 안	
통 제	

STATE DEPARTMENT REGULAR BRIEFING   BRIEFER: RICHARD BOUCHER
12:22 P.M. EST   FRIDAY, JANUARY 17, 1992

    The United States government, represented by Undersecretary of State for Political Affairs Arnold Kanter, will meet with a North Korean delegation headed by Korean Workers Party Secretary Kim Il-Sung in New York on January 22nd to discuss issues of concern.

Q   January --

MR. BOUCHER: January 22nd in New York.

    Are these exclusively nuclear issues of concern?

MR. BOUCHER: The issues that we expect to discuss, I don't have a full agenda for you here. Let me say two things about that. First of all, we will be discussing the nuclear issue, as well as other concerns. The context is what we've said previously, that we are prepared to improve our relations with North Korea in the context of their addressing a number of concerns, most immediately the nuclear issue and progress in the North-South talks, which remains the primary means for resolving the problems on the Korean Peninsula.

    Q   Do you want to touch on any of those other issues --

MR. BOUCHER: I don't want to at this point. We've stated in the past what the various issues and concerns were and those certainly still apply.

    Q   Does the meeting with North Korea means that the United States is going to have closer relation with North Korea from now on?

    MR. BOUCHER: I wouldn't necessarily put it in that context. At thi point there are no specific follow-up meetings planned. This is a meeting to discuss

(**0320 - 2 - 1**)

의신 1과	
통 제	

issues of concern, and I gave you the general (context of it ?) --
(inaudible) -- go farther than that.

Q   (Are ?) these takes substituting the Beijing contact
between consular -- political consulars, or it's going on separately
from the Beijing contact?

MR. BOUCHER: Since October '88, I think we've had 18 of those
meetings at the political consulor level in Beijing. I expect that
those meetings would continue. I'm not aware of anything specific
scheduled at this point, though.

Q   Richard, is this the highest level meetings ever held
between North Korean and American officials that you recall?

MR. BOUCHER: That I recall, yes. (Laughter.) That other
people who've worked on this recall, I think I'd better doublecheck
that.

Q   (Off mike)?

MR. BOUCHER: The spelling I have is Kim, K-i-m, Young,
Y-o-u-n-g, and Sun, S-u-n.

Q   Will this meeting be one time or not?

MR. BOUCHER: As I said, at this point, we have no further
meetings scheduled or planned. We'll see what happens.

Q   Did you have a consultation on these talks with the South
Korean government?

MR. BOUCHER: We've been in very close contact with our South
Korean ally on a whole number of issues recently. I'll just leave
it at that.

Q   Including this meeting?

MR. BOUCHER: Including this, yes.

0320-2-2

0087

공　　　란

공   란

공   란

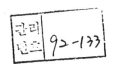

報 告 事 項

報 告 畢

1992. 1. 20.
外交政策企劃室
特殊政策課 (9)

題 目 : 북한, 일본의 핵위협 대두 주장

> 북한의 노동신문은 우리민족에 대한 일본의 핵위협이 현실적인 문제로 되어가
> 고 있다면서 이를 막기위해 남북이 힘을 합쳐 노력해야 된다고 주장함.

1. 주장 내용 (1.18, 노동신문 논평원의 글)

   o 우리 공화국의 반핵.비핵정책과 이의 관철 노력으로 한반도에서의 핵문제는
     해결 전망이 열리고 우리민족의 머리위에 드리워졌던 핵위협이 일단 제거됨

   o 그러나 한반도비핵화선언이 합의된 지금 우리민족에 대한 일본의 직접적인
     핵위협이 현실적인 문제로 되어 가고 있음. 지금 일본은 필요이상의 핵물질을
     축적하는등 핵계획을 맹렬히 추진하고 있음.
     - P. Leventhal 미 핵통제연구소장에 의하면 일본은 2000년대 초까지 100톤의
       플루토늄 확보 계획이며 1995년에는 핵재처리능력을 보유하게 됨.
       가상 미, 불의 이어 세번째 국으로 세계 3위의

   o 일본의 핵위협으로부터 우선 피해를 볼 것은 전체 우리민족인 만큼, 어떻게
     하든지 이를 막기위해 남북이 힘을 합쳐 함께 노력해야 함.
     - 합의서 채택과 비핵화공동선언 합의는 함께 노력하면 민족적 단결이 가능
       하며 단결된 힘으로 일본의 핵위협을 막을 수 있음을 보여줌.

2. 분 석

   o 일본의 핵위협 문제를 우리민족 공동의 과제로 내세우고 이를 위해 남과
     북이 힘을 합쳐 함께 노력해야 한다고 주장한 점이 주목되며, 향후 일.북
     수교회담등 기회에 대일카드로 활용할 의도가 있는 것으로 보여짐

   o 또한 북한이 핵문제 해결을 지연시키고자 할 경우, "일본의 핵위협"을 이유
     로 삼을 가능성도 있음.

   검 토 필 (1992. 6. 10.)

3. 언론대책 : 대외 보안
4. 조치사항 : 관계국(아주,미주,국제기구)에 통보. 끝.

예 고 : 발행처 : 92.12.31. 일반
        접수처 : 독후파기

일반문서로 재분류 (1993. 6. 30 자)

0091

분류번호	보존기간

발 신 전 보

번   호 : _____   종별 : _____

수   신 : 주   수신처 참조   대사//총영사

발   신 : 장   관   (정특)

제   목 : 북한, 일본의 핵위협 대두 주장

북한은 ~~대신~~ 노동신문 논평원의 글(1.18), 조선반핵평화위 백남준 부위원장
담화(1.19), 외교부 대변인의 중앙통신 기자와의 회견(1.20)등을 통해 우리민족에
대한 일본의 핵위협이 현실적으로 대두되고 있다면서 남북이 힘을 합쳐 대처 ~~되어야~~
해야 된다고 주장하고 있는 바, 아래 ~~관련내용~~ 참고바람.

1. 주장 내용

o 우리 공화국의 반핵.비핵정책과 노력으로 한반도 핵문제 해결 전망이 열리
   고 ~~우리~~민족의 머리위에 드리워졌던 핵위협이 일단 제거됨

o 그러나 남북간 비핵화공동선언이 합의된 지금, 우리민족에 대한 일본의 직접적
   핵위협이 현실적인 문제로 대두됨. 지금 일본은 필요이상의 핵물질 축적등
   핵계획 맹렬 추진중
   - P. Leventhal 미 핵통제연구소장에 의하면 일본은 2000년대 초까지 100톤의
     플루토늄 확보 계획이며 1995년에 가서는 미.불에 이어 세계3위의 핵재
     처리능력 보유

o 일본의 핵위협으로부터 우선 피해를 볼 것은 전체 우리민족인 만큼, 어떻게
   하든지 이를 막기위해 남북이 힘을 합쳐 ~~노력~~ 노력해야 함.
   - 합의서 채택과 비핵화공동선언 합의는, 함께 노력하면 민족적 단결이 가능
     하고 단결된 힘으로 일본의 핵위협을 막을 수 있음을 보여줌.

/ 계 속 /

참조 아주국장: 국기국장:
      미주국장:

보 안	
통 제	

앙고재	82년 1월 21일	통수정책과	기안성자명 박동상		과 장	심의관	국 장	실 장 전결	차 관	장 관 전결		외신과통제

0092

2. 분 석

   ㅇ 일본의 핵위협 문제를 우리민족 공동의 과제로 내세우고 이를 위해 남북이
      힘을 합쳐 함께 노력해야 한다고 주장한 점이 주목되며, 향후 일.북
      수교회담등 기회에 대일카드로 활용할 의도가 있는 것으로 보임

   ㅇ 북한이 핵문제 해결을 지연시키고자 할 경우, "일본의 핵위협"을 이유
      로 삼을 가능성

                    (외정실장 이 시 영)

수신처 : 주미 ,일 ,러 ,유엔 ,제네바 ,카다나 ,영 ,독 ,불 ,오지리 ,호주 대사
          주북경 대표 , 주홍콩 총영사

예 고 : 92.12.31. 일반

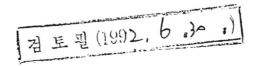

0093

공   란

공 란

공   란

공   란

공   란

공 란

공 란

공   란

공 란

공   란

공   란

공   란

공   란

공   란

공　　　란

공   란

공   란

공 란

공   란

공   란

공　　란

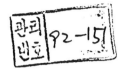

국　　　　방　　　　부

(795-7462)

대미 24103-7　　　　　　　　　　　　　　　1992. 1. 27

수신 외무부 장관

참조 미주국장

제목 주미대-릴리차관보 면담관련 국방부 입장 (통보)

　　　1. 관련근거 : USW-0327 ('91.1.21)

　　　　　　　　　　　　" Lilley차관보 면담"

　　　2. 북한 핵/MTCR 문제 관련, 릴리 미 국방부 국제안보담당차관보
의견에 대한 국방부 입장을 첨부와 같이 통보하니, 필요한 조치를 취해
주시기 바랍니다.

첨　부 : 릴리 차관보 면담관련 국방부 입장 1부.　　끝.

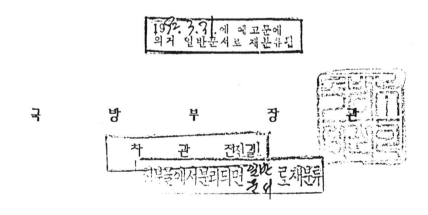

국　　　방　　　부　　　장　　　관

공 란

공   란

공   란

공　　　란

공   란

核武器제조기술관련
이란, 旧蘇학자 모집

[런던·新華] 이란은 核무기제조를 돕을 旧소련의 과학자들을 모집중이라고 선데이 타임스가 보도했다.

이 신분은 이들이 지않은 이란내 정치및 과학계 소식통들의 말을 인용, 이란이 「旧소련의 일부 최고급 두뇌들」에게 36만달러의 자금을 제시하고 있다고 전했다.

이 신문은 일부 소련과 학자들이 이미 이란을 방문했지만 이들이 계약까지 체결했는지 여부는 밝혀지지 않았다고 말했다.

조선 (92. 1. 28)

이란, 舊蘇핵학자 모집

[런던·新華] 이란은 核무기제조를 도울 舊소련의 과학자들을 모집중이라고 英國선데이 타임스가 26일 보도했다.

이 신분은 舊소련의 일부 최고급 두뇌들에게 36만달러의 해외 자금을 제시하고 있다고 전했다.

동아. (92. 1. 27)

이란 舊蘇과학자 고용
핵무기 조립위해 50명 유치

[런던·본 AP·UP·로이터=]

英선데이타임스 보도

서울조약기구 (나토) 사무총장 25일 참가국들에 핵무기가 이 타임스紙는 25일 이란이...

중앙 (92. 1. 27)

---

hired by 3rd World countries: NATO head

BONN (AFP) — Nuclear experts from the former Soviet Union have already been recruited by countries that want to build atomic bombs, according to NATO Secretary General Manfred Woerner.

Without naming specific countries, Woerner told the German magazine Bunte: "I have information that they have tried to recruit specialists with atomic know-how from the former Soviet Union. Several have already been recruited."

A number of Western leaders have expressed fears of a nuclear brain-drain to Third World countries.

On Friday, the United States acknowledged it was considering hiring nuclear experts from the former Soviet Union to prevent this from happening.

Woerner said the migration of such specialists was even more dangerous than the presence of nuclear arms in the Commonwealth of Independent States, which replaced the Soviet Union.

Iran recruiting Soviet scientists

LONDON (AP) — Iran is recruiting former Soviet nuclear scientists to help build an atomic bomb, according to a report published in the Sunday Times.

The newspaper, quoting unnamed Iranian political and scientific sources, said Iran was offering $360,000 to "some of the top brains in the former Soviet Union."

K. H (92. 1. 28)

0121

주 미 대 사 관

USW(F) : **457**   년월일 : **92. 1. 27** 시간 : **09:15**

수 신 : 장 관 (미일. 미이. 정특. 정안. 정홍. 해신)

보	안	
통	제	

발 신 : 주 미 대 사

제 목 : **북한**

(출처 : USA TODAY)
4A · MONDAY, JANUARY 27, 1992 ·

NORTH KOREAN MESSAGE: In a policy shift signaling a new opening to the outside world, North Korean President Kim Il Sung sent a message to the leaders of six Southeast Asian nations meeting in Singapore. He asked for closer ties in the region.

배부처	장관실	차관실	一차관보	二차관보	기획실	의전실	아동신	미주국	아주국	미주국	구주국	통아국	국기국	경제국	통상국	문화국	영교국	총무과	감사관	공보관	외연원	청와대	총리실	안기부	공보처	경기원	상공부	해신
	/	/	/		/	/			○															/	/	/		/

3   2   13 M

. (457 - 2 - 1)

외신 1과	
통 제	

0122

47-2

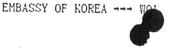

The Washington Times
PAGE A4 / MONDAY, JANUARY 27, 1992 ★

Electronic spying reoriented at NSA

By Bill Gertz
THE WASHINGTON TIMES

The supersecret National Security Agency has combined several units of its signals intelligence collection division to better focus electronic spying in the post-Cold War era, according to U.S. officials.

Officials, who spoke on condition of anonymity, described the shift as a "major reorganization" intended to adjust to the changing international scene.

Some officials said the changes were aimed at pre-empting attempts by Congress to force a reorganization of the entire U.S. intelligence community, which includes the NSA, CIA and other military and civilian intelligence agencies.

The NSA's headquarters, located at Maryland's Fort George G. Meade, recently shuffled three electronic intelligence-gathering groups by eliminating the Soviet and East European division, known as A Group, and reorienting those spying activities to include all operations against European nations.

The A Group was the largest and most prestigious of NSA's collection operations divisions and one that occupied a large percentage of NSA funds and personnel.

The NSA's B Group, once limited to spying exclusively on Asian communist communications — those from China, North Korea and Vietnam — was combined with the signals intelligence group that spies on the rest of world, known as G Group.

NSA spokesman Michael S. Conn said NSA organizations "are created and dissolved on a fairly routine basis."

But Mr. Conn declined to comment on any specific changes within the NSA's office of signals intelligence operations, one of the largest and most prestigious bureaus within the agency.

The NSA uses an international array of electronic listening posts, ships and satellites to listen in on foreign communications. It collects diplomatic, military, scientific and commercial links, and monitors nuclear-related tests or movements.

Its budget, estimated at more than $3 billion annually, is expected to decrease only slightly as part of the Bush administration's proposed fiscal 1993 intelligence budget of about $30 billion, government sources said.

President Bush told NSA employees in a speech last year that "signals intelligence is a prime factor in the decision-making process by which we chart the course of this nation's foreign affairs."

With between 20,000 and 40,000 employees, the NSA is one of the largest employers in Maryland.

According to the officials, one of the NSA's top priorities since the breakup of the Soviet Union has been to collect information on former Soviet scientists who have been involved in building nuclear weapons and who want to work for Third World governments seeking nuclear arms.

The NSA also is on the lookout for information about illicit sales or thefts of nuclear weapons or components from among the 30,000 nuclear arms in the new Commonwealth of Independent States.

CIA Director Robert Gates said U.S. intelligence is leading an international effort to monitor the 1 million people who have worked on Soviet nuclear arms, including about 2,000 scientists who are skilled enough to design a nuclear weapon.

So far, reports of nuclear scientists from the former Soviet republics selling information or expertise have not been confirmed, Mr. Gates said in Senate testimony last week.

However, NSA has picked up information that indicates Russian nuclear scientists are assisting North Korea with its secret nuclear weapons development program, according to intelligence sources.

457-2-2

0123

"舊蘇과학자 北韓핵개발 지원"

워싱턴타임즈 보도

[워싱턴=金喆濟특파원] 미국의 촘단급비밀을 취급하는 정부기관인 국가안전국(NSA)은 러시아연방의 핵과학자들이 북한의 핵무기개발을 돕고있다는 정보를 입수했다고 워싱턴 타임즈가 27일 이 신문은 전했다.

美정보관리들의 말을 인용, 보도했다.

닥냉전시대를 맞은 美국가안전국의 최우선임무가 진전하고 있으나 당사자들이 하고있어 결과가주목된다.

옛소련의 제3세계 국가들에게 핵무기제조기술을 판매하거나 유출시키는 것을 추진하는 것이라고 늦것으로보였다.

러聯 核과학자들 北무기 개발지원

WT紙보도

[워싱턴=聯合] 美國의 국가안보국(NSA)은 러시아의 핵과학자들이 北韓의 핵무기개발계획을 지원하고 있음을 시사하는 정보를 입수했다고 워싱턴 타임스紙가 27일 보도했다.

타임스紙가 27일 정보소식통을 인용 보도했다.

반대한 전자스파이활동 전세계에 걸쳐 수집 분석하는 NSA는 소련연방 붕괴이후 그동안 핵무기개발에 관여해온 과학자 그중에서도 제삼세계국가들의 핵개발을 원하고 있다.

보버트 게이츠 중앙정보국(CIA)국장은 지난주 상원기자회견에서 미국의 관련정보기관이 핵무기를 설계할수 있는 2천여 과학자와 과거핵무기개발에서 일한바 있는 1백만명의 소련인에 대한 정보를 수집하려는 국제적 노력을 선도하고 있다고 말한바 있다.

동아 (82. 1. 28)

경향 (82. 1. 28)

0124

분류번호	보존기간

발 신 전 보

번 호 : WUS-0424   920129 1052 WG   종별 :

수 신 : 주 미 대사. 총영사

발 신 : 장 관 (미이)

제 목 : 북한 핵개발

연 : WUS-137

대 : USW-171

1. 구 소련 핵과학자들의 해외유출 또는 핵기술 판매우려와 관련, 워싱톤 타임즈지(1. 27자)는 미국가안보처(NSA)가 러시아 연방 핵과학자들이 북한의 핵무기 개발 계획을 지원하고 있다는 정보를 입수한 것으로 보도하고 있는바, NSA 측과 접촉, 관련정보 내용을 파악보고 바람.

2. 연호 Bartholomew 국무차관의 CIS 4개국 순방 결과도 파악 보고 바람.
끝.

(미주국장 반기문)

예 고 : 92. 12. 31 일반

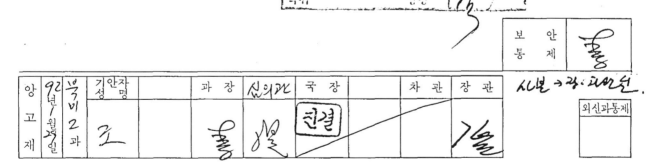

검토필(1992. 6. 30.)

예고문에 의거 재분류(1992.12.31.)

앙 고 재	92년 1월 29일		기안 책임		과 장	심의관	국 장		차 관	장 관	

전결

보 안 통 제

신본 →과 : 과장원

외신과통제

0125

공   란

공   란

외 무 부

종 별 :

번 호 : USW-0520   일 시 : 92 0131 0848

수 신 : 장 관 (해외,해신,문홍)

발 신 : 주 미 대사

제 목 : 북한 핵개발 저지대책

1. HERITAGE FOUNDATION 은 1.29. 북한의 핵무기보유는 동북아 안보에 위협 요인이 됨은 물론 미국의 안보에도 영향을 미친다고 설명하고 북한의 확실한 핵사찰 절차 이행과 북한내 핵무기 생산시설의 완전한 폐기를 확인하는 절차가 필요함을 지적하면서 북한이 이를 거부하거나 약속을 위반할 경우에 대비하여 미국은 정치.경제적제재조치 또는 군사적 조치까지 검토해야 한다는 동재단 RICHARD D. FISHER 연구관의 정책 건의를 담은 BACKGROUNDER 2,000 부를 발간, 행정부,의회, 언론, 외교단등 배포처에 배포하였음. (전문 별전 USW(F)-0546 송부)

2. 주요 내용

(서론)

- 북한은 92년 중반까지 플루토늄 생산이 가능하고 93년 중반까지 핵폭탄을 제조할 것으로 예상되는바, 북한의 핵보유는 한국, 일본은 물론 미국과 우방의 안보에 위협 요인이됨.

- 북한의 핵보유를 저지하기 위해 한.미 양국은 91년 미국의 전술핵 철거(9.27), 한반도 비핵화 선언(11.8), 팀스피리트 훈련 중지결정(1.7)등 양보조치를 취했음.

- 이에대해 북한은 12.31. 한반도 비핵화 공동선언에 서명하고 91.1.30.까지 IAEA 사찰 서명3.19.까지 핵통제 공동위 설치를 약속했음.

(남은 과제)

- 41년간 대남 적대행위를 해왔고 테러,강압정치및 110만명의 중무장 병력을 보유한 북한은 항상 국제적 위협요인이 되어 왔음.

- 남.북간에 합의된 한반도 비핵화 공동선언만으로는 북측의 확실한 약속이행을보장하는 것이 아님(IAEA 사찰을 받아온 이라크의 예가 있음)

- 남.북한간 협의 진행중인 상호 사찰로서 92.6.까지 평양의 약속이행을

공보처	장관	차관	1차보	1차보	문협국	의정실	분석관	정와대
안기부	국방부	공보처						

PAGE 1

확인해야하고 추가해서 미국과 한국은 핵무기 제조시설의 완전한 폐기를 주장,
92년말까지 북한이 핵무기 제조시설을 폐기하지 않을 경우에 대비해서 외교적 경제적
조치를 준비해야 하고 나아가 군사적 조치까지 검토해야 할 것임.

(회유책)

- 한.미 양국은 북의 핵개발 저지를 위해 정치.경제적 회유책을 견지해 왔음.

- 한국은 12.13. 합의한 남북 화해 불가침및 교류협력의 합의로 문화, 정치,
경제적 교류를 증대하고자 하고 있음.

- 미국은 북한과의 관계개선과 연계하고 41년간의 무역제재 조치를 완화하고자
하며, 일본도 핵개발을 중단하지 않으면 관계 정상화 않겠다 하고 있음.

- 중국은 북한 핵개발 관련 압력을 가하지 않고 있음.

(향후 단계적 조치)

- 제 1단계: 199년말까지 시한을 정해서 핵무기 제조시설을 완전히 폐기하고 이의
입장을 촉구하는 미행정부의 성명 발표

. 분명히 1992년말 까지라는 시한을 명시해야함.

. IAEA 와 남한측 조사관이 북한의 핵재처리시설 파괴를 확인해야함.

- 제 2단계: 북한이 4월까지 IAEA 와 남한측 조사관의 입국, 사찰을 허용할 경우
미.북한관계 격상 제시

. 한반도 비핵화 선언에 의하면 4월까지 남한조사관이 북한에 들어가는 것으로
되어 있으므로 IAEA 조사관도 입국해야함.

. 지금까지 미.북한 접촉은 북경에서 있었고1.22. 뉴욕 접촉이 있었는바,
북한내핵사찰이 시작된후 미 국무부 차관은 평양을 방문할 수도있고 41년간 지속되어
온 무역제재 조치도 농산물분야부터 해제할 수 있음.

- 제 3단계: 북한 핵무기 제조시설의 완전 폐기가 확인될때 까지 정상적인
외교통상관계 수립보류

. IAEA 조사관이나 한국 조사관이 북한내 핵제조 시설 폐기를 확인하기 까지 정상
외교.통상관계 수립 보류해야함.

. 중.소로 부터 경제지원이 단절된후 외국기술과 자본을 필요로 하는 북한에 대해
약속을 이행하는 묘약이 될것임.

- 제 4단계: 중국에 대해 북한의 핵개발 저지압력을 가하도록 함.

. 북한의 주요 우방으로 남아있는 중국을 움직여서 핵개발 계획을 중단토록 촉구

PAGE 2

. 일본도 핵개발 중단이 확실시 될때까지 북한과 관계 정상화를 보류토록 해야함.

- 제 5단계: 주한미군의 존속

. 미의회의 감축 압력이 있더라도 주한미군은 37,000명선을 유지해야함.

. 북한의 핵무기 제조시설 폐기를 입증할수있을때 한해 주한미군 감축 가능

- 제 6단계: 북한이 1992년말까지 핵무기 제조시설을 폐기하지 않을 경우 한국과 협의,적절한 정치.경제.군사적 수단을 강구할 것

. 중.일.소련등을 동원, 북한의 핵개발계획을 비난하는 국제적 캠페인을 벌이거나 UN안보리 결의안을 유도할 수 있음.

. 이렇게 해도 말을 듣지 않으면 한.미 양국은 북한에 대한 국제적 경제제재를 선도해야함.

. 영변이나 북한내 다른 핵연구 시설에 대한 공중 폭격같은 군사조치는 북한으로 하여금 남한에 대한 보복 또는 제 2의 한국전쟁을 유발할수 있음을 들어 마지막 수단으로 고려되어야함.끝.

(공보공사-해공관장)

정 리 보 존 문 서 목 록

기록물종류	일반공문서철	등록번호	32693	등록일자	2009-02-26
분류번호	726.61	국가코드		보존기간	영구
명　　칭	북한 핵문제, 1992. 전13권				
생 산 과	북미1과/북미2과	생산년도	1992~1992	담당그룹	
권 차 명	V.2 2-3월				
내용목차	* 2.7-18 Kartman 미국 국무부 한국과장 방한 　2.22-25 Paal 미국 대통령 NSC 아시아담당 수석보좌관 방한 * 북한 핵관련 대책, 한.미국간 협의, 미국의 사찰과정 참여 요구 등				

0001

공   란

공 란

공   란

공   란

공   란

공   란

원 본

외 무 부

종 별 :

번 호 : USW-0581 일 시 : 92 0204 1843

수 신 : 장관(미일,미이,정특,정안)사본;통일원장관,청와대 외교안보수석)

발 신 : 주 미 대사

제 목 : 북한 핵 문제 세미나

1. 본직은 금 2.3 당지 WCNP(WASHINGTON COMMITTEE ON NON-PROLIFERATION)가 주관한 북한 핵문제에 대한 세미나에 참석, 기조 연설을 갖고 이어서 참석자들과 약 2 시간에 걸쳐 질의.응답을 가짐(당지 COSMOS 클럽에서 개최된 금일 세미나에는 JAMES GOODBY 대사, ARTHUR HUMMEL 대사, SAIS 의 RALPH CLOUGH, 및 DOAK BARNETT 교수, 카네기 재단의 SELIG HARRISON 및 LEONARD SPECTER 연구원등 각계 전문가가 참석하였음)

2. 금일 기조 연설을 통하여 본직은 아직 북한의 진의를 단정적으로 확인할수는 없으나, 북한이 비핵 공동 선언에 합의하고 IAEA 안전 협정에 서명한것은 그 자체로 큰 의미가 있는것이며, 이는 한국정부의 주도하에 미국및 여타 우방국과의 협력이 성공적이었음을 나타내는것이라고 설명함.

이와같은 북한의 태도 변화에는 1)남.북대화, 2) IAEA 를 통한 압력, 3)한.미 협력,4)일.북한 수교 협상을 위요한 한. 미 일간의 협의등 4 개 주요 압력 수단(QUADRIAD)이 유효하였음을 지적하고, 그러나 북한이 아직 IAEA 사찰, 남. 북 시범 사찰 실시 제의에 소극적인 태도로 일관하고 있으므로, 금후 핵 문제에 대한 북한의 성실한 협력을 얻어내기 위해서는 이러한 4 개 수단을 중심으로 북한에 계속적인 압력을 경주하는것이 중요함을 강조하였음.

3. 이어 계속된 질의, 응답중 특기 사항은 하기와같음.

가. O (카네기 재단 의 SPECTER 연구원, WCNP 소장 JAMES LEONARD, HUBERMANCONSULTING 의 HUBERMAN 회장)

- 한국이 최근 영국과 체결한 원자력 협정에 따르면 한국이 영국에서 핵 연료를 재처리할수 있는 수단(OPTION)을 보유하는것으로 되어있음.

- 한국이 이에 따라 플루토늄을 보유하게되면, 형평의 원칙상 북한이

미주국	장관	차관	1차보	2차보	미주국	외정실	외정실	분석관
정와대	안기부	통일원						

92.02.05 10:52

외신 2과 통제관 CH
0008

플루토니움을 갖게 되는것도 막을수 없으므로 핵비확산 노력을 위해 큰 문제를 제기하게될것임.

- 이는 또한 한. 미간에는 물론, 미. 영간에도 큰 문제를 야기하게될것으로 봄.

0 본직은 답변을 통해 노 대통령의 11.8 선언을 통해 핵문제에 대한 아국의입장은 명백히 밝혀진것을 설명하고, IAEA 규정을 철저히 준수하고 있는 아국에 대해서 핵확산의 의구심을 갖는것은 근거가 없음을 강조하였음.

나. 핵 사찰에 대한 북한의 태도와 관련, SAIS의 CLOUGH 교수는 영변에 소재한 3MW 발전소가 IAEA 의 관할하에 있어왔음을 지적하면서, 이들을 통해 과거 사찰에 대한 북한의 태도를 감지할수 있을것이라는 의견을 제시하였음.

다. 0 (GOODBY 대사)

- 비핵선언과 남. 북 대화의 상관관계및 비핵 선언 내용에 국제적 보장 문제가 포함되어 있는지에 대하여 질문

0 본직은 답변을 통해 비핵 선언 채택을 위해서는 남북한간에 긍정적인 분위기 조성이 중요하였는바, 그러한 점에서 남북대화가 필수적이었음을 강조하고 일부에서는 한국정부가 국내 정치적 고려에서 남북 대화를 졸속히 추진하였다는 시각도 있어 왔으나, 여당이 내각 책임제로의 개헌이 없을것임을 확약하고 있는 현재로서는 이러한 주장은 설득력을 상실하였음을 설명하였음.

0 비핵선언의 국제적 보장 문제와 관련, 본직은 한반도 문제의 당사자 해결원칙(SUPREMACY)을 강조하고 실제상의 문제로 일정한 단계에 이르면 주변국의 협조가 필요할것이나 이 경우에도 한국내에 일본의 정치적, 군사적 역할 비대화에 대한 유보적 여론이 있는것도 고려해야할것이라고 부연하였음.

라. 0 (HUMMEL 대사)

-북한의 유엔 가입 결정, 남. 북 기본합의서 체결시에 북한내에서 비준 동의 절차 문제가 제기되었는지를 질문하면서 북한이 유독 IAEA 핵 안전 협정에 대해서만 비준 동의 절차를 강조하는데 대하여 의문을 제기

0 본직은 답변을 통하여 북한 헌법에 따르면 최고 인민회의의 동의없이 조약 비준이 가능하다는것이 우리의 해석이라고 하면서, 북한이 국내 절차를 이유로 IAEA 비준을 지연시키는것은 법률적 문제가 아니라 정치적 결단의 문제이며, 이러한 배경에서 북한의 비준 지연은 극히 우려되는 사태라고 답변

마. 0 (SAIS 의 BARNETT 교수)

PAGE 2

0009

- 북한의 핵 개발의 초기 단계에 있다면 한국이 지금까지 취해온 조치가 유효할것이나, 이것이 완성 단계에 있다면 현재와같은 조치로는 미흡한것으로 본다고 하면서, 북한 핵개발 현황에 대한 정보 평가를 문의

0 본직은 북한의 핵개발이 임박하였다는 우려때문에 아측이 비핵선언 발효 이전이라도 핵통제 공동위 를 구성하는등 남. 북 공동 사찰과 IAEA 사찰의 조속한(SOONER, RATHER THAN LATER)실시를 위해 노력하고 있고, 이와함께 시범 사찰도 강력하게 요구하고 있음을 설명함.

바. 카네기 재단 HARRISON 연구원은 북한은 핵문제를 남. 북한 관계, 미.북한관계, 남북 통상무기 군축 문제등과 연관하여 가장 큰 양보를 얻어내기 위해 노력하고 있으므로 기존합의의 이행과정에서도 지연전술(CAT AND MOUNE GAME)을 쓸것으로 보인다고 하면서, 북한이 한국에 대한 핵우산 철회 문제를 더이상 고집하지 않고 있으나, 적절한 시기에 가서는 북한에 대한 핵 불사용 보장을 명확히 해 주어야할것으로 본다고 종래 입장을 반복하였음.

4. 금일 세미나는 북한 핵문제에 대한 주재국 각계의 관심이 고조된 계기에동문제에 대한 OPINION-LEADER 들을 상대로 지금까지의 성과를 분석하고, 금후의 과제및 접근 방식에 대한 방향을 제시하는 좋은 기회였던것으로 평가됨.

(대사 현홍주-국장)

예고:92.12.31 일반

관리 번호	92-320

외 무 부

종 별 :

번 호 : USW-0634　　　　　　　　　일 시 : 92 0206 1815

수 신 : 장관(미일,미이,통일)

발 신 : 주 미 대사

제 목 : 백악관 인사 방한

　　1. 백악관 NSC 아시아 담당 수석 보좌관인 DOUGLAS PAAL 은 2.14 부터 호주,싱가폴 및 아세안국가 순방후 2.22-25 방한 예정인바, 체한중 미주국장과의 면담및 청와대 외교 안보수석및 경제수석을 각각 예방하기를 희망한다고함.

　　2. 아직 항공일정등은 미정이라고 하는바, 상세 추보 위계이며, 동인의 금번 순방활동을 감안, 동인의 면담 희망 인사외에 외무부 고위급 간부와의 면담 주선을 건의함.

　　(대사 현홍주-국장)

　　92.12.31 까지

미주국	장관	차관	1차보	2차보	~~구주국~~	통상국	외정실	분석관
정와대	안기부							

PAGE 1　　　　　　　　　　　　　　　　　　　92.02.07　　10:17

분류번호	보존기간

발 신 전 보

번 호 : WUS-0574   920208 1055 DQ   종별 : _____

수 신 : 주   미   대사,총영사

발 신 : 장 관(미 일)

제 목 : 백악관 인사 방한

대 : USW - 0634

대호 Paal 보좌관 방한시 면담주선 결과는 아래와 같으며 순방 및 방한
관련 상세사항 파악 보고 바람.

    2. 24(월)   11:00   미주국장

             15:00   외교안보수석

             15:30   경제수석   끝.

(미주국장   반기문)

예 고 : 92.12.31. 일반

	기안자 성명	과 장	국 장	차 관	장 관
양 고 재 92년2월8일 북미1과		심의관	저런		

보 안
통 제

외신과통제

0012

Kartman 국무부 한국과장 체한일정(안)
======================================

2. 8(토)

18:30   김포착(동경발 NW 29편)

        숙소 향발(Hilton Hotel)

2. 9(일)

12:15   박정수 국회 외무.통일위원장 주최 오찬

2.10(월)

09:00   Gregg 대사 면담

10:00   Hendrickson 정무참사관 면담

11:00   Morford 경제참사관 면담

12:15   임동원 통일원 차관 주최 오찬

14:00   Garza 총무참사관 면담

15:00   Wilkinson 총영사 면담

16:00   Frederick 상무관 면담

0013

2.11(화)

10:00	반기문 외무부 미주국장, 송민순 북미1과장 면담
12:15	도영심 의원 면담(조선호텔)
14:30	김동근, 김종필 민자당 최고위원 보좌관 면담
16:00	정태익, 이량, 민병석, 변종규 비서관 면담
17:30	박준규 국회의장 면담(롯데 커피숍)

2.12(수)

11:15	McCullough gregg대사특보 면담
12:15	박태준 의원 주최 오찬, Gregg대사 동석(관저)
16:00	Gregg 대사의 초임 및 재임직원 간담회 배석
17:00	반기문 외무부 미주국장 주최 만찬(항원)

2.13(목)

09:30	미상공회의소 간부회의 참석(무역회관)
10:00	Jeffrey Cliber 오산비행장 부사령관 면담
	Fogelman 중장 주최 오찬
18:30	김영삼 민자당 대표최고위원 주최 만찬(상도동)

2.14(금)

오 전	이동복 안기부장 특보주최 조찬
오 전	과천 정부 제2청사 방문
19:30	Burghardt 공사주최 경제지도자들을 위한 만찬 배석(관저)

0014

2.15(토)

정몽준 의원 면담

2.16(일)

18:30   Gregg 대사 주최 만찬

2.17(월)

4인 위원회 조찬 배석

Burghardt 공사주최 이종찬의원을 위한 만찬 배석

2.18(화)

14:00   김포 항발

0015

공   란

공   란

공   란

공 란

공   란

공   란

공   란

공   란

공　　란

공   란

공 란

공   란

공   란

공   란

공   란

공　　　란

공   란

공　　　　　란

발 신 전 보

번 호 : WNY-0270   920213 1729   FL종별 :

수 신 : ~~주~~ 장관   ~~대사.//총영사~~ (주 뉴욕 총영사 경유)

발 신 : 장 관   (정특)

제 목 : 남북정상회담 관련 대언론 브리핑

    최근 국내외언론의 남북정상회담과 관련한 추측 및 억측보도에 대해 2.13(목) 남북고위급회담 대변인이 발표한 표재 브리핑 요지를 아래 보고함.

ㅇ 노대통령은 평화통일을 위하여는 쌍방 최고 당국자간의 회담이 가장 확실하고 실질적인 방법이라는 확신하에 취임이래 정상회담의 조속개최를 희망해옴.

ㅇ 북측도 이 문제가 고위급회담의 성과에 달려있다고 한 바 있어, 남북기본합의서 등이 채택된 현상황에서 정상회담개최문제가 논의된다면 자연스러운일임.

ㅇ 그러나 그간 어떤형태로도 남북간 공식적인 협의는 없었으며 따라서 정상회담 3월 개최 보도는 낭설임. 최근 정세로 볼때 우리보다도 북측이 정상회담 개최를 필요로 하고 있어, 그 여부는 북측에 달려있으며 우리측이 서두를 일이 아님.

ㅇ 금번 6차 고위급회담 대표단은 남북기본합의서등의 발효문제 이외에도 특히, 핵통재공동위 발족, 북한의 IAEA 핵안전협정 조기 비준.발효 및 시범 핵사찰 문제등의 타결에 총력을 집중할 것임. 이와 같은 주요현안의 타결도 정상회담 실현 ~~여부에 영향을 미칠 것임.~~ 이도움이될것임   끝.

(차 관)

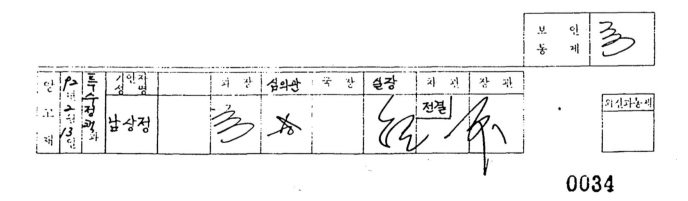

	특수정리과	기안자 성 명		과장	심의관	국장	실장	차관	장관		외신과 접수
안 고 재	92 2월 13일	남상정						전결			

보안 통제	33

0034

공   란

공   란

공   란

공   란

공   란

공　　　란

공 란

발 신 전 보

번 호 : WUS-0685 920214 1134 FE 종별 :

수 신 : 주   미   대사. 총영사

발 신 : 장 관 (미 일)

제 목 : 남북정상회담 관련 대언론 브리핑

분류번호	보존기간

최근 국내외언론의 남북정상회담과 관련한 추측 및 억측보도에 대해
2.13(목) 남북고위급회담 대변인이 발표한 표제 브리핑 요지를 아래 보고함.

    ㅇ 노대통령은 평화통일을 위하여는 쌍방 최고 당국자간의 회담이 가장
       확실하고 실질적인 방법이라는 확신하에 취임이래 정상회담의 조속
       개최를 희망해 옴.

    ㅇ 북측도 이 문제가 고위급회담의 성과에 달려있다고 한 바 있어, 남북
       기본합의서등이 채택된 현상황에서 정상회담 개최문제가 논의된다면
       자연스러운 일임.

    ㅇ 그러나 그간 어떤형태로도 남북간 공식적인 협의는 없었으며, 따라서
       정상회담 3월개최 보도는 낭설임. 최근 정세로 볼때 우리보다도 북측이
       정상회담 개최를 필요로 하고 있어, 그 여부는 북측에 달려 있으며
       우리측이 서두를 일이 아님.

    ㅇ 금번 6차 고위급회담 대표단은 남북 기본합의서등의 발효문제 이외에도
       특히, 핵통제 공동위 발족, 북한의 IAEA 핵안전협정 조기 비준.발효 및
       시범 핵사찰문제등의 타결에 총력을 집중할 것임. 이와 같은 주요현안의
       타결이 정상회담 실현에 도움이 될 것임. 끝.

(미주국장   반기문)

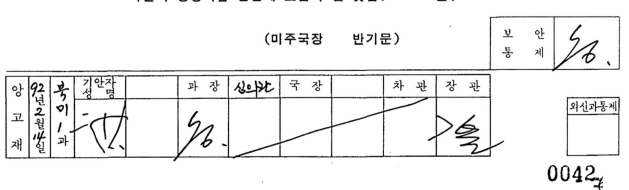

보 안
통 제

앙 고 재	92년 2월 14일	북미 1과	기안 자성 명		과 장	심의관	국 장		차 관	장 관

외신과통제

0042

공 란

공   란

공 란

공   란

공   란

공 란

공 란

북한 핵문제, 1992. 전13권 (V.2 2-3월) 185

공   란

공   란

공　　　란

공   란

발 신 전 보

번 호 : WUS-0750 920218 1617 CJ   종별 :

수 신 : 주 　미 　대사. 총영사

발 신 : 장 관 (미일)

제 목 : Kartman 국무부 한국과장 방한

　　　　표제관련, 동인의 주요 체한일정을 아래 통보하며 미주국장 면담시 면담
요록은 정파편 송부 예정이니 참고바람.

　　　　　o 2. 8(토)　　18:30　　　김포 착(동경발 NW 29편)

　　　　　o 2. 9(일)　　12:15　　　박정수 국회 외무.통일위원장주최 오찬

　　　　　o 2.10(월)　　09:00　　　Gregg 대사 면담, 주한미대사관
　　　　　　　　　　　　　　　　　　부서장과의 개별 면담

　　　　　o 2.11(화)　　10:00　　　반기문 외무부 미주국장 면담

　　　　　　　　　　　　12:15　　　도영심 의원 면담

　　　　　　　　　　　　14:30　　　김동근, 김종필 민자당 최고위원 보좌관
　　　　　　　　　　　　　　　　　　면담

　　　　　　　　　　　　16:00　　　정태익, 이량, 민병석, 변종규 비서관
　　　　　　　　　　　　　　　　　　면담

　　　　　　　　　　　　17:30　　　박준규 국회의장 면담

/계　　속/

보 안 통 제	

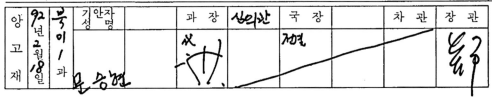

외신과통제	

0054

o 2.12(수)   11:15   McCullough Gregg대사특보 면담

             12:15   박태준 의원 주최 오찬, Gregg대사 동석

             16:00   Gregg 대사의 초임 및 재임직원 간담회
                      배석

             17:00   반기문 외무부 미주국장 주최 만찬

o 2.13(목)   09:30   미 상공회의소 간부회의 참석

             10:00   Jeffrey Cliber 오산비행장 부사령관
                      면담, Fogelman 중장 주최 오찬

             18:30   김영삼 민자당 대표최고위원 주최 만찬

o 2.14(금)   오 전   이동복 안기부장 특보주최 조찬
             오 전   과천 정부 제2청사 방문
             19:30   Burghardt 공사주최 경제지도자들을
                      위한 만찬 배석(관저)

o 2.15(토)   정몽준 의원 면담

o 2.16(일)   18:30   Gregg 대사 주최 만찬

o 2.17(월)   Burghardt 공사주최 이종찬의원을 위한
                      만찬 배석

o 2.18(화)   이 한   - 끝 -

                              (미주국장   정태익)

0055

POL15591

EAP/K KARTMAN VISIT TO KOREA
FEBRUARY 7-18, 1992.

SATURDAY, FEBRUARY 8

6:30 PM   ARRIVE SEOUL FROM TOKYO VIA FLT NW 29
            MET BY EMBASSY CAR, PROCEED TO HILTON HOTEL

OPEN

SUNDAY, FEBRUARY 9

12:15   LUNCH WITH FOREIGN AFFAIRS COMMITTEE CHAIRMAN
            PARK CHUNG-SU AT HILTON (AL O'NEILL)

REMAINDER DAY FREE - PERSONAL KOREAN FRIENDS

MONDAY, FEBRUARY 10

8:30   DEPART HOTEL

9:00   AMBASSADOR

10:00   POL - HANK HENDRICKSON

11:00   ECON - DICK MORFORD

2:00   ADMIN - O.P. GARZA

3:00   CONS - ED WILKINSON

4:00   FCS - PETER FREDERICK

TUESDAY, FEBRUARY 11

ROKG MEETINGS:

NUB VMIN LIM
NUB KANG KEUN-TAIK
MOFA DG BAN KI-MOON
MOFA DIR SONG MIN-SOON
MOFA DIR LEE HO-JIN

BLUE HOUSE: CHUNG TAE-IK
             KIM JAE-SUP'S REPLACEMENT
             MIN BYUNG-SOOK

7:30 Kim Dong-Kun at 10:00

Do answer from Wash w/ Kim Jae-sup

0056

192 북한 핵 문제 총괄 1

WEDNESDAY, FEBRUARY 12

POSSIBLE BREAKFAST WITH DB LEE

11:15   SAA - JIM MCCULLOUGH

12:15   AMBASSADOR'S LUNCH WITH PARK TAE-JUN

4:00   ATTEND AMBASSADOR'S MEETING WITH FIRST AND
          SECOND TOUR (FAST) OFFICERS

(DINNER WITH ACADEMICS - HOST? - INCLUDING CHANG
DAO-CHOONG, CHUNG CHOONG-WOOK, ET AL)

THURSDAY, FEBRUARY 13

(?? 9:30 AMCHAM BOG MEETING AT TRADE CENTER)

10:00   OSAN AB - BG JEFFREY CLIBER VICE COMMANDER,
          7TH AIR FORCE (POC: MRS. FUENTES)
          LUNCH AT OSAN WITH LTG RON FOGELMAN

PM? - USFK

6:30 - DINNER WITH KIM YOUNG-SAM (TED KLOTH)

FRIDAY, FEBRUARY 14

DAY AT KWACHON -ECONOMIC/TRADE-RELATED MEETINGS TBD (ECON)

?LUNCH WITH GENERALS

?6:30   DINNER HOSTED BY DCM WITH BUSINESS LEADERS

0057

SATURDAY, FEBRU## 15

?MEETINGS WITH POLITICIANS TBD

(PARK JUNE-KYU, DOH YOUNG-SHIM, CHUNG MONG-JUN)

SUNDAY, FEBRUARY 16

6:30   AMBASSADOR'S SMALL IN-HOUSE GET-TOGETHER AT
          RESIDENCE

MONDAY, FEBRUARY 17 (U.S. HOLIDAY, EMBASSY CLOSED)

(NB: BIG 4 BREAKFAST)

?POSSIBLE DINNER WITH LEE CHONG-CHAN HOSTED BY DCM

TUESDAY, FEBRUARY 18

2:00 PM   DEPART EMBASSY FOR KIMPO AIRPORT

(SUGGEST INFORMAL/OFF-RECORD DINNER WITH JOURNALISTS - TED
KLOTH CAN ARRANGE/HOST)

0058

관리 번호	92-93

원 본

외 무 부

종 별 :

번 호 : USW-0870

일 시 : 92 0220 1928

수 신 : 장 관 (미이,정특,국기)

발 신 : 주 미 대사

제 목 : 고위급 회담 핵문제 협의

1. 미 국무부는 제 6 차 고위급 회담에서의 핵문제 협의와 관련, 하기 요지의 PRESS GUIDELINE 을 준비하였다고 알려왔음.

(질문) 제 6 차 회담의 핵문제 합의 도출 실패에 대한 평가

(답변)

- 2 개 협정 발효및 3 개 분과위 구성 합의를 환영함.

- 북한이 특히 핵사찰에 조속히 호응해 올 것을 기대함.

- 이와함께 북한이 더 이상의 지체없이 IAEA 핵안전협정을 조속히 이행하는것이 중요함.

(질문) IAEA 핵 안전협정의 지연 가능성에 대한 질문

(답변)

- 지난 1 월 북한 대변인은 서명후 곧(SOON) 핵안전협정을 비준할 의도임을밝힌바 있으며, 서명은 지난 1 월에 이루어짐.

- 최근 남. 북한간의 2 개 협정은 서명후 수주만에 비준이 이루어진바, 북한이 약속(COMMITMENT)을 준수할 것을 기대함.

2. 상기 GUIDELINE 을 FAX 송부함(USW(F)-0959). 끝.

(대사 현홍주-국장)

예고: 92.12.31. 일반 고문에
                               재분류 됨

검토필(19 P. 6.30.)

미주국 안기부	장관	차관	1차보	2차보	국기국	외정실	분석관	청와대

0059

주 미 대 사 관

USF(F) : 0959   년월일 :92. 2. 20   시간 : 19:28

수 신 : 장 관 (메, 경축. 국기)

발 신 : 주 미 대 사

제 목 : 침부물   (출처 : 외무부)

보	안	✓
동	제	

(0959 - 3 -1)

외신 1과	
동 제	

0060

FINAL VERSION

EAP Press Guidance
February 20, 1992

KOREA: NORTH-SOUTH TALKS

Q: Could you give us a read-out or assessment of the sixth
Prime Ministerial meeting between North and South Korea,
particularly their apparent failure to agree on a nuclear
inspection program?

A   AS WE HAVE NOTED PREVIOUSLY, WE WELCOME THE COMING

    INTO EFFECT OF THE TWO NORTH-SOUTH ACCORDS AND THE

    AGREEMENT BY THE TWO SIDES TO HOLD MEETINGS BEGINNING

    IN MARCH OF SUB-COMMITTEES TO IMPLEMENT THE

    "RECONCILIATION, NON-AGGRESSION, AND EXCHANGES" ACCORD.

    THE TWO SIDES HAVE ALSO AGREED TO MEET IN PANMUNJOM ON

    FEBRUARY 27 FOR DISCUSSIONS ON FORMING THE COMMITTEE

    WHICH WILL IMPLEMENT THE NON-NUCLEAR ACCORD.

    WE LOOK FOR NORTH KOREA'S FULL AND PROMPT

    IMPLEMENTATION OF THESE ACCORDS, PARTICULARLY ITS

    AGREEMENT TO EARLY INSPECTIONS OF DPRK NUCLEAR

    FACILITIES.

    JUST AS IMPORTANTLY, WE BELIEVE IT ESSENTIAL THAT

    NORTH KOREA MOVE QUICKLY TO FULFILL ITS PUBLIC

    PROMISES TO RATIFY AND IMPLEMENT ITS IAEA SAFEGUARDS

    AGREEMENT WITHOUT FURTHER DELAY.

0959-3-2   0061

- 2 -

Q: What is your response to press reports indicating that the North may insist on submitting its IAEA safeguards agreement to its Supreme National Assembly and that this may delay ratification for two more months?

A: WE HAVE SEEN A PRESS REPORT TO THAT EFFECT. WE NOTE,

HOWEVER, THAT IN JANUARY DPRK SPOKESMEN EXPRESSED

NORTH KOREA'S INTENTION TO RATIFY THE IAEA AGREEMENT

SOON AFTER SIGNATURE, WHICH TOOK PLACE LAST MONTH.

IN THE CASE OF ITS TWO RECENT AGREEMENTS WITH THE ROK,

THE NORTH COMPLETED RATIFICATION IN A FEW WEEKS. OUR

HOPE AND EXPECTATION REMAINS THAT THE NORTH WILL HOLD

TO THE COMMITMENTS IT HAS MADE.

0062

0959-3-3

공 란

공   란

공   란

공 란

공 란

공 란

공   란

공   란

공 란

공　　　란

공   란

공   란

공 란

공   란

공   란

공   란

공   란

공   란

공   란

북한 핵문제, 1992. 전13권 (V.2 2-3월) 217

공   란

공   란

공   란

공   란

공   란

공   란

공　　　란

외 무 부

관리
번호 92-109

증 별 :

번 호 : USW-0927   일 시 : 92 0225 1601

수 신 : 장 관 (해신,미일,문홍)

발 신 : 주 미 대사

제 목 : NYT 사설 대응

1. NYT 는 2.24. 북한의 핵문제 관련 'HOLD THE FIRE ON PYONGYANG'S NUKES' 제하 아래 요지의 사설을 게재함.

   - 한. 미 양국에는 북한이 지연 전술을 벌리고 있다는 경종이 울리고 있으나, 지금은 북한이 조만간 핵시설에 대한 사찰을 허용할 것이라는 기대를 갖고 냉정히 대처하는 것이 바람직함.

   - 지금은 '여유를 갖고 응수하는 것이 옳바른 대응책'('THE GENTLER GAMESTER IS THE SOONEST WINNER')임.

2. 위 관련 당관은 아래 요지의 LETTER TO THE EDITOR 를 작성, 2.24. 동사LEON SIGAL 논설위원 앞으로 송부함(동 기고문 별전 USW(F)-1053 송부함)

   - 북한이 IAEA 에 핵시설 사찰 대상 리스트를 제출했다는 귀지의 보도는 사실과 다른 것이며 우리는 현재 북한이 핵안전 협정을 조속 비준하고 IAEA 에 의한 최초 사찰에 앞서 북한이 사찰대상 시설 리스트를 제출하기를 기다리고 있는 중임. IAEA 는 과거의 경험에 비춰 북한이 성실하게 약속을 이행하지 않을 경우, 이 복잡한 사찰과정이 북한의 조작으로 더욱더 지연될수도 있음을 인식하고 있음.

   - 귀지는 한. 미 양국이 보다 인내심을 갖고 북한의 핵문제에 대응해 줄것을 권고하고 있으나, 핵문제에 관한한 시간은 결정적 요인(CRUCIAL FACTOR)이며 이미 얼마남지 않았음.

   - 북한은 이미 핵폭탄을 제조할수 있는 농축 핵원료를 생산할수 있는 단계에 까지와 있을 수도 있음. 관측통들은 북한이 광범위한 사찰이 시작되기 전에 핵폭탄 제조용 농축 원료를 생산한뒤 이를 은닉하기 위한 시간을 벌려하고 있다고 추정하고 있음.

   - IAEA 의 사찰민 한국이 제안한 남북한 상호 사찰은 더이상 지체되어야할 이유가

공보처 정와대	장관 안기부	차관	1차보	2차보	미주국	문협국	외정실	분석관

PAGE 1

없는 것임. 문제는 국제사회가 인내를 보이도록 할 것이 아니라 북한에 대해 자신의 약속을 신속히 이행토록 책임을 부과하는 것이 마땅함. 그간의 경험은 국제사회의 계속적 압력만이 북한으로 하여금 약속을 끝까지 이행하도록 납득시킬수 있을 것임을 보여 주고 있음.

3. 공보공사는 동 필자 LEON SIGAL 과 접촉, 동인이 범한 사실상의 오류에 대해 상기 요지로 설명하고 동 기고문의 게재를 요청했음. 끝.

(공보공사 - 해공관장)

예고: 92-6.30. 일반[   ]
의거 인반문서로 재분류[ ]

주 미 대 사 관

USW(F) : *1053*   년월일 : *920225*   시간 : *1604*

수 신 : 장   관(해신·미일·분홍)

발 신 : 주 미 대 사

제 목 : 첨부물   (출처 :   )

| | 보 안 통 제 | *시* |

1053 - 3 - 1 | 외신 1과 통 제 |

THE NEW YORK TIMES   *MONDAY, FEBRUARY 24, 1992*   A18

Hold the Fire on Pyongyang's Nukes

The Bush Administration's sound strategy of coaxing North Korea to give up its nuclear ambitions seems to be succeeding. Alarmist voices in Seoul and Washington claim that Pyongyang is just stalling. But they'd do better to keep cool for now in the expectation that North Korea will soon open its nuclear sites to inspection.

At the same time the Administration is right to register displeasure over Pyongyang's delivery of Scud missiles to Syria. While such sales violate no commitments by North Korea, they irresponsibly increase risks in the Middle East.

North Korea has now moved rapidly toward compliance with the Nuclear Nonproliferation Treaty. Last month it signed a safeguards accord with the International Atomic Energy Agency, which it says will be ratified "in the shortest possible time." It has submitted its list of facilities to be opened for inspection, including the reprocessing plant at Yongbyon. And its talks with Seoul on a Joint Nuclear Control Commission to conduct mutual inspections are moving ahead.

Yet sources in Seoul, opposed to accommodation with the North, are voicing suspicions. So are some in the U.S. intelligence community. And these voices are being amplified by chest-pounding Democrats eager to show how tough they can be on arms proliferators. If Pyongyang's progress should slow, tough measures could be justified. But for now, the gentler gamester is the soonest winner.

1053-3-2

0092

EMBASSY OF THE REPUBLIC OF KOREA

SHINIL PARK
MINISTER

2320 MASSACHUSETTS AVE. N.W.
WASHINGTON, D.C. 20008
(202) 939-5682, FAX (202) 387-4695

February 24, 1992

Dear Mr. Sigal:

Your February 24 editorial ("Hold the Fire on Pyongyang's Nukes") stated that North Korea has "submitted its list of [nuclear] facilities to be opened for [international] inspection." But, it has not. Now, we are waiting for the North first to officially ratify the International Atomic Energy Agency's safeguards agreement, and then to submit its list of proposed inspection sites in advance of actual IAEA inspections. The IAEA knows from experience that, unless the North is sincere in its commitment, this complex process could be manipulated by Pyongyang to stall for even more time.

You counsel Seoul and Washington to be patient. But, time is a crucial factor and may be running out. The North could well be on the verge of producing enriched, weapons-grade nuclear fuel. Some observers have speculated that North Korea is stalling in order to give itself time to produce and then conceal enough enriched fuel to build bombs before comprehensive inspections commence.

Regarding both IAEA scrutiny as well as mutual South-North inspections recently proposed by South Korea, Seoul sees no reason for further delay. The burden should not be placed upon the international community to be patient but rather upon the North to be expeditious in fulfilling its commitments. While you suggest that the "gentler gamester" will be the "soonest winner," Seoul's experience is that only constant pressure will convince the North to follow through on its pledges. And, in this high-stakes gamesmanship, we are fast approaching the final buzzer.

Sincerely,

Park Shinil

Mr. Leon Sigal
Editorial Board Member
The New York Times
229 West 43rd Street
New York, New York 10036

0093

10/3 - 3-3

외 무 부

종 별 :

번 호 : USW-0940   일   시 : 92 0225 1828

수 신 : 장관(미이,미일,정안,기정)

발 신 : 주미대사

제 목 : 국방부 브리핑

　　금 2.25 국방부 정례브리핑시 언급된 북한핵개발 관련 내용을 하기 보고함.(전문은별 전 USW-1073 편 송부함.)

　　(질문) GATES CIA 국장이 금일 하원외무위 청문회에서 북한의 핵개발이 빨리는 2개월정도 밖에 남지 않았으며, 이미 플로토니움 처리시설을 보유중에 있다고 증언하는 것에 대해 국방부도 동일한 의견을 갖고 있는지?

　　(답) - 북한 핵개발 시점(TIME FRAME)에 관한 GATES 국장의 언급은 그의 판단에 맡겨두고자함.

　　- 우리는 북한이 현재 핵무기 개발 능력을 보유하고 있다고 보지는 않으나, 계속해서 그들의 핵무기 개발 노력을 지대한 관심을 가지고 지켜보고 있음.

　　- 우리는 북한이 이미 서명한 협정에 따라 그들의 핵시설에 대한 국제사찰에 신속히 응해야 한다고 거듭 강조해 왔음.

　　- 최근 언론에 보도된 미정부관리의 사찰시한 (DEADLINE) 설정 운운은 근거없는것임. 미국은 북한에 대해 특정시한(A SPECIFIC DATE)을제시한 적이 없으며 다만그들이 신속히 국제사찰에 응할 것을 계속 강조하였음.

　　(질문) 주한 미군 2단계 감축 재개 여부가 북한의특정 행동에 따른 CONTINGENCY PLAN 인지 ?

　　(답) 우리는 북한 핵개발 계획의 위험과 불확실성이 완전 제거될 때 까지 주한 미군2단계 감축을 중단한 것임. 이는 북한의 특정행동(SPECIFIC ACTION)에 연계되는 것이아님.

　　(질문) 국제 핵사찰이 북한의 핵개발 계획을 밝혀낼 수 (REVEAL) 있다고 확신하고 있는지?

　　(답) CHENEY 장관도 언급한바 있듯이 걸프전교훈의 하나가 국제 핵사찰의

미주국   미주국   외정실   정와대   안기부

PAGE 1   92.02.26   09:06 FE 0094

　　　　　　　　　　　　　　　　　　　　　　　　　외신 1과 통제관

제한성임. 우리는 동 사찰이 북한 핵개발 계획의 전모 ENTIREEXTENT를 폭로(
DIVURGE) 할 것이라는 확신은갖고 있지 않음

　　(대사 현홍주-국장)

주 미 대 사 관

USW(F) : *1093*   년월일 : *92.2.25* 시간 : *18:28 PM*

수 신 : 장 관 (머이, 니인, 정안, 기2b)

발 신 : 주 미 대사

제 목 : 국방부 브리핑   (출처 : *FNS*)

┌──────────┐
│ 보   안 │
│ 통   제 │
└──────────┘

DEFENSE DEPARTMENT REGULAR BRIEFING   BRIEFER: PETE WILLIAMS
.12:02 P.M.. EST   TUESDAY, FEBRUARY 25, 1992

    Q   Gates is up on the Hill saying that North Korea could be
as little as two months away

from having a nuclear weapon and it already has a plutonium
processing facility. Is that a view shared by here, and what's
happened to collapse the time frame in which the North Koreans might
get a nuclear weapon?

    MR. WILLIAMS: I have not seen the -- whatever estimate the
Director has given the Congress. I would obviously defer to him
on his judgment of what the time frame is. We don't believe that
the North Koreans currently, right now today have the capacity to
produce a nuclear weapon, but we obviously are keeping a very close
eye on their efforts to, we believe, continue work in that
direction, which is of great concern to us.

    We have repeatedly said that North Korea should expeditiously
submit to international inspection of its nuclear facilities as it's
required to do under the very treaties that North Korea has already
signed. We welcome the work that North Korea has made with South
Korea. They, for example, together have both signed a mutual
declaration saying that the Peninsula should be nuclear free, and we
welcome that, but now North Korea has to complete this process by
submitting to international inspection as it's required to do.

    I would note some reports I've seen in the last day or so in
newspapers saying that some sort of deadline has been set by an
official of the US government. That is not the case. There has
been no formal deadline set. No date has been given to North Korea
by which it must submit to the inspections. But rather I would
simply say again that we have repeatedly said that North Korea
should submit to expeditious inspections. But Dave, I don't have
anything further to offer on whatever Mr. Gates' testimony is.

(*1093 - 3 - 1*)

┌──────────┐
│ 외신 1과 │
│ 통   제 │
└──────────┘

0096

Q   Well, have you defined what expeditious is?

MR. WILLIAMS: No, we've never put a deadline on it.

Q   So, June is just a bogus month?

MR. WILLIAMS: Well, it's a perfectly fine month in and of itself, but we've never conveyed that date to the North Koreans.

Q   Pete, Les Aspin --

MR. WILLIAMS: But I just want to be clear on this. We have never given them a specific date, but we have repeatedly said that they must expeditiously submit to international inspections. They well know their responsibilities under the protocols that they, themselves have signed. They have taken on this obligation voluntarily to submit to international inspections, but they have yet to do so, and they need to do it quickly.

Q   Well, is there any concern that if they are, in fact, only a couple of months away from having a bomb, that the inspections could be kind of moot?

MR. WILLIAMS: Well, they need to submit to the inspections as soon as possible. I don't know any other way to answer the question. Obviously, we're eager for them to do so quickly, but we have not given them any deadline.

Q   Is that what phase two of the withdrawal from Korea is -- South Korea is contingent upon?

MR. WILLIAMS: No. The contingence -- we have never linked the withdrawal for phase two under the Southeast Asia troop deployment plan to any specific action by the North Koreans. We have never said, for example - I would say again we have never said -- that if they do X, that if they submit to inspections, then we will go ahead with phase two of the drawdown. What we have said is that we are suspending the drawdown based on our assessment of the security environment on the Peninsula, and when we believe it is prudent to continue with it, we will. But we have never made it contingent on any specific action.

Q   Have you -- when you tell them they have to submit or they must submit expeditiously, have you -- what is the term of art? Do you say serious consequences or --

MR. WILLIAMS: I don't believe we've ever -- all we've done is point out to them their own obligation under the protocols that they've signed. I don't believe we've given them any kind of quid pro quo.

Q   And what's been their response?

MR. WILLIAMS: Well, they haven't submitted to inspections yet. They say they will, they say they're getting ready to do so, they keep putting sort of contingencies on it that they will do it if

1093 - 3 - 2

/ 0097

South Korea will take certain steps, or they will do it if the
United States will take certain steps. Of course, the protocols
that they signed aren't contingent upon anything. They have an
obligation to do so all entirely on their own, and they need to
submit to inspections.

Q   What's the incentive?

MR. WILLIAMS: They have signed up to do so automatically. You
might ask them why they signed it, but they're the ones who signed
it, and they need to do so.

Q   We're not --

MR. WILLIAMS: As a responsible nation, if you sign something
that says you will submit to inspections, you have to submit to
inspections, all by youself, without anybody holding something over
your head.

Q   But there have been things held over other nations' heads,
such as Iraq -- international sanctions, things of that sort.

MR. WILLIAMS: Well, that's a different matter. That's an
entirely different category. The point is that North Korea
voluntarily said they would do this, and they need to do it.

Q   New subject?

MR. WILLIAMS: Anything else on this one?

Okay. Yes, sir.

Q   How is your contingent plan in the East Asia, if North
Korea has definitely procured nuclear weapons in the --

MR. WILLIAMS: Well, the Department's long-standing practice is
that we never discuss contingency plans.

Q   One other question on that.

MR. WILLIAMS: Sure.

Q   Are you confident that international inspection would
reveal a nuclear weapons program if there were one?

MR. WILLIAMS: Ah, well, as the Secretary has said before, one
of the lesson we learned from the Persian Gulf War is that there is
a limit to how much you can learn under international inspections.

Q   So, you're not confident.

MR. WILLIAMS: So I don't believe we have complete confidence
that that would divulge the entire extent of their nuclear efforts.
And let me see; as I look at -- here in my notes, David, I see the
specific term that we used in announcing the second phase. We said
they'd been postponed until the dangers and uncertainties of the
North Korean nuclear program have been thoroughly addressed, but
it's not tied to any specific action by them.

1093-3-3

0098

234 북한 핵 문제 총괄 1

북리 2과강

外務部 情報狀況室
受信日時 92. 2. 26. 09:00

美CIA 국장, 수개월내 北韓 核무기 개발 가능성 議会 증언

CIA CHIEF SAYS NORTH KOREA NEAR WEAPON
(Eds: edits, adds details, Pentagon comments)
By Jim Adams
WASHINGTON, Feb 25, Reuter - U.S. Central Intelligence
Agency Director Robert Gates said on Tuesday that North Korea
could have a nuclear weapon as soon as a few months under its
present programme.
Gates told the House of Representatives Foreign Affairs
Committee that North Korea is nearing completion of two
facilities for producing plutonium but said additional steps
would be needed to produce nuclear weapons.
"We think a few months to as much as a couple of years --
to have a nuclear weapon," Gates replied when asked how long
that would take.
Gates said the CIA has information suggesting that North
Korea has a deception plan for hiding its nuclear efforts.
But a senior North Korean official said in Vienna that his
country expects to ratify a nuclear safeguards agreement in
April and will probably open its secret nuclear sites to
international inspectors by June.
Foreign Ministry official O Chang Rim said he expected his
country's Supreme Assembly would approve at its next meeting
in April the agreement Pyongyang signed last month at the
International Atomic Energy Agency (IAEA).
"If it's ratified by April, the inspections will most
probably take place at the begining of June," O told a news
conference at the IAEA headquarters in Vienna.
Gates said one reactor at Yongbyon has been operating for
four years and its sole purpose appears to be to make
plutonium. He said a second, larger reactor may start up this
year to make plutonium.
Gates said another facility there is nearly completed that
can reprocess reactor fuel to recover the plutonium.
The CIA director also told the committee, "North Korea
constitutes one of the world's major proliferation threats."
At the Defence Department, spokesman Pete Williams said
that even international inspections in North Korea may not
tell the whole nuclear story.
"One of the lessons we learned from the ... Gulf War is
that there is a limit to how much you can learn under
international inspections," Williams told reporters. "I don't
believe we have complete confidence that that would divulge
the entire extent of (North Korea's) nuclear efforts."
On other regions, Gates said the CIA believed Iraqi
President Saddam Hussein would have had a nuclear weapon by
now if the Gulf War had not stopped him, and would have been
inclined to use it.
"We believe that he would have had a workable nuclear
device this year," Gates said. Asked if Saddam would have used
it, Gates said, "I think so. Given the attitude and approach
that he took over the past year and a half, I think that's a
distinct possibility."
REUTER JX RRO LD
Reut20:50 25-02

0099

主要外信隨時報告

美국방부, 북한 핵사찰 6월시한 통보설부인

소식통, 6월 IAEA회의 對北조치 경고

外務部 情報狀況室
受信日時 92. 2 .26. 09:00

(워싱턴=聯合) 박정찬특파원=美국방부는 25일 미국이 북한의 핵사찰 시기와 관련 시한을 정한바 없으며 이를 북한에 통보한 적도 없다고 밝혔다.

국방부의 피트 윌리엄스 대변인은 이날 정례 브리핑에서 "미국정부가 어떤 종류의 시한을 정했다는 보도를 봤다"고 말하고 "이는 사실이 아니다"고 해명했다.

그는 "공식 시한이 정해진 바가 없으며 사찰을 언제까지 받아야 한다는 날짜를 북한에 제시한 적이 없다"고 말하고 "그러나 우리가 북한에 대해 조속히 사찰을 받을것을 되풀이 촉구해 왔다는 것을 말하고 싶다"고 설명했다.

그는 또 "6월이 그 자체로는 매우 좋은 달이지만 우리가 북한에 그같은 시기를 전달한 적이 없다"고 말했다.

한편 워싱턴의 한 고위 소식통은 "오는 2월 27일의 판문점 접촉 결과를 한미 양국이 매우 주의깊게 주시하고 있다"고 말하고 이 접촉에서 북한측의 긍정적인 반응이 없을 경우 "북한의 핵개발 의도에 대한 미국의 의심이 깊어질 것"이라고 강조했다.

익명을 요구한 이 소식통은 "6월이라는 시점이 나오고 있는 것은 국제원자력기구의 이사회 시점과 결부돼 있는 것으로 본다"고 말하고 "그전에 북한이 사찰을 받지 않을 경우 한반도 핵문제는 국제적인 무대로 옮겨질 것"이라고 말해 북한이 사찰에 응하지 않을 경우 6월 국제원자력기구 이사회를 계기로 對북한 조치가 제기될것임을 시사했다.

이 소식통은 "최근 영변 핵시설 주변에서 작업이 계속되고 있는 상황이 美정보기관에 의해 포착됐다"고 전하고 "만일 북한이 지금처럼 부정적인 태도를 계속 취한다면 불행히도 유엔에서 한반도 핵문제가 논의될 상황이 벌어질 것"이라고 덧붙였다.(끝)

(YONHAP) 920226 0827 KST

0100

공   란

공   란

정. 특. 2.

長 官 報 告 事 項

報告畢

1992. 2. 26.
外交安保研究院
企劃調査課(92-06)

題目 : 시거 博士와 金英鎭 敎授 초청 세미나 開催 結果 報告

당 연구원에서는 2. 25(화) 前 美국무부 東亞·太 차관보 개스턴 시거 박사
와 조지 워싱턴大 金英鎭 敎授를 초청, "北韓의 核問題와 南北高位級會談
관련 韓半島 情勢"에 관하여 세미나를 개최하였는 바, 同 要旨를 아래와
같이 보고합니다.

1. 시거 博士

가. 蘇聯·東歐를 비롯한 공산체제의 붕괴에 따라 세계는 정치·경제적인
    평화와 안정 그리고 민주화를 중심으로 하는 새로운 世界秩序 형성을
    위한 歷史的인 變革期를 맞고 있슴. 러시아의 옐친, 중국의 鄧小平
    등의 지도자들도 이러한 추세에 부응, 經濟改革과 더불어 민주화의
    필요성을 절감하고 있슴.

나. 美國의 대내외 정책도 새로운 방향을 모색해야 할 단계에 이르렀슴.
    왜냐하면 제2차 세계대전 이래 엄청난 비용을 투입해 온 미국의 외교

// 계   속 //

안보정책 분야에 대한 예산지출이 더이상 美議會에서 정당화되기
어렵게 되었을 뿐만 아니라, 美國政府도 이제 국민복지를 비롯한 국내
경제적 측면에 더욱 관심을 기울여야 할 입장에 처해 있기 때문임.

다. 이러한 국제적 환경 변화속에서 韓半島 또한 종래와는 다른 독특한
상황을 맞고 있습. 한국의 정치적 발전과 경제적 성공은 미국을
비롯한 서방의 각국으로부터 찬사를 받고 있는 바, 현재 경제적 침체
로 體制的 危機에 봉착해 있는 북한과의 교섭에 있어서 前向的 姿勢를
취할만큼 강력한 입지를 구축하였습. 이와 함께 1991년 南北韓 유엔
同時加入은 분단이래 수십년간 지속되어온 韓半島의 緊張緩和에 크게
기여할 것으로 평가되고 있습.

2. 金英鎭 敎授

한편 김영진 박사는 최근 미국내 언론과 전문가들의 견해를 바탕으로
남북한 관계에 대한 미국측 시각에 대하여 다음과 같이 언급함.

가. 미국의 전문가들간에는 東北亞 地域 뿐만 아니라 세계적으로도 중대한
문제로 등장하고 있는 북한의 核開發 問題에 대한 한국정부의 태도에
대하여 우려하는 의견이 지배적임. 韓·美 관계는 미국의 對亞·太
外交政策의 핵심요소로 간주되고 있는 바, 북한의 핵개발 문제는 사안
의 중요성을 고려할 때 양국의 협의를 통한 공동대처가 바람직할 것임.

나. 최근 IAEA 문제에 관련한 미국의 對北韓 政策은 종래의 소극적 접촉의
원칙에서 적극적인 자세로 변화의 양상을 보이고 있는 바, 이는 남북
한간의 급속한 관계진전과 관련되는 것임. 즉 한국정부는 그동안 美·
北韓간의 대화를 반대해 왔고 미국정부는 이를 존중하여 그동안 소극적
인 對北韓 접근 원칙을 견지해 왔으나, 1991년 말 한국정부의 과감한
對北韓 政策으로 한국정부는 더이상 미국과 북한간의 직접대화 움직임
에 반대할 근거를 상실했다고 할 수 있습.

0104

2

다. 따라서 미국의 직접적인 對北韓 접촉 시도에는 한국정부의 對북한 정책에 대한 불만이 하나의 요소로 작용했다고도 볼 수 있음. 즉 對북한 접촉과 관련 미국정부는 남한의 입장만을 고려하기보다는 자국의 입장을 분명히 표명하는 것이 미국의 國家利益에 부합하는 것이라고 생각하게 되었으며, 최근의 美·北韓間 고위급 접촉이 이러한 한국의 정책에 대한 지렛대(leverage)로 작용할 것이라고 인식했을 가능성이 있다고 미국 전문가들은 지적하고 있음.

라. 「南北合意書」, 「非核化宣言」이 결정되어 가는 과정에서 남한정부가 보여준 태도는 미국측이 가장 중요한 문제라고 생각하는 북한의 핵개발 문제를 다소 경시하면서 북한에 접근을 시도했다는 인상을 주었음. 미국의 전문가들은 북한이 금년 1. 30 서명한 IAEA 핵안전협정이 3~4월경 북한 최고인민회의에서 비준되고 이후 상당한 시간이 지나 핵사찰이 이루어진다고 하더라도, 북한의 핵개발 저지를 위한 그 실효성에 대하여 상당한 懷疑를 가지고 있음.

마. 즉 1991년 말 아무런 실천조치나 조건이 고려되지 않고 불가침선언에 조인하는 등 남한의 성급한 대북한 정책은 궁지에 빠진 북한으로 하여금 핵무장을 하도록 시간을 주고 입지를 강화시켜주는 역할을 했다고 하는 것이 미국 전문가들의 다수 의견임. 이러한 맥락에서 미국 전문가들은 한국의 對北韓 政策이 북한의 핵개발 문제 해결에 기여하는 방향으로 韓·美간에 충분한 협의를 통해 추진되어야 한다고 지적하고 있음. 끝.

3

0105

외 무 부

종 별 : 지 급

번 호 : USW-0961   일 시 : 92 0226 1848

수 신 : 장 관(미이,미일,정특,국기,기정)

발 신 : 주 미대사

제 목 : 북한 핵 문제

1. 북한 핵 문제와 관련, 국무부는 하기와 같은 PRESS GUIDANCE 를 발표하였음.

가. 문: 북한 핵기발 저지를 위한 다음 단계 조치는 무엇인지 ?

답: O 북한이 국제적 우려를 해소(ADDRESS) 할수있는 유일한 방법은 안전 협정을신속히(PROMPTLY) 를 비준하고, 비핵 공동선언에 따라 남.북한간에 신뢰할수 있는 상호사찰을 실시하는것임.

O 북한이 핵 안전 협정을 충실히 이행하지 않을 경우에는 IAEA는 이를 유엔 안보리에 제기(REFER)할수 있는 권한(EMPOWERED) 을 갖고 있음. 북한이 그 의무를충실히 이행하여 이러한 조치를 취하지 않을수 있기를 기대함.

나. 문: 북한에 대해 제재 조치나 무력을사용할 계획은 없는지 ?

답: 우리는 외교적 노력을 강조하고자 함.

다. 문: IAEA 가 북한 핵 시설 사찰을 곧 실시할수 있을것으로 보는지 ?

답: O 북한은 어제 IAEA 이사회에서 4월 비준, 6월 사찰 계획을 밝힌바 있음.

O 2.25 이사회에서 KENNEDY 대사는 북한이 가능한 조속한 시일내에(AS SOON AS POSSIBLE) 협정을 비준, 시행할것과, BLIX 총장의 권고에 따라 협정비준 이전이라도IAEA 에 필요한 정보를 제공할것을 강력히 요구(URGE) 한바, 이를 다시한번 강조(SECOND) 하고자 함.

2. 상기 내용 전문은 FAX(USW(F)-1083) 송부함.

(대사 현홍주-국장)

미주국	1차보	미주국	국기국	외정실	분석관	청와대	안기부

주 미 대 사 관

USW(F) : *1083*   년월일 : 92. 2. 26   시간 : *18:48*

수 신 : 장 관 (미, 미안, 구아주, 제1, 기안)

발 신 : 주 미 대 사

제 목 : USW-0961의 청부물

보 안 통 제	

(출처 :   )

(1083 - 3 - 1)

외신 1과 통 제	

0107

EAP PRESS GUIDANCE
February 26, 1992

NORTH KOREA'S NUCLEAR PROGRAM

Q: Given what CIA Director Gates said yesterday, what will be
    our next step in countering North Korea's nuclear program?
    Will the U.S. go to the UN? Impose sanctions? Use
    military force?

    -- AS WE HAVE SAID REPEATEDLY, NORTH KOREA CAN ONLY

        ADDRESS INTERNATIONAL CONCERN ABOUT ITS NUCLEAR PROGRAM

        BY PROMPTLY RATIFYING ITS IAEA SAFEGUARDS AGREEMENT,

        ACCEPTING INSPECTIONS OF ALL ITS NUCLEAR FACILITIES

        UNDER THAT AGREEMENT, AND BY NEGOTIATING AND

        IMPLEMENTING WITH THE ROK A CREDIBLE BILATERAL

        INSPECTION REGIME UNDER THE JOINT DECLARATION ON A

        NON-NUCLEAR KOREA.

    -- (IF PRESSED) IF NORTH KOREA FAILS TO ACCEPT ITS

        OBLIGATIONS UNDER THE NPT TO FULLY IMPLEMENT A

        SAFEGUARDS AGREEMENT, THEN THE IAEA IS EMPOWERED TO

        REFER THE CASE TO THE UN SECURITY COUNCIL. WE HOPE

        NORTH KOREA WILL FULLY MEET ITS OBLIGATIONS IN WHICH CASE

        THIS STEP WILL BE UNNECESSARY.

    Q: Do you plan to impose sanctions or use military force?
    A: -- WE ARE EMPHASIZING DIPLOMATIC EFFORTS.

                    1083-3-2

                                            0108

Press Guidance
February 26, 1992

North Korea and IAEA Inspections

Q: Are we confident that the IAEA will be able to conduct inspections of North Korean nuclear facilities soon?

A: -- NORTH KOREA, YESTERDAY, INFORMED THE IAEA BOARD OF

   GOVERNORS THAT IT WOULD PLACE THE FULLSCOPE SAFEGUARDS

   AGREEMENT, WHICH IT SIGNED JANUARY 30, BEFORE ITS SUPREME

   PEOPLE'S CONGRESS FOR RATIFICATION IN APRIL, AND THE

   NORTH KOREAN REPRESENTATIVE IN VIENNA SAID THAT

   INSPECTIONS COULD BEGIN IN EARLY JUNE. YESTERDAY,

   FEBRUARY 25, AT THE IAEA'S BOARD OF GOVERNORS MEETING,

   AMBASSADOR KENNEDY URGED NORTH KOREA TO RATIFY AND

   IMPLEMENT THE AGREEMENT AS SOON AS POSSIBLE, AND TO

   ACCEPT DIRECTOR GENERAL BLIX'S INVITATION TO PROVIDE

   NECESSARY INFORMATION TO THE IAEA EVEN BEFORE THE

   AGREEMENT IS RATIFIED, AND WE STRONGLY SECOND THESE

   COMMENTS.

1083-3-3

0109

STATE DEPARTMENT REGULAR BRIEFING   BRIEFER: RICHARD BOUCHER
1:19 P.M. EST   THURSDAY, FEBRUARY 27, 1992

    Q   Do you think that the present international intelligence
information, like CIA Director Gates' allegation that North Korea
has some hidden facilities, that can be -- (inaudible) -- to have
that kind of challenging inspection treaty in North Korean
facilities?

    MR. BOUCHER: The North Koreans have signed but not yet
ratified.

    Q   It's ratified.

    MR. BOUCHER: -- (inaudible, cross talk) --safeguards agreement
that is similar to that signed by the other non-nuclear weapons
states that are party to the NPT. Under this agreement, like all
other NPT parties it would be subject to the special inspection
regime.

(1127 - 1 - 1)   외신 1괴
                                통   제

                                                        O

0110

종 별 :

번 호 : USW-0993

일 시 : 92 0227 1925

수 신 : 장관(<u>미일</u>,미이,중동일,정총)

발 신 : 주 미 대사

제 목 : 북한 핵관련 HERITAGE 재단 관계자 발언

연;USW-0827

연호 한. 미 우호 협회의 대표단을 위한 HERITAGE 재단 주최 오찬 간담회시북한 핵무기 문제가 주요 거론되었는바, 동 재단 관계자 주요 발언 내용을 아래 보고함(당관 박인국 서기관 참석)

1. SETH CROPSEY, HERITAGE 재단 ASIAN STUDIES CENTER 소장

0 북한에 대한 미국의 제재 전망에 대한 해답을 얻기 위해서는 유사한 상황에서의 미국의 정책 결정 형태를 연구해볼 필요가 있느나, 파나마와 이락이 좋은예가 된다고 봄.

0 미국의 파나마와 이락 개입은 각각 1 개월과 1 년간에 걸쳐 여러 차례의 과정을 통해 결국은 군사력 행사로 외교적 목적을 달성 하였음. 결국 북한에 대한 규제도 이범주를 크게 벗어나지 않을것으로 보이며, 북한 입장에 근본적인 변화가 없다고 판단될때는 일정 단계를 거쳐 군사력 개입의 형태를 띄게 될것으로 생각함.

2. DARYL PLUNK 연구원

0 대북한 핵 규제 문제는 가벼운 경고 단계는 이미 넘어선것이 확실하며 미국은 동 문제를 곧 유엔으로 옮겨 미국의 문제가 아닌 세계의 문제로 발전시켜 범세계적인 비난과 규제를 시도할것으로 보임.

3. RICHARD FISHER 연구원

0 북한의 핵무기 개발 시점에 관해서는 수개월에서 부터 수개년까지 논쟁이분분하나 이제 북한 핵무기 개발 저지를 위해서는 시간이 얼마남지 않았다는 사실에는 의견의 일치를 보고 있음.

0 SOLARZ 의원은 대표적인 비관론자인데 북한의 어떤 조치에 대해서도 불신하는 입장으로 당장 내일이라도 구체적인 규제를 실행에 옮겨야 한다는 주장임.

미주국	장관	차관	1차보	2차보	미주국	중아국	외정실	분석관
정와대	안기부							

PAGE 1

92.02.28 10:03 0111

외신 2과 통제관 BX

O SOLARZ 의원이 강경론을 띄고 있는것은 북한이 중동 제국에 대한 주요 미사일등 핵관련 시설 공급원이 되고 있어 이스라엘의 안보에 직접적인 위협을 가하고 있다고 판단한 때문인것으로 관측됨.

4. 상기 대표단은 금일 GERALD SOLOMON(공화, 뉴욕) 하원의원및 BENJAMIN GILMAN(공화, 뉴욕)하 원 의원과도 면담하고 양국 민간 레벨의 우호 증진 방안에관해 협의하였음.

(대사 현홍주-국장)

92.12.31 까지

외   무   부

종   별 : -

번   호 : CGW-0160   일   시 : 92 0228 1700

수   신 : 장 관(해신,미일,문일)

발   신 : 주 시카고총영사(공)

제   목 : 사설게재 보고

　1. CHICAGO TRIBUNE 은 2.28 'A NEW ALARM ON N. KOREA'SNUKES' 제하 사설을 게재함.(FAX 송부)

　2. 동 사설은 북한이 핵확산 방지 조약에 조인하고 남북한간 불가침 및 핵무기 금지에 합의 했으면서도 실제 사찰을 수용하지 않는것은 지연전술을 통해 자신들의 사악한 계획을 추진시키려는 강한 의심을 불러 일으킨다고 지적함. 또한 북한이 핵관련 활동을 숨기려는 의도를 갖고 있다는 게이트 미국 CIA 국장의 미하원 내발언과 함께 한국은 3월말까지 핵사찰 일정을 밝히지 않을 경우 대우그룹의 대북투자를 연기하기로 했다고 소개함. 동 사설은 김일성이 핵개발을 포기하지 않을 경우, 온세계가 그를 저지시킬 책무가 있다고 주장함.

　3. 필자 STEPHEN CHAPMAN 논설위원은 당관측과 협의, 6공 4주년, 남북대화 전망및 북한 핵문제를 적절히 연계한 사설 혹은 논설게재를 추진해 왔으나 여건상 핵문제에 중점을 두게 되었음을 양지해 달라고 2.26 당관측에 알려 왔음을 참고바람.끝

　　(총영사 김정기-부장)

공보처　　미주국　　문협국

PAGE 1   92.02.29   08:29 WH
                                                   외신 1과 롱제관   0113

CGW(F)-5   20228 1700
장란(해선, 미안, 문안)
CGW-0160 의 첨부 (총 1매)

A new alarm on North Korea's nukes

Saddam Hussein's plan to become a nuclear power is now in ruins, but the day is steadily approaching when the United States and its allies will face the question whether to let nuclear weapons come into the hands of another bellicose dictator: Kim Il Sung, ruler of North Korea.

The United States and South Korea have tried to coax the North into abandoning this ambition by agreeing to a withdrawal of all American nuclear weapons from the South. So far, though, there are more reasons for doubt than for hope.

The Bush administration has been raising concerns about North Korea's activities for several months. The testimony given Tuesday by CIA director Robert Gates ought to impress the world and the American people that the danger is not just serious but urgent.

In the past, it was believed that Pyongyang was at least a year away from being able to make a nuclear weapon. But Gates said that North Korea might become a nuclear power within a few months.

Some observers have been encouraged by Pyongyang's willingness to sign the Nuclear Non-Proliferation Treaty, which would oblige it to allow international monitors to inspect its nuclear facilities. They have also taken comfort in the treaty signed by the two Koreas in January disavowing aggression and nuclear weapons.

But the North-South treaty is largely a symbolic gesture, and Kim Il Sung's regime has repeatedly stalled on actually admitting inspectors, raising strong suspicions that it is merely stalling for the time it needs to carry out its sinister plans.

Gates shares those suspicions. He told a House committee that North Korea is concealing its nuclear activities, despite its promises, and questioned the sincerity of a government that "has not yet even admitted the existence of, much less declared, the plutonium production reactors and a reprocessing facility."

He said the usual international monitoring, which involves inspections of admitted facilities, is probably not enough in the case of North Korea; inspectors need the right to investigate any facility they choose.

The State Department says the United States isn't prepared yet to recommend international sanctions against North Korea, much less consider military action. South Korea, however, has suspended the plans of its Daewoo corporation to invest in the North unless Pyongyang schedules nuclear inspections by the end of March.

It should be increasingly obvious that there are few greater dangers to world peace than this one. If Kim Il Sung isn't willing to stop his march toward nuclear weapons, the world will have a duty, sooner or later, to stop him.

Chicago Tribune
92. 2. 28. p 1-20
(사설)

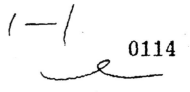

0114

공   란

외 무 부

종 별 :

번 호 : LAW-0254   일 시 : 92 0228 1540

수 신 : 장 관(미일,정북,정보,해신,해기)

발 신 : 주 라성 총영사

제 목 : 북한핵사찰 촉구관련 LA TIMES 사설 보도

　　금 2.28.LA TIMES 지는 사설난에 '북한의 핵개발 너무 가까이 다가와' 제하 아래요지 보도함

　　- 아 래 -

　　0 북한이 핵무기를 개발하는데 수개월 내지 길어야 2년 정도 걸릴것이라고한 게이츠 CIA 국장의하원 청문회 발언은 북서태평양 세력균형이 심각하게 붕괴될 수 있는 시기가 빠르게 닥아오고 있음을 시사하고 있음

　　0 빈약한 부존자원속에서 절대적인 통제력을 행사하는 김일성 정권은 북한을 몇안되는 핵보유국에 가까이 접근시켜 놓았음

　　0 북한은 4월에 핵안정협정을 비준할 것이라고 밝히고 있으나, 남북한 핵사찰 협상에서는 장애조건만 제시하고 있음

　　0 게이츠 국장은 북한이 경찰위성이나 현지사찰단이 탐지할 수 없도록 많은 시설을 지하로 숨기는 작업을 열심히 진행하고 있다고 말함

　　0 게이츠는 더욱 소름끼치는 가능성을 제기하고 있는바, 외화가 부족한 북한이 리비아와 같은 나라에 핵관련 기술, 심지어는 무기까지 판매할수도 있을 것이라함

　　0 북한의 핵개발 위협은 지역적일 뿐 아니라전 세계적인 위협도 함축하고 있으므로 간주되므로, 모든 핵시설에 대한 완전한 국제 사찰에의 개방을 위해 북한에게 계속적인 압력을 가하는것이 시급함

　　0 미국이 앞장서서 폭로하고 있는 북한의 핵위험은 전세계에 대한 위험이므로 미국은 우방국들에게 이러한 노력에 대한 도움을 요청할 필요조차 없을 정도임.끝

　　(총영사 박종상-국장)

미주국	1차보	외정실	외정실	분석관	정와대	안기부	공보처	공보처	외연회

PAGE 1   92.02.29   10:15 WG

　　　　　　　　　　　　　　　　　　　　　　　　외신 1과 통제관

252 북한 핵 문제 총괄 1

공   란

공　　　　　　란

외 무 부

종 별 : -

번 호 : UNW-0585   일 시 : 92 0302 1800

수 신 : 장 관(국기, 연일, <u>미의,</u> 기정) 사본:유종하 대사

발 신 : 주 유엔 대사대리

제 목 : 북한핵관련기사

   북한 핵관련 금 3.2.(월)자 NYT 지 사설을 별첨 FAX 송부함

   (대사대리 신기복-국장)

    첨부: UNW(F)-0212

국기국   미주국   ∵∵ | 국기국   안기부   차관실

UNW(주)-0 지/지   20-302 1800
(국제, 연일, 이이, 기제)

92. 3. 2. (月)   NYT 사설

Fearing North Korea Too Fast

Is North Korea rushing to develop nuclear arms while deceitfully fending off international inspection with promises? That suspicion gained a little altitude last week after testimony by Robert Gates, the Director of Central Intelligence. It was possible to infer that the North Koreans are within a couple of months of nuclear pay dirt.

But that's not what Mr. Gates said and that's not what the intelligence community judges to be the fact. Even if North Korea bargains hard in the talks with South Korea to resume tomorrow, it is nowhere near building The Bomb.

Scaremongers failed to convince the intelligence community that North Korea was about to get a nuclear device. In his carefully cleared statement, Mr. Gates said, "Even after North Korea accumulates enough plutonium, making a device would require several additional steps that could require months or even years." It won't begin amassing that plutonium unless a reprocessing plant at Yongbyon starts operating.

That means there's plenty of time to gauge whether Pyongyang intends to live up to its obligations. It knows what it has to do: ratify the nuclear safeguards accord it signed with the International Atomic Energy Agency and open all suspect sites to intrusive inspection. And it could allay suspicion by advancing the date for ratification to late March and expediting the start of inspection.

Some intelligence analysts, having underestimated Iraq's nuclear program, may be particularly edgy about North Korea. But Pyongyang has been keeping its promises to Washington. If it is proceeding on course, premature pressure could backfire. If it is not, there will be plenty of time for Washington to prepare the way for stern international sanctions.

UNW-0585 전달

2/2 -1-1

0120

UNW (ㅎ)-2/2

의 추가분

The Washington Post

AN INDEPENDENT NEWSPAPER

North Korea's Run for a Bomb ...

THE AMERICAN government has now gone public with its concern over secret nuclear-bomb development in Communist North Korea. The chief of intelligence discloses indications of a nuclear "deception plan" and suggests a bomb could be as close as a "few months" away. North Korea is a completely closed society with a notoriously treacherous government—and a legendary tunnel-digging capacity. Its recent diplomacy of smile and maneuver has encouraged the hope, especially in South Korea, that it was exchanging its go-it-alone nuclear ambitions for broader security guarantees that would integrate it in its region. But its diplomacy is also consistent with a policy of nuclear concealment. Particularly disturbing is its evasion of the prompt and full international inspection that would ease, though it would not end, anxieties about its nuclear intentions.

What this means is that a major crisis is building in east Asia precisely at a moment when most people elsewhere are still relaxing in the glow of the end of the Cold War. For even the strong suspicion of North Korean accession to nuclear status would be taken as menacing not simply by South Korea but also by nearby Japan, China and Russia and by remote America as well. That North Korea might be able to sneak-build a nuclear force over the active objections of all of them would be a stunning blow to regional stability. It would give Kim Il Sung or a successor dangerous new options of nuclear diplomacy and nuclear threat, not to speak of commercial sale. For the first time, American troops protecting South Korea would be under a direct nuclear gun.

North Korea has no security justification for a bomb. The United States squeezed South Korea out of its nuclear program years ago. More recently, in a so-far unreciprocated gesture of strategic respect for North Korea, Washington withdrew its own nuclear weapons from the peninsula. The North's reach for a bomb, while pretending to reach for regional accommodation, could only be regarded as intimidating and hostile.

Perhaps the North's nuclear works can still be brought under effective inspection—although whether intelligence is good enough to make inspection foolproof is a question. Otherwise, it becomes necessary for the countries that deal with North Korea to isolate it with tough Security Council sanctions. A new collective guarantee of South Korea would be in order. So would a collaborative military option, although again much depends on the intelligence. Every nation everywhere has a powerful interest in halting a rogue regime's run to nuclear daylight.

0121

외 무 부

종 별 :

번 호 : SFW-0193

일 시 : 92 0302 1600

수 신 : 장관(해신, <u>미북</u>, 문홍)

발 신 : 주 상항 총영사

제 목 : 북한핵사찰 수락촉구사설

1. 3.2 자 당지 S.F. 크로니클은 북한이 남북한의 한반도 비핵화 합의사항 이행을 기피, 방해하고 있다고 지적하면서 북한은 지상 및 지하의 모든 핵시설에대해 즉각적이고도 철저한 국제 핵사찰을 받아야 한다고 요지 사설을 게재함

2. 동지 THOMAS BENET 주필, MICHAEL BIGELOW 외신부장과 접촉, 6 차 고위급회담결과 관련 자료등 제공하고 북한 핵사찰 수락의 필요성에 관한 논설게재를 협의한바 있음

3. 동사설 FAX 송부함

(공보관)

예고;92.6.30 까지

공보처   장관   차관   1차보   2차보   미주국   문협국   외정실   분석관
청와대   안기부

PAGE 1

92.03.03   10:20 0122

외신 2과   통제관 BX

258   북한 핵 문제 총괄 1

공 란

공 란

공   란

공   란

공   란

공   란

공 란

외 무 부

종 별 :

번 호 : USW-1131   일   시 : 92 0305 1935

수 신 : 장 관(미이,미일,동구일,정안,정북)사본: 주미대사

발 신 : 주 미 대사대리

제 목 : 북한 핵문제등 관련 워포비츠 국방 차관 발언

　　　월포 비츠 국방 차관은 금 3.5 SIPE DEFENSE WRITERSGROUP 주관 간담회에 초청 연사로 참석, 북한 핵문제 및 구 소연방 문제등에 관한 질의에 답변한바, 주요 발언 요지 아래 보고함.

　1.북한 핵문제

　(북한의 핵 개발 진척사항을 질의한데 대해)

　　0 정확한 평가를 내리기는 어려우나 북한이 핵개발계획에 많은 진척을 이루고 있으며 핵 개발에 매우 근접해 (MUCH TOO CLOSE) 있다고 봄.

　　0 북한이 잘못된길을 가고 있음을 설득하고 핵무기 계획을 포기토록할 유인들은 많음. 예를들어 핵 개발을 포기치 않을 경우 북한은 일본등을 비롯 비중 있는 나라들과의 관계 정상화를 기대할수 없을것임.

　(북한의 핵 개발 포기 의사 여부)

　　0 북한은 희망적인 말들을 해왔으나 막상 이행하고 확인하는 절차에 있어서는 계속 지연 전술을 펴고 있으며, 북한이 핵 개발 계획을 전환했다는 아무런 징후도 찾아 볼수 없음.

　(북한이 핵 개발을 하고 있다는 구체적 증거가있느냐는 질의에 대해)

　　0 북한이 원자력 발전과 거의 관계가 없는 핵계획을 가지고 있는 플루토늄 추출외에는 별용도가 없는 재처리 시설을 보유하려는 것이 그증거임.

　　0 북한은 핵무기를 독자적으로 개발할 능력이 있는 것으로 추정됨.

　(북한에 대한 군사적 해결 방안 검토 여부)

　　0 미국은 정치적인 해결을 원하며, 지금은 군사적 대안을 논의할때가 아님.

　(북한의 핵무기 보유시 일본에 미칠 영향)

　　0 북한의 핵무기 보유는 일본에게 불안을 조성하게 될것이나, 일본이 이에

미주국　1차보　미주국　미주국　구주국　외정실　외정실　분석관　청와대
안기부

대응하여 핵무기 개발등 재무장을 추진할지 여부는 미국의 방위 역할에대한 일본의 관점에 좌우될것임. 그러나 일본이 중국및 러시아의 위협 뿐만 아니라 5류 국가인 북한의 위협에 대해서까지 미국의 방위에 의존해야하느냐 하는 의문에 봉착하게 될것임.

0 북한의 핵무기 보유는 북한이 이를 사용치않는다 하더라도 위험한 것이나, 랑군사태, 칼 폭파사건등의 예에 비추어 볼때 북한이 핵 무기를 사용치 않을것이라는 가설은 타당치 않음.

2.구 소연방 문제

가. CIS 에 대한 평가

0 최근 러시아및 우크라이나를 방문 SHAPOSHNIKOV원수 및 GRACHEV CIS 통합군 부사령관과의 면담시, 이들은 CIS 체제가 적어도 과도적인 중요 문제들을 처리해 나가는데 매우 중요하며 이러한 과도적 문제들이 단시일내에 해결되지는 않을 것으로 생각하고 있었음. 이러한 과도적 문제의 해결이후에도 CIS 의 존속이 계속 필요한지에 대해서는 CIS 공화국내에서도 의견이 갈리고 있음.

0 CIS 체제는 구소련의 엄청난 부담으로 부터 벗어남으로서 공화국간의 갈등 , 특히 러시아, 우크라이나간의 문제 해결을 용이하게 하는 한편 나아가서 구소련의 원만한 해체를 도모할수 있는 매우기발한 발상 이었음.

나. 대러시아 관계

0 러샤아의 당면 과제는 민주제도와 시장 경제의 정착이며, 특히 경제 문제의 해결이 급선무임.러시아가 민주 제도를 정착해 나가는데는 아직 많은 세월이 소요될 것이나, 그간 거의 폭력이 없는 가운데 놀라운 개혁을 이루었으며, 동 개혁의 성공시 가장 평화적인 혁명으로 역사에 기록될것임.

0 러시아에 대한 기술 유출 통제와 관련 민간경제 개발에 필요한 기술에 대한 통제는 거의 해제 되었으며,첨단 군사 장비에 사용될수 있는 기술에 대한 통제만 계속되고 있음. 러시아의 민주주의 추구에도 불구 상황의 변화가능성에 대처해야 할 필요성이 있으며, 핵무기및 ICBM 등을 개선할수 있는 첨단 기술을 계속 통제해 나가야 할것임.끝

(대사 대리 김봉규-국장)

공 란

공 란

공   란

5. 北韓 核問題에 대한 美政府內 意見對立 報道 관련   노

 ㅇ 3.10 美 國務部 關係官은 3.10자 뉴욕 타임스紙가 北韓
    核問題와 관련, 美 行政府內에 상당한 異見이 있는 것처럼
    報道한 것은 게이츠 CIA局長에 대한 政治的 攻擊의 성격이
    강한 誇張된 記事라고 논평함.   (駐美大使代理 報告)

0135

공   란

공   란

主要外信隨時報告

北韓 核지연전술 계획완료등 3가지 분석
레민, 美군축국장 외신기자 간담회

外務部 情報狀況室
受信日時 92. 3. 12. 09:00

(워싱턴=聯合) 박정찬특파원=로널드 레먼 美국무부 군축국장은 11일 美國은 핵문제 해결을 위한 남북한 대화를 지지하고 있으나 북한이 새로운 문제들을. 제기하고 있는데 대해 크게 우려하고 있다고 말하고 이 문제는 남북한이나 美-북한간의 문제가 아니라 세계적인 문제라고 강조했다.

레먼국장은 이날 워싱턴 포린 프레스 센터 오찬 간담회에서 이같이 말하고 앞으로의 대응책과 관련 "지난번 국제원자력기구 이사회에서 많은 나라들이 매우 강한 입장을 표시했다"고 상기시켰다.

그는 북한이 핵안전협정 서명후 "각 단계마다 시간을 끌고 있으며 우리는 그 의도에 대해 매우 우려하고 있다"고 말하고 북한의 이같은 입장을 *협상을 위한 지렛대 *사찰에 대비한 정리 *핵개발의 완료등 세가지 측면에서 분석하고있다고 밝혔다.

그는 또 북한에 대한 효과적인 사찰을 위한 기술적 수준에 관해 한국에도 우수한 많은 전문가들이 있고 미국이 한국과 긴밀히 협의하고 있기 때문에 별 문제가 없을 것이라고 내다봤다.

레먼국장은 북한의 핵개발 단계에 대한 美행정부내 상이한 평가에 대한 질문을 받고 이라크의 핵능력에 대해서도 여러 상이한 시각이 있었으나 실제 사찰 결과 이라크의 핵개발 단계가 예상보다 진전돼 있었던 점을 상기시키면서 최악의 상황까지를 염두에 둔 평가를 도외시할수 없다고 덧붙였다.(끝)

0138

공   란

공   란

외 무 부

종 별 : 지 급

번 호 : USW-1285 일 시 : 92 0312 1904

수 신 : 장관(미일,미이,정안)

발 신 : 주미대사

제 목 : 닉슨 도서관회의 (GATES 국장연설)

연: USW-1266

금 3.12. GATES CIA 국장은 연호 표제세미나에서 ' THE GLOBAL ASSESSMENT' 제하의 연설을 행하였는 바, 북한 관련부분 주요 내용을 하기 보고함. (연설문 전문은USWF-1474 편 송부)

가. 북한 미사일 수출

. 북한은 제3국에 사정거리 확장 미사일(EXTENDED-RANGE MISSILES) 및 동 제조기술을 수출,중동 및 서남아시아 지역에 있어서 이미 진행중인 군비경쟁을 가속화 시키고 있음.

. 이란은 북한으로 부터 정규 및 사정거리 확장 스커드 미사일을 구입하고 있으며, 중국은 전장미사일 (BATTLEFIELD MISSILES), 크루즈미사일,장거리미사일 부품 및핵 기술을 수입하고 있음.시리아도 북한으로 부터 사정거리 확장 스커드를 구입하고있음.

. 북한은 주된 무기 확산 위험국(MAJOR PROLIFERATION THREAT) 들중의 하나가 되었으며,중동에 소련형 스커드 미사일 및 사정거리 확장스커드미사일을 판매하였고, 현재는 사정격리 1,000KM 정도의 대형 미상일을 개발중에 있음.

나. 북한 핵무기개발

. 북한은 무기제조 가능 핵분열 물질 (WEAPON-GRADE FISSILE MATERIAL) 을 생산할 수 있는 시설(INFRASTRUCTURE) 을 외부 도움없이 갖추었음. 북한에는 우라늄광산이 있으며, 영변에는 오로지 플로토니움 생산을 목적으로 하고 있는 것으로 보이는 2개의 원자로가 있음.그중 하나는 4년째 가동중이며, 두번째 원자로는 금년중 가동될 것으로 보임. 또한 풀로토니움 추출을 위한 핵연료 재처리 시설을 거의 완성하였음.

. 북한이 충분한 풀로토니움을 축적한 이후,핵폭발 장치를 만드는데 까지는 몇가지 단계가 더 필요하며 이에는 수개월 내지 2년의 기간이 소요될것임.

미주국	1차보	미주국	외정실	분석관	정와대	안기부

0141

PAGE 1

92.03.14   00:34 DQ

외신 1과 통제관

공   란

공   란

공　　란

공   란

공　　　　　란

공   란

공   란

공   란

공   란

공   란

공　　　란

공 란

공 란

공 란

공　　　　란

공　　　　　란

공　　　　란

공 란

공   란

공   란

공   란

공   란

공 란

공   란

공 란

공   란

공   란

공   란

공   란

공   란

관리번호 92-144

외 무 부

종   별 : 지급

번   호 : USW-1364

일   시 : 92 0317 2045

수   신 : 장관(미이,미일,정특,기정)

발   신 : 주미대사

제   목 : 북한학자 참석 학술회의

1. 금 3.17 당지 CSIS 가 주관하고 있는 한.미 관계회의 (CSUS US-KOREA TASK FORCE)가 미의사당내 소회의실을 빌려 개최된바, 금일 회의에는 현재 CSIS 초청으로 당지를 방문중인 북한 학자 4 인(USW-1176 참조), 일.북한회담 일본측 수석대표 나까히라대사 (USW-1252 참조), 당관 임성준참사관을 비롯 약 50 명의 정부, 의회, 학계, 업계 이사등이 참하였음.

2. 금일회의는 재무성 과장 (OFFICE OF FOREIGN ASSTS CONTROL REGULATION)인 NEWCOMB, 상무성 과장 (OFFICER OF TECHNOLOGY AND POLICY ANALYSIS) 인 SCHLECTY6 가 '적성국 교역법 (TRADING WITH ENEMY ACT)에 따른 북한과의 교역제한에대하여 설명하고, 이어서 북한 문제를 중심으로 북한 군축평화연구소 부소장인송락은, 나까히라대사, 당관 임성준참사관 및 당지 러시아대사관 아파나시에프참사관이 발표하고 이어서 질의, 응답을 갖는 형식으로 진행되었음.

3. 금일 회의중 주요 토의내용을 하기보고함.

가. 송낙은 부소장

0 북한은 미국과의 교역확대를 희망하는바, 미국은 대북한 금수관련 규정등시대에 맞지않는 법과 제도를 고려야함.

0 지난 1 월 미.북한 고위접촉에 이어 이제 미의회와 교역문제에 대해서 까지 논의하게 된것에 만족함.

0 핵문제는 잘 해결되고 있으며, 일.북한관계, 미.북한관계도 진전되고 있는바, 미의회의 협조를 기대함.

나. STANLEY ROTH(SOLARZ 의원 보좌관)   검토필 (1992. 6. 30.)

0 북한의 핵이행은 말뿐인바, 북한은 핵사찰 이행이 이렇게 지연되고 있는데대해 명확한 설명을 해야함.

미주국 안기부   장관   차관   1차보   2차보   미주국   외정실   분석관   정와대

PAGE 1

0172

92.03.18   13:11

외신 2과   통제관 BZ

다. 백봉환 (평화군축연구소)

0 북한은 핵사찰을 받지 않겠다고 한적은 없고, 공정하게 받겠다는것임.

0 남한이 핵무기가 철수되었다고 하고 미국이 이를 확인함으로서 핵사찰을 받을수있는 분위기가 조성되었음.

0 그러나 핵사찰은 일정한 국내법절차에 따라 이루어져야 하는바 법의 적용에는 일정한 시간이 소요되게 마련임.

라. 나까히라 대사

0 일본은 북한을 외부에 개방시켜야 한다는 취지에서 일.북한관계 개선을 추진하고 있음.

0 북한은 일본이 관계개선을 제의했다고 선전하고 있으나 이는 사실이 아님.

0 일.북한관계 정상화의 가장 큰 난관은 북한 핵문제이며 두번째 문제는 1,800명에 달하는 북송교포의 일본인 처 문제임.

0 핵문제와 관련 북한은 지연 전술을 쓰고있는바, 이는 현명하지 않음.

마. 임성준참사관

0 핵문제와 관련, 북한이 지금까지 취해오고 있는 태도에 비추어 아직은 의혹을 풀기에 미흡함.

0 북한은 미.북한관계, 일.북한관계, 국제협력등에 있어 핵문제 해결이 큰 기회 (OPPORTUNITIES)를 줄수도 있고 큰 좌절 (CHALLENGES)을 줄수도있는 관건임을 이해야함.

바. 아파나시에프 참사관

0 러시아는 모든 가능한 채널을 통해 북한 핵문제 해결을 위해 협조할 용의가 있음.

4. 관찰 및 평가

0 북측대표단은 동인들의 금일 행사참석이 CSIS 주관 학술회의 참석이며 그장소가 의회 건물임에도 불구하고 금일 회의을 미의회와의 접촉으로 부각시키고자노력하였음 (이와관련, 금일 임성준참사관이 접촉한 KARTMAN 과장과 안호영 서기관이 접촉한 정보사국 MERRILL 담당관은 북한 대표들이 자신들의 방미 성과를크게 부각시키고자 노력하는것은 이해할 만한 반응이라고 하면서, 이러한 분위기가 오히려 핵문제등에 대한 북한 태도의 유연화를 불러올수있는 효과도 기대한다는 반응을 보임).

0 북한대표단은 미국이나 아국에 대한 비난을 적극 자제하였으며, 핵문제와관련 큰

진전이 있을것이라는 점을 부각시키고자 노력하였음.

0 한편 핵문제와 관련 북한을 제외한 모든 참석자들의 강경한 입장
표시는북한대표단에게 나름대로의 교육적 효과가 있었을 것으로 기대됨.

0 송락은 부소장은 91 년까지 북한외교부 미.일 담당국장을 역임하였고, 개별
접촉시 한난열 (쿠바 및 인니 근무), 조경환(방글라데쉬 근무)도 외교부 직원을
역임하였음이 확인되었음. 끝

(대사 현홍주-국장)

예고문: 92.12.31 일반

외 무 부

종 별 : 지 급

번 호 : USW-1383   일 시 : 92 0318 1848

수 신 : 장관(미일,미이,정특,기정)

발 신 : 주 미 대사

제 목 : 북한학자 참석 CSIS 간담회

연: USW-1364

1. 금 3.18 당지 CSIS 는 연호 북한 평화군축연구소 송락은 부소장등 북한학자 4
명을 초빙한 가운데 CSIS 회의실에서 WILLIAM TAYLOR CSIS 부소장의 사회로 조찬
간담회를 개최한 바, 동 간담회는 송락은 부소장이 1 시간내외 (통역시간제외하면 25
분 정도)로 북한의 대내외 정책에 관한 주제 발표를 하고 이어서 약 30 분간
질의.응답을 갖는 형식으로 진행되었음. 동 간담회에는 CSIS, 국방부관계자 및 당관
박흥신 서기관등 30 여명이 참석하였음.

2. 송락은 부소장의 발표요지는 다음과 같음.

가. 핵사찰 문제

. 북한은 핵사찰을 성실, 당당하게 그리고 의심없게 받자는 입장임. 이는 남한으로
부터의 핵무기 철수, 팀스피리트 중단, 남북동시 사찰 합의등 그간 핵문제 해결의
여러 전제조건이 대부분 충족되었기 때문임.

. 3.8 최고인민회의에서 IAEA 안전협정을 비준하고 곧이어 IAEA 와 사찰 절차를
마련 예정이며, 이와 별도로 남. 북한간에 6 월중 사찰실시에 합의한바 있음.

. 북한은 뉴욕 고위급회담에 따라 성실히 합의사항을 이행중에 있음. 일부
미언론과 계층에서 북한을 의심하고 비난하는 언행은 문제의 진전에 아무런 긍정적
역할도 하지 못함.

나. 북한 경제

. 동구권 미 구소련의 붕괴이후 다음 차례는 북한이라고들 말하고 있으나 이는
잘못된 견해임. 이러한 예고와는 달리 북한 체제는 계속 유지될 것인바, 이는 북한이
러시아, 중국, 동구권과는 다른 독자적인 사회주의를 추구하기 때문임.

. 경제 위기는 없으나 경제발전을 해나가는 가운데 난관이 없는 것은 아님.또한

검토필(1992. 6. 30.)

미주국 청와대	장관 안기부	차관	1차보	2차보	미주국	외정실	외정실	분석관

PAGE 1

0175

92.03.19   09:54

외신 2과   통제관 BZ

민족경제 건설을 추구한다고 해서 외국과의 경제관계 개선에 반대하는 것은 아님.
(선봉 경제특구, 합영추진 예시)

　　다. 승계문제

　.　북한의 권력승계는 이미 70 년대 부터 차근차근 진행되어 왔으며, 이제 김정일은
(비서동지라고 지칭) 온 나라의 모든 분야를 영도하고 있음.

　.　작년 12 월 최고사령관 추대 이전에도 김정일은 이미 군대에 대한 실질적권한을
행사해 왔으며, 승계가 계속 확고하게 이루어지고 있는바, 이를 놓고 구구한 추측을
할 필요가 없음.

　.　라. 미.북관계 개선

　.　주체를 견지한다고 해서 대외관계를 폐쇄적으로 하겠다는 것은 아니며, 미. 일
등과도 관계개선을 추진하고 있음. 일부에서 북한의 대외관계 개선이 원조를 받기
위한 것으로 오해하고 있으나, 북한은 평등, 주권존중에 입각하여 대외관계를 추진할
것임.

　.　1 월 미.북한 고위급 회담은 김정일의 영단에 의해 실현된 것인바, 북한은
고위급 회담의 만족스러운 합의를 존중, 이행할 것임.

　3. 이어 진행된 질의응답에서는 북한의 핵사찰 문제, 한반도 군축문제등이 거론
되었는바, 대부분 틀에 박힌 답변에 그쳤으며, 다만 한반도에서의 미국의 역할을
질의한데 대해 한난열이 답변한 내용을 참고로 아래 보고함.

　.　한반도는 열강에 의해 분열 되었으며 남. 북분단에 미국도 책임이 있으므로
통일을 이루어 나가는데에 적극 협조해 나가야 함.

　.　냉전구조가 깨지고 구소련이 붕괴된 이후 미국의 역할이 더욱 강화된 바,미국이
남. 북 평화 장치의 마련에 기여해야 함.

　.　이를 위해 정전협정을 평화협정으로 대체하고, 주한미군의 지위를 변경하는
문제가 검토되어야 함. 주한미군을 단시일내에 철수하기는 어렵겠지만 점차적으로
단계적 감축을 해나가기 바람.

　.　미국은 이제 남. 북한 균등정책을 실시할 때가 되었음. 하루아침에 동등한
관계를 바라지는 않치만 북측은 적대시하고 남측은 맹목적으로 지지하는 일방적
정책은 중단해야함.

　4. 당관 관찰

　.　<u>핵사찰 문제와 관련, 남. 북한이 6 월중 사찰실시에 합의했다는 송락은의발언은</u>

PAGE 2　　　　　　　　　　　　　　　　　　　　　　　　0176

핵봉제공동위 구성 공동 발표문에 언급된 사찰 시한을 대외적으로 인정했다는 점에서 관심을 끌었음.

. 한편 승계문제와 관련, CARLIN 미국무부 정보조사국 동북아과장은 박서기관과 접촉시 북한이 승계문제를 대외적으로 언급한 것은 새로운 사실로서 김정일의 권력승계를 대외적으로 기정사실화 하려는 움직임으로 추정된다고 하면서, 70 년대 부터 승계작업이 진행되어 김정일이 거의 모든 국정을 맡아보고 있다는 발언은 정보조사국의 그간 분석과도 맥락을 함께하고 있다고 평가하였음.

(대사 현홍주-국장)

92. 12. 31 까지

가. 질문 : 최근 남.북한의 동시사찰 문제에 대한 한.미간 이견 여부

　　　　- 한국측이 대화 계속에 치우친 나머지 Strict 하지 않다는

　　　　　시각 (3. 18자 NYT)

ㅇ 한.미 양국은 북한의 핵개발이 한반도의 안보뿐만 아니라

　　동북아지역 전체의 평화와 안정에 중대한 위협이 된다는 점에

　　인식을 같이 하고 있음.

ㅇ 한.미 양국은 핵문제를 포함한 주요 안보 문제에 관해 긴밀히

　　협조 및 협의를 하여 왔으며 핵문제를 해결하는 기본 인식과

　　전략에 있어서 아무런 이견을 보이고 있지 않음.

0178

ㅇ 미국은 북한 핵문제 해결 노력과 남북 대화 노력을 병해하면서
　가능한 국제적 압력 수단 동원등 외교적으로 북한의 핵개발
　문제를 해결하려고 노력하고 있는 우리정부의 입장을 지지.지원
　하고 있음.

ㅇ 우리정부는 핵문제 해결이 없는 남북 관계의 실질적 진전은
　어렵다는 기본적 입장에서 대북 협상을 계속하고 있음.

나. 질문 : 한국측이 종국적으로 강제사찰 내지 안보리 제재를 검토하고
　　　　　있는지 ?

ㅇ 우리는 북한 핵문제를 최대한 당사자간에 자주적으로 해결하려고
　노력하고 있음.　다시말해 계속적인 북한과의 대화와 설득 및
　협상을 통하여 이를 해결하려고 노력하고 있음.

ㅇ 지난 3. 14자 「공동발표문」을 통하여 남.북한은 3. 18로부터
　대략 2개월 정도의 기간안에 상호사찰규정을 채택하고 그후
　20일안에 제1차 상호사찰을 실시하기로 양해하였는바, 현재
　우리는 남북간의 상호사찰이 국제적으로 신뢰받을 수 있는 사찰이
　될 수 있도록 포괄적이고 강제적 성격의(comprehensive and
　intrusive) 사찰규정을 북측에 제의해 놓고 있음.

ㅇ 위에서 언급한 시기까지 우리의 노력에도 불구하고 북한이
　남.북한 상호사찰 실시를 계속 지연, 거부하거나 또는 IAEA에
　의한 핵사찰 수용도 어느 일정시기 까지 계속 거부할 경우
　한국정부는 미국을 비롯한 우방국들과 협의, 국제사회에 의한
　해결 방안등에 관해 협의할 것임.

/계속/

0179

다. 질문 : 최근 언론보도등을 보면 한.미 양국이 북한의 핵개발 능력을
       의도적으로 과대평가하는 것이 아닌지 ?

  ○ 북한은 영변지역에 핵개발 단지를 조성하고 이미 4MW 급과 30MW 급
    연구용원자로를 가동중에 있으며 최대 200MW 급 제3의 원자로를
    건설중(93년 가동 목표 추정)에 있는 것으로 파악되고 있으며
    그외에 핵무기 개발에 사용될 플루토늄 축출이 가능한 핵재처리
    시설을 건설중인 것으로 파악됨.

  ○ 특히 최근 핵재처리시설에는 계속 기자재가 투입되고 있는 것으로
    파악되고 있고 Cold Test가 진행중인 것으로 보여저 금년 5∼6월
    경에는 동 시설이 가동될 가능성이 높은 것으로 판단되고 있음.

  ○ 북한의 경우에는 발전용 원자로가 없으므로 핵연료 recycling을 위한
    핵재처리시설을 건설, 가동할 아무런 경제적 정당성이 없다고 할 수
    있으므로(일반적으로 700MW 급 발전용 원자로를 대략 10기 이상
    보유하는 경우에 생성되는 spent fuel이 있을때 이를 재처리하여
    다시 핵연료로 사용할 경제적 타당성이 있는 것으로 알려짐),
    북한의 재처리시설은 핵무기 개발을 위한 플루토늄 추출이 목적
    이라는 의심을 받을 수 밖에 없음.

  ○ 더구나 북한은 핵무기를 개발할 의사도 능력도 없다고 하면서
    핵사찰 수용을 지연시키고 있으므로 핵무기 개발의 의심을 더욱
    짙게 하고 있는바, 여러가지 상황 증거와 정황에 근거할때 북한의
    핵개발 능력을 과대평가하는 것은 아니라고 생각함.

라. 질문 : IAEA 사찰 및 남.북한 동시사찰 실현 전망 평가 및 실효성
       여부

/계속/

0180

o 북한에 대한 IAEA 사찰은 북한이 NPT 당사국으로서 당연히 수용
   하여야 할 의무인 것이며, 남북간 상호사찰도 남북간에 합의되고
   지난 2. 19자로 발효된 「한반도 비핵화에 관한 공동선언」에
   따라 남.북한이 모두 이를 이행하여야 할 법적 의무를 지고 있으므로
   북한은 남북 상호사찰을 받을 의무가 있음.

o 북한이 IAEA 사찰이든 남북 상호사찰이든 어느 사찰을 먼저 수용할
   것인가와 그 시기에 대해서는 전망하기 어려운 상황이나, 북한의
   핵개발 정도에 대한 국제적 평가에 기초해 볼때 금년 6월경까지
   북한은 사찰을 받아야 될 것임.

o 북한의 핵개발에 대한 국제적 의혹을 불식시키기 위하여는 IAEA
   에 의한 사찰과 남북간 상호사찰이 반드시 실현되어야 하는바,
   IAEA 사찰이 기본적으로 북한이 신고하는 대상에 대하여 사찰이
   실시되는 것임을 감안할 때 남북간 상호사찰을 한반도 비핵화
   이행 여부를 검증하는 장치가 되어야 하므로 보다 실효성 있고
   완벽한 것이 되어야 함.

마. 질문 : 북한이 지연책 내지 HIDE AND SEEK 게임을 하고 있다고 보는
            근거

o 북한은 핵무기를 개발할 의사도, 능력도 없다고 주장하면서도
   핵사찰을 언제 받겠다는 의사를 표명한 적이 없음. NPT 조약상
   의무와 관련하여 북한은 그동안 미루어오던 IAEA 핵안전협정에
   지난 1. 30. 겨우 서명은 하였으며 4. 8자로 소집되는 최고인민
   회의에서 비준 문제를 심의하겠다고 하면서도 언제 사찰을
   받겠다는 공식적 약속은 표명하지 않고 있는 상황임.

/계속/

0181

o 우리의 작년 12. 18자 노대통령의 핵부재선언과 관련하여 북한은
   IAEA 핵사찰을 지연 또는 회피할 구실은 없어졌으며 국제적인
   의혹의 강도를 감안, IAEA Process상 기한을 채우지 않고라도
   최단시일내 해당되는 절차를 밟아 사찰을 받을 수 있음에도
   불구하고 모든 절차를 계속 지연시키고 있는 것은 핵무기 개발
   또는 은닉에 필요한 시간을 벌기 위해 안간힘을 쓰고 있는 것이
   분명함.

o 남.북한간 핵문제 접촉에서도 핵사찰 규정 채택 시한을 정하자는
   우리측 주장을 계속 거부해 왔으며 현재 핵통제공동위원회(JNCC)가
   개최되어 남북상호사찰 실시를 위한 사찰규정을 토의하는 과정에서도
   사찰의 전제조건으로서 여러가지 불필요한 합의서 채택을 주장하고
   있는 것도 핵사찰 수용을 계속 회피하기 위한 전술임.   끝.

예고 : 독후 파기

0182

92. 3. 18.
북/4/4

o Basic Approach

- Our policy toward North Korea is a classic mixture of "carrot and
  stick".

- Dealing with an unpredictable and unidentifiable regime, armed with
  belligerent communism, creates inevitable contraditions.

- We have been pursuing the reduction of tension on the Korean peninsula
  by opening up dialogue with North Korea. At the same time, we have
  demonstrated our firm determination to dissuade North Korea from doing
  anything to destabilize the precarious peace on the peninsula.

- So far our government has been successful in drawing North Korea into
  an institutional negotiation. In January, the "Basic Agreement"
  between the South and the North was put into force. This agreement
  includes programmes for human and economic exchanges and for political
  and military confidence building measures.

- However, we made it clear to North Korea that there would be no
  implementation of the Agreement unless North Korea takes necessary
  measures to allow int'l and bilateral inspections of its nuclear
  facilities. Our negotiators have been tough. They didn't budge an
  inch from this firm postion.

0183

- On March 14, North Korea largely accepted our demand for setting a specific schedule for mutual inspection. The South and the North adopted a joint statement which commits the two sides to work out an inspection regime and to implement it within a period of 80 days.

- It remains to be seen whether North Korea would be cooperative enough to allow inspections by some time in June as assumed in terms of the joint statement.

- There have been some concerns both within and outside Korea that the ROK government might not have been assertive enough in dealing with North Korea. This criticism has been amplified by the North Korean tactic of delaying inspections as long as possible.

- However, we believe that maintaining pressure on North Korea on the nuclear issue while not destroying the framework of negotiation itself is important and has been effective so far.

- Our policy towards North Korea reflects the complex nature of the negotiations. Many scholars, including critics of government policy, admit that the recent progress and stalemate between the two parties is a part of long involved process of expectation and frustration.

o The US-NK relations

    - The US government has refrained from engaging in direct negotiations with North Korea and has maintained a set of conditions to be met before it will engage in improving relations with North Korea.

0184

- We strongly believe this policy has been right and is bearing fruit because North Korea seems to be unable to find any way-out of its self-imposed isolation other than through dialogue with South Korea. The ongoing process of the South-North negotiation has been greatly helped by the firm stance of the United States and other friendly governments.

- The Int'l community is very concerned over the North Korean nuclear programme and its continued violation of the Int'l regime for arms exports.

- The fact that the South Korean government is engaged in dialogue with North Korea does not necessarily require that the governments of our allies engage in parallel dialogue with North Korea especially at a time when the South-North negotiation are approaching a critical juncture.

- However, the ROK government and the US government have shared a view that limited contacts between the US and North Korea might help encourage the latter to act more constructively.

- We know that a number of scholars and experts have advocated that expanded and upgraded conversation with North Korea would help to elicit a more positive North Korean reaction.

- We don't underestimate the benefits of that policy. Under-secretary Kanter met Kim Yong Soon at New York in January. We understand that Kim's reaction was quite constructive.

0185

- However, North Korea's subsequent action has not been consistent with its words. Even though South Koreans continue dialogue with North Koreans, we are extremely careful not to misread their intentions.

- We are grateful to the US gov't and public for supporting the South-North dialogue. We also appreciate the firm stance of the US gov't and experts outside the gov't on this issue. We hope that a time will arrive soon when the United States can open up full-scale dialogue and exchanges with North Korea. But North Korea may not be the same by that time.   – end –

0186

주 미 대 사 관

USW(F) : *1667*   년월일 : *92.3.19* 시간 : *1840*

수 신 : 장 관 *(미.미, 정특)*

발 신 : 주미대사

제 목 : *북한 核문제 국방부 브리핑*   (출처 : *7NS*)

보안
통제

DEFENSE DEPARTMENT REGULAR BRIEFING   BRIEFER: PETE WILLIAMS
THURSDAY, MARCH 19, 1992

Q   On Korea, on **North Korea**, there was a report that United
States and **South Korea** government have some difference of opinion
how to deal with the North Korean nuclear facilities. For example,
is it necessary to hit the -- execute the so-called surgical
operation on the North Korean Yongbyon site, or if then, when? You
have some difference of opinion, United States and South Korean
government --- do you have such kind of difference?

MR. WILLIAMS: No, I'd say the best way to describe it is that
we're very pleased, we think President Roh has shown extraordinary
leadership in his declaration earlier of a nuclear-free peninsula.
We think that was a very important step. And we are working closely
with the republic of Korea on ways to make sure that in fact is
carried out and we think they're doing just fine.

0187

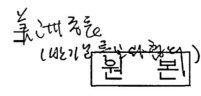

판리 번호	82-349

외 무 부

종 별 :

번 호 : CPW-1142

일 시 : 92 0320 1830

수 신 : 장관(친전)

발 신 : 주 북경 대표

제 목 : 정주영 회장 발언

　　1. 최근 정주영 회장이 공개 석상에서 "현대 건설에서 핵무기를 저장하는 공사를
했다"라고 한 발언은, "핵무기 공격에 지탱할 수 있는 대피시설 또는 창고건설 공사를
했다"라는 표현을 부정확하게 표현한 것으로 사료됨.

　　2. 그러나 북한측이 동 발언을 핵사찰 연기를 위한 선전목적에 사용하고 있고,
한반도의 핵문제가 국제적으로 민감한 문제가 되어 있는 만큼, 정부로서는 국제여론의
오해를 불식시키기 위해 재외 공관에서 사실 설명을 하도록 조치해 주시는 것이 좋을
것으로 사료됨. 끝.

　　(대사 노재원-장관)

　　예고:92.12.31 일반

검토필(19 92. 6. 30.) 박

예고문에 의 ...... 5(92. 3)
직위　　　　　　성명

장관

0188

PAGE 1

92.03.20　　21:21

외신 2과　통제관 CE

	분류번호	보존기간

발 신 전 보

번 호 : WCP-0655   920323 1724 FO   종별 :

수 신 : 주 ~~북경대표~~ ~~~~ 대사. 총영사

발 신 : 장 관 ~~~~ (미비)

제 목 : 정주영 회장의 핵관계 발언

1. 지난 3. 5. 정주영 국민당대표(전 현대그룹 회장)는 롯데호텔에서 열린
   한국인간개발연구원 초청간담회에서 다음과 같은 발언을 하였음.
   "우리나라는 수의 계약하고 전부 돈받는다.   군대 공사는 기밀이기
   때문에 수의 공사한다고 그러는데 미국은 수의공사가 없다.   미국이
   원자탄 저장고를 만드는데 이는 극비중의 극비로서 깊은 산속에 있는
   건설 현장에 미국 감독관도 자기 터널만 들어간다.   6개 업체에서
   공개 경쟁 입찰하여 현대가 수주하였는데 그 현장을 나는 가보았다.
   수의 계약은 정치자금을 받아 들이기 위해서 하는데 나는 정경유착의
   고리를 반드시 끊겠다."

2. 상기 발언 관련, 북한은 이를 기회로 하여 마치 남한에 핵기지가 존재하고
   있는 것으로 대내외 선전에 이용하고 있는바, 이에 대한 정부의 입장을
   아래 통보하니 귀 주재국 또는 언론으로부터의 문의가 있을 경우 또는
   북측의 선전 책동에 반박할 필요가 있을 경우 활용바람.

검토필(1992. 6. 30.)
/계속/

예고문에 의거 재분류(19)
직위   성명

| | 보안통제 | |

앙고재	92년 3월 23일	북미2과	기안자 성명	조	과장	심의관	국장	차관보	차관	장관 X		외신과통제

0189

ㅇ 정주영씨는 국민당 대표로서 국회의원 총선거를 앞두고 정부의 건설
   실태를 비판하여 국민의 정치적 지지를 유도할 목적으로 이와 같은
   발언을 한 것인바, 국민에게 극적인 비교 감각을 충격적으로 전달하기에
   급급한 나머지 나온 사실무근의 엉뚱한 예시에 불과함.

ㅇ 정주영씨는 동 발언에 대해 회의 참석자들로부터 사실 확인을 요구받자
   현장에서 자신의 발언이 잘못된 것이라고 하면서 본인이 직접 발언을
   취소한 바 있음.

ㅇ 우리정부는 노 대통령의 91. 11. 8. 비핵화선언 및 12. 18. 핵부재
   선언등을 통하여 우리 영토내에는 일체의 핵무기가 존재하지 않음을
   대내외에 천명한 바 있음.

ㅇ 그럼에도 불구하고 북한이 이와같은 우리의 입장에 대해 의심을 갖고
   있다면 우리도 북한의 핵개발에 대해 의혹을 갖고 있으니 만큼 이미
   남북이 비핵화 공동선언에서 합의한대로 조속히 상호사찰을 실시하여
   이와같은 불신을 제거하자는 우리의 제안에 응해야 할 것임.

3. 본 건과 관련하여 미측은 한국대통령이 12. 18. 핵부재선언을 한바에 따라
    핵무기가 한반도에 존재하고 있지 않기 때문에 정 회장 발언은 문제될 것이
    없으며 북한의 의심은 상호사찰 실시를 통해서 해소될 문제라는 인식을
    가지고 있음을 참고바람.   끝.

예고 : 92. 12. 31. 일반

(차관)
(장관 이상옥)

수신처 : 주미, 영, 러, 일, 오지리, 유엔, 호주, 카나다, 제네바대사,
       주북경대표.

0190

공   란

공   란

공 란

공   란

공   란

공 란

외 무 부

관리번호 B2-160

종 별 :

번 호 : NYW-0418

일 시 : 92 0324 1630

수 신 : 장관(해신,정홍,미북,기정)

발 신 : 주 뉴욕 총영사(문)

제 목 : WNET 북한 핵문제 특집 좌담 프로

연:NYW-0380

1. 연호,3.23. 방영 예정이었던 북한 핵개발 관련 좌담프로는 북한 핵문제가 최근의 HOT ISSUE 가 되고 있지 못하다는 방송국측의 판단에 따라 4 월 초순경으로 연기되었음.

2. 일자 확정되는 대로 추보하겠음. 끝

(문화원장 김준길-해공관장)

예고 92.12.31. 까지

검토필(1992. 6.30.)

예고문에 의거 재분류(19)

공보처	차관	1차보	2차보	미주국	문협국	외정실	분석관	청와대
안기부								

공　　　란

공 란

공　　　란

공   란

공　　　란

공 란

공　　　　란

공   란

공   란

공　　　　　란

공   란

공   란

공 란

공   란

공 란

공   란

공   란

공　　　　　란

공   란

공   란

외 무 부

종 별 :

번 호 : USW-1561   일   시 : 92 0327 1902

수 신 : 장관(미이, 미일, 중동일, 정특, 기정)

발 신 : 주 미 대사

제 목 : 하원 군사위 청문회

1. 하원 군사위 국방정책 연구반(반장: LES ASPIN 의원, 민주-위스콘신)은 "지역위협 및 1990 년대 국방 대책" 제하 일련의 청문회를 개최하고 있는바, 금3.27(금)에는 ROBERT GATES CIA 국장을 증인으로 출석시켜 중동 및 한반도의 정세에 관하여 청문회를 개최하였음. (당관 김형진 서기관 참석)

2. 동 청문회는 GATES 국장의 증언(증언문은 USWF-1863 로 FAX 송부함) 부분은 공개로, 이후 질의.응답은 비공개로 진행되었는바, ASPIN 의원과 BILL DICKINSON 의원(공화-알라바마)은 모두 발언에서 냉전이후 분쟁 발발의 위험이 가장높은 지역으로 중동과 한반도를 지적하고 동 지역에서의 안보위협 및 미군의 역할에 대한 GATES 국장의 견해를 요청한바, GATES 국장의 주요 증언 내용은 하기와 같음.

가. 중동은 향후 수년내 미국이 군사적으로 개입하게될 가능성이 가장 높은지역으로 특히 이락과 이란이 큰 위협이 되고 있는바, 이락은 걸프전 패배 및 UN 의 제재에도 불구하고 화학무기 원료 및 상당규모의 군사력을 보유하고 있으며, 제한낮적이나마 무기생산을 재개하고 있고 이란은 북한으로 부터의 스커드 미사일 구입등 90-94 년간 20 억불 상당의 무기를 외국으로 부터 구입할 계획으로 있으며 핵무기, 화학무기등 대량살상 무기개발 노력을 강화하고 있음.

나. 한반도는 미군의 실제의 적과 대치하고 있는 유일한 지역으로 북한은 병력의 전투준비도, 공군력, 병참등에는 약점이 있으나 남한에 대한 대규모 기습공격에 적합한 병력을 휴전선 바로 이북에 유지하고 있으며, 최근 기동력을 증강시켜 더욱 큰 위협이 되고 있음.

다. 더우기 북한은 핵무기 원료를 자체 생산할 수 있는 시설을 개발중에 있으며, 영변에 플로토늄 생산만계획위한 것으로 보이는 원자료 2 기를 건설, 1 기는 4 년전부터 가동중이며 보다 용량이 큰 1 기는 금년도 가동예정인바, 플로토늄 추출을

미주국	장관	차관	1차보	2차보	미주국	중아국	외정실	분석관
청와대	안기부							

0218

PAGE 1   92.03.28   10:25
                                          외신 2과   통제관 BX

위한 핵연료 재체리 시설도 거의 완공단계에 있음.

　　라. 북한은 91.12 월 한반도 비핵화 선언에 합의하였음에도 불구하고 영변의 원자료 및 핵재처리시설의 존재 자체를 부인하고 있고 핵안전 협정을 상금 비준하지 않는등 핵개발을 계속할 조짐이 있어 제 3 국의 의심을 불식시킬만한 사찰을 받아들일 것인가에 대하여는 의구심이 있는바, <u>북한의 핵무기 개발은 임박하였으며 그것도 매우 임박(CLOSE, PERHAPS VERY CLOSE) 하였다고 봄.</u> 북한의 핵무기 개발은 동북아 안보에 위협이 될뿐 아니라 북한이 외화를 얻기위해 핵물질 및 관련 기술을 외국에 수출할 가능성이 있기 때문에 더욱 우려가됨.

　　마. (장기적으로는) 북한에 대해 과거 소련이 공급한 신무기 및 연료공급의 중단, 경제적 어려움등으로 북한의 남한에 대한 군사적 우위가 감소될 것이나, (단기적으로는) 북한의 전략가들이 북한이 우위에 있을 때 남한을 공격하도록 권고할 수 있고 북한이 재래식 무기의 유지 및 현대화의 어려움으로 오히려 핵무기및 미사일 개발 노력을 강화할 수 있으므로 더욱 위험한 상황을 맞이하게 될 것임.

　　　(대사 현홍주-국장)

<u>92.12.31 까지</u> 해분류(19 ． ． ．)
제외

주 미 대 사 관

USE(F) : *1863*   년월일 : *920327* 시간 : *1440*

수 신 : 장 관 (미이, 미일중동일, 가정)전특)   봉안제 *82*

발 신 : 주 미 대 사

제 목 : 미하원 국방위 청문회시 Gates 증선문   (출처 :   )

STATEMENT OF

THE DIRECTOR OF CENTRAL INTELLIGENCE

BEFORE

THE U.S. HOUSE OF REPRESENTATIVES

ARMED SERVICES COMMITTEE

DEFENSE POLICY PANEL

27 MARCH 1992

(*1863 - 26 - 1*)

외신 1과 봉제

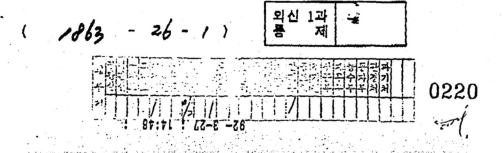

0220

Mr. Chairman, and members of the Defense Policy Panel:

I am happy to come before you again to discuss emerging trends in parts of the world where the United States has manifest and enduring security interests. You have suggested I focus on the Middle East and Persian Gulf, as well as on the Korean peninsula, and I will do so. I would be remiss, however, if I did not first at least allude to other parts of the world where our interests are at stake and our military forces might be needed, though not necessarily to fight.

When I was here last December, I ended my statement with a caution about the unpredictability of the future. I suggested we think about:

--- How fast events are moving.

--- The prospects for turbulence and instability in heavily armed Central Eurasia.

--- The problematic disposition of nearly the 30,000 nuclear weapons of the former Soviet Union.

0221

UNCLASSIFIED

--- The volatility of the Middle East and South Asia.

--- The proliferation of weapons of mass destruction,
    particularly the nuclear development programs in countries
    hostile to our interests.

--- The centrifugal forces of nationalist and ethnic hostility that
    threaten instability or even civil war on several continents.

During the ensuing three and a half months some disquieting
trends have been evident. Unrest is worse, for example, in parts
of the former Soviet Union than when I last stood here before you.
Conflict is deepening between Soviet successor states such as
Armenia and Azerbaijan. While the CIS has helped cushion the
collapse of the Soviet empire, it is facing increasing strains that it
may not survive. It is not hard to find other disquieting news:

--- Ukraine has suspended the transfer of tactical nuclear
    weapons to Russia for dismantling.

--- Ratification and implementation of the CFE Treaty appears
    increasingly complex and problematic.

1863- 26-3

--- Arms races are heating up in the Middle East and Southeast Asia, among other regions.

--- Despite significant -- and costly -- counternarcotics achievements, narcotics trafficking shows no sign of abating.

--- The devastating explosion in Buenos Aires shows that international terrorism is still of grave concern.

On the other hand, I can point to some positive developments and trends, as well:

--- White citizens in South Africa voted strongly in favor of continuing political reforms. A cease-fire is in effect in El Salvador, and the prospects that the contending factions can work out their differences peacefully have improved. Democracy has begun to make progress even in Albania and Romania. The unrest in Yugoslavia has abated, if perhaps only temporarily.

--- Transforming centrally planned economies into market economies continues to be wrenching and destabilizing. But the worst predictions -- about massive starvation, hypothermia, and civil unrest in Russia, for example -- have so far failed to materialize. And Yel'tsin is still holding firmly to the course of economic reform.

We may no longer need to fear a nuclear holocaust, but the famous Chinese curse appears to have come true. We are truly living in interesting times. With those thoughts in mind, I will devote the balance of my presentation to the regions you have asked me to cover.

THE MIDDLE EAST AND PERSIAN GULF

If in the next few years it again becomes necessary to deploy US combat power abroad, the strategically vital region encompassing the Middle East and Persian Gulf is at the top of the list of likely locales.

Among the several countries in this region that are hostile to US interests, two -- Iraq and Iran -- continue trying to rebuild their military power to enhance their influence. Let me say a few words about each, starting with Iraq.

IRAQ: WEAKENED BUT STILL FORMIDABLE

Operation Desert Storm greatly reduced Iraq's ability to conduct large-scale offensive military operations. The UN sanctions have impeded Saddam's efforts to reequip his forces. Preoccupied with defending the regime and putting down local insurgencies, the Iraqi military is currently capable of conducting only small-scale offensive operations with limited objectives.

Nevertheless, the size and equipment of Iraq's military forces remain formidable, especially in comparison with those of most of its neighbors. Let me give you some figures:

--- Iraq's ground forces number about two dozen divisions, though they are on the whole smaller and much less capable than the prewar divisions. The Army still has more than 3,000 armored personnel carriers, 2,000 tanks, and 1,000 artillery pieces.

--- We believe Iraq also retains some mobile Scud missile launchers and as many as several hundred missiles.

0225

--- The Iraqi Air Force probably still has about 300 combat aircraft, though many are not operational. Because the Air Force has been grounded for over a year, it would need at least a month of intensive training and maintenance to become even minimally combat-ready.

--- Although a large quantity of Iraqi nuclear-related equipment has been identified and destroyed, we suspect Iraq has managed to hide some equipment from the UN inspectors. And, of course, Iraq's nuclear scientists and engineers retain their expertise.

--- Baghdad surrendered thousands of chemical munitions, tons of chemical agents, and considerable production equipment, but we believe the regime still has more of everything -- more precursor chemicals, more bulk agent, more munitions, more production equipment.

--- The regime never admitted having a biological weapons program and never surrendered any toxins or weapons. But we know the Iraqis had such a program, and we are

convinced they have been able to preserve some biological weapons and the means to make even more.

HOW LONG TO RECOVER?

The restoration of Iraq's defense industries is one of Saddam's main postwar goals. Notwithstanding UN-imposed inspections and sanctions, Iraq claims to have partly repaired nearly 200 military-industrial buildings and to be in the process of repairing many others. We can confirm that significant reconstruction has been taking place at least two dozen military-industrial sites.

Limited production of artillery and ammunition has resumed at some weapon production facilities damaged during the Gulf war. Despite these efforts, total arms production will remain significantly below prewar levels as long as sanctions remain in force and inspections continue.

If the sanctions were removed, we estimate it would take Iraq at least three to five years to restore its prewar conventional military inventories. Long before then, Iraq's forces could be strong enough to threaten its neighbors.

More important, however, is how fast we think Iraq could restore its special weapons capabilities. We believe Baghdad has been able to preserve significant elements of each of its special weapons programs. Once it is free to begin rebuilding them, its scientists and engineers will be able to hit the ground running.

--- The nuclear weapon development program would need the most time to recover, because much of the infrastructure for the production of fissile material would need to be reconstructed. (This judgment would be reinforced if equipment at certain only recently identified nuclear research sites is destroyed, as UN inspection teams have demanded.) The time Iraq would need to rebuild its nuclear capability could be shortened dramatically if it could somehow procure fissile material from abroad.

--- Much of the chemical weapons production infrastructure would have to be rebuilt before the Iraqis could reestablish the prewar level of production. However, we believe they could quickly resume limited production of such weapons using covert stocks of precursor chemicals, undeclared chemical process equipment, and unfilled munitions.

--- Because it doesn't take much equipment to make biological warfare agents, we estimate the Iraqis could resume production within weeks. They have retained microbial fermentation equipment and pathogen cultures; we remain convinced they also have a stockpile of biological weapons.

--- Finally, we judge that the Iraqis could soon restore their capability to produce Scud-type missiles, though they might need some help from abroad.

WHAT IF SADDAM WENT AWAY?

How might Iraq's internal politics and external behavior change if Saddam Hussein left the scene?

As Saddam's decades of repressive rule demonstrate, he will do whatever it takes to cling to power. No succession mechanism is in place, nor are there any obvious candidates to replace Saddam -- Iraq is one of those countries where being the number-two man is unnerving, not to say life-threatening.

Consequently, we judge that if Saddam left the scene, it would be because of a coup or other violent act. How likely this is to happen, I cannot say, though we have evidence that Saddam's power base is shrinking and that dissatisfaction with his leadership is growing even among his core supporters -- chiefly, among Iraq's Sunni Muslims.

A likely successor to Saddam would be someone from the current, Sunni-Arab-dominated ruling circle -- someone who shares Saddam's perspectives, especially his belief in the political efficacy of ruthless violence. Such a successor might think pretty much like Saddam. Even so, whoever Saddam's successor was, he would lack a broad power base and could face immediate and serious challenges from other contenders.

A successor regime might be a little less hardnosed, both toward Iraqi Shi'ites and Kurds and toward Iraq's external adversaries. While it would continue efforts to restore Iraq's military capability, it might shift some resources from military to civilian reconstruction. The new regime could anticipate a quick end to the UN sanctions as well as recognition and support from the international community. In the short run, then, Iraq might present a lower threat to its neighbors. Still, any successor to Saddam is likely to share his regional aspirations, and over the

0230

longer term we could expect Iraq to try to regain its position as the dominant Arab military power.

If a successor regime begins to have trouble maintaining Iraq's unity or territorial integrity, its immediate neighbors, particularly Iran, Turkey, and Syria, will be strongly tempted to intervene. They all fear that an unstable Iraq would threaten their own national interests and might lead to an undesirable shift in the regional balance of power. None wishes to see Iraq break apart into independent Kurdish, Shi'ite, and Sunni states.

IRAN'S REARMAMENT PROGRAM

While Iraq struggles to recover from the Gulf War, Iran is determined to regain its former stature as the preeminent power in the Persian Gulf. Tehran's reformulated national security policy has three main goals:

--- Guarantee the survival of the regime.

--- Project power throughout the region.

--- Offset US influence in the Middle East.

0231

UNCLASSIFIED

To achieve these goals, Iran has undertaken diplomatic measures to end its international isolation, is purchasing weapons from a variety of foreign suppliers, and is developing a capability to produce weapons of mass destruction. During the period 1990-94, Iran plans to spend $2 billion in hard currency annually on foreign weapons.

--- Already, Tehran has purchased significant numbers of advanced warplanes and antiaircraft missiles from Russia and China. It has bought some extended-range Scud missiles from North Korea and is building a factory to manufacture its own.

--- As part of its upgrade of naval forces Iran has also contracted to buy at least two Kilo-class attack submarines from Russia.

--- Even after Operation Desert Storm, Iraq still has three times as many armored vehicles as Iran. To reduce that gap, Tehran is attempting to purchase hundreds of tanks from Russian and East European suppliers.

In the Iran-Iraq war, Iraq's chemical weapons were decisive factors in several important engagements, a lesson not lost on Iran.

--- We judge that Tehran is seeking to acquire a nuclear weapon capability. Barring significant technical input from abroad, however. the Iranians are not likely to achieve that goal before the year 2000.

--- Although extensive and improving, Iran's chemical weapon program remains relatively crude. Nevertheless, we expect Iran to develop chemical warheads for its Scud missiles within a few years.

--- We also suspect that Iran is working toward a biological warfare capability.

IRAN AND THE ARAB STATES

Tehran is rebuilding its military strength not only to redress the military imbalance with Iraq but also to increase its ability to influence and intimidate its Gulf neighbors -- though in the near term Tehran's desire to reduce US involvement in the region will probably lead it to court the Gulf States rather than bully them.

0233

Tehran is also trying to improve its relations with Arab states outside the Gulf, stressing Muslim solidarity and Islamic principles. In countries with Islamic opposition movements, Iran hopes to increase its influence among local fundamentalists without damaging its relations with these governments. For example, in Algeria Tehran wants to maintain ties with the new regime but continue its political and financial support for the Front for Islamic Salvation, which the Algerian Government is in the process of banning. Trying to have it both ways has been difficult: Algiers recalled its Ambassador in Tehran recently to protest Iran's continued support for the FRONT.

Iran's growing support of radical Palestinian groups may bring it closer to some Arab states, such as Libya. This support reflects Tehran's antipathy toward Israel, which it regards as both a US ally and a strategic threat. We expect Iran to continue to strongly oppose the peace process and probably to promote terrorism and other active measures aimed at undermining progress toward Israeli-Palestinian reconciliation.

Tehran's main surrogate in the Arab world will continue to be the radical Lebanese Shi'ite group Hizballah, which is the leading suspect in the recent horrific bombing of the Israeli Embassy in Argentina. To ensure that its links to Hizballah are preserved, Tehran will be careful to stay on the good side of the Syrian Government, which controls access to the territory occupied by Hizballah.

IRAN AND THE NEW ISLAMIC REPUBLICS

Tehran considers developments in the region to its north to be vital to its national interests. It wants both to fill the void caused by the collapse of the Soviet Union and to prevent the United States and regional rivals, especially Turkey, from gaining dominant influence there. Tehran's diplomatic efforts to improve its own influence in the new Islamic states of the region have included sponsoring them for membership in various regional and international organizations.

In addition, Tehran is trying to forge cultural and religious ties to the new republics. It remains to be seen how successful Tehran will be, given that these peoples are mostly Turkic, not Persian, and mostly Sunni Muslims, not Shi'ites.

We see no evidence of Iranian efforts to subvert the secular governments of the new states or to alienate them from Russia and the other non-Muslim members of the CIS. For now, at least, Iran seems to want to preserve amicable relations with Russia, which has become a major source of its arms. Furthermore, Iran must be cautious about instigating instability along its northern border, lest nationalist sentiment be aroused among its own Azeri and Turkmen minorities. Indeed, with regard to the conflict between Azerbaijan and Armenia, Tehran has tried to exert a moderating influence on the Azerbaijani Government.

While pursuing military reconstruction, President Rafsanjani is trying to create an Iranian image of responsibility and respectability -- both to reassure foreign investors and the Gulf Arab states and to maximize Iran's leverage in Afghanistan and the Central Asian republics. Moreover, Tehran wants to avoid providing the United States with an excuse to extend its presence in the Gulf. Tehran's current approach appears pragmatic and patient, but its clerical leadership has not abandoned the goal of one day leading the Islamic world and reversing the global dominance of Western culture and technology.

0236

HAS CHANGE PASSED BY THE MIDDLE EAST?

What about the impact of recent military, political, and economic trends in the region? Haven't these trends reduced the capability and inclination of Iran, Iraq, Libya, and Syria for military conflict and terrorism?

It is true that these states have suffered some major setbacks:

--- Iraq's military forces were devastated during the Gulf War and are encountering difficulties in rebuilding because of international sanctions. The Iraqi regime is likely to find itself in nearly continuous military conflict, at least against Kurdish and Shi'ite dissident groups.

--- Iran has still not recovered from the destruction suffered during its long war with Iraq, and its military reconstruction is being hampered by the poor state of its economy.

--- Meanwhile, having seen its hope of achieving strategic parity with Israel dashed by the collapse of its Soviet sponsor, Syria may have difficulty finding a reliable source of

0237

advanced conventional weaponry. Damascus will find it even harder to pay for such weaponry.

--- The Libyan regime is currently preoccupied with the fear of UN sanctions and the possibility that the United States and Britain will launch military action in punishment for its bombing of Pan American Flight 103. As a consequence, its perpetual subversion machine is barely ticking over.

Still, such developments have not led these governments to abandon their objectives -- we see no evidence of that -- only to alter their strategies and timetables. In particular, the escalating cost and difficulty of building first-rate conventional forces have increased the attractiveness of weapons of mass destruction. The evident determination of all four states to acquire special weapons suggests that they view such weapons as force multipliers capable of compensating for inadequacies in conventional forces and perhaps deterring future Desert Shield/Desert Storm campaigns.

0238

THE KOREAN PENINSULA

I'll turn now to the second part of the world you asked me to focus on, namely the Korean peninsula -- the one place in the world where US forces remain deployed opposite the forces of an avowed adversary.

STATUS OF THE NEGOTIATIONS

Since initialing agreements on Nonaggression/Reconciliation and the denuclearization of the Korean peninsula last December, North and South Korea have engaged in a series of negotiations and discussions, some at very high levels, to implement the accords. These discussions have achieved some concrete results, particularly the formation on 19 March of a Joint Nuclear Control Commission with a mandate to set up bilateral inspections of nuclear facilities.

For the most part, however, the two sides have so far produced a framework for but not the substance of reconciliation. They remain far apart on critical issues, such as frequency, thoroughness, and basic ground-rules for nuclear inspections. They also have major differences about the people-to-

people exchanges and military confidence-building measures called
for in the reconciliation agreement.

THE THREAT FROM THE NORTH

Until they are much farther along in this process, we must
continue to be wary and respectful of the military threat from
North Korea It is hard for me to say very much about this in open
session, however. North Korea is the most secretive state on
earth. Much of what we know about that country and the threat it
poses to South Korea comes from sensitive sources, and I must
wait until we get into closed session to go into some details.

I can say this much, however. The North maintains enormous
ground forces just north of the Demilitarized Zone. They are in
formations optimized for a sudden, massive strike southward
toward Seoul. In recent years, these forces have increased their
mobility and flexibility, improving their capability to threaten
prepared defenses. They considerably outnumber the opposing
Southern forces in both men and weapons. Notwithstanding the
recently signed Korean nonaggression pact, until these forces go
away, the threat they present is real and serious.

0240

It is not a question of fearing an attack from the South. The South Korean forces are deployed to defend Seoul. They present no countervailing threat to North Korea -- and P'yongyang knows it.

I don't want to exaggerate this threat. North Korea's armed forces suffer from many deficiencies. Their training and, consequently, combat readiness are questionable. They have weaknesses in air defense and logistics. They could not count on much if any support from erstwhile allies.

Furthermore, as Operation Desert Storm demonstrated, US airpower is highly effective against massed ground forces. The prospect that South Korea would receive extensive combat air support as well as other support from US forces is a potent deterrent, even to forces as strong as those North Korea has concentrated along the border.

NORTH KOREA'S NUCLEAR WEAPON PROGRAM

P'yongyang has been building an infrastructure that, without input from abroad, will be able to produce weapons-grade fissile material from scratch. It has domestic uranium mines. At

Yongbyon it has constructed two nuclear reactors whose sole purpose appears to be to make plutonium. One of these reactors has been operating for four years; the second, much larger reactor, may start up this year. Nearly completed is another facility at Yongbyon that will be able to reprocess reactor fuel to recover the plutonium.

Last December, North and South Korea negotiated an agreement-in-principle for a nuclear-free peninsula. Each side has committed itself not to "test, manufacture, produce, receive, possess, store, deploy, or use" nuclear weapons. Both sides also agreed not to have nuclear reprocessing or uranium enrichment facilities. There are grounds for questioning the North's intentions, given that it has not yet even admitted the existence of, much less declared, the plutonium production reactors and reprocessing facility at the Yongbyon nuclear research center.

Moreover, verification procedures remain to be worked out -- agreement was reached only his month that a joint committee should be formed to do that. The validity of the North-South nuclear accord depends on the inspection regime P'yongyang ultimately accepts.

Historically, North Korea has not been forthcoming in this area. It signed the Nuclear Nonproliferation Treaty in December 1985, and was thereby obligated to declare and place all nuclear facilities under safeguards. We are still waiting for P'yongyang's promised ratification of a safeguards agreement. Because some aspects of P'yongyang's behavior so far could be interpreted as an effort to continue nuclear weapon development, we wonder whether the North Koreans will accept meaningful on-site inspections that could allay our suspicions.

We believe P'yonguang is close, perhaps very close, to having a nuclear weapon capability. Where North Korea is concerned, moreover, we have to worry not only about the consequences for stability in Northeast Asia if it acquires nuclear weapons, but also about the possibility that P'yongyang might put nuclear materials and related technologies on the international market. In the past, the North Koreans have been willing to sell anything that could earn hard currency.

TRENDS UNFAVORABLE TO THE NORTH

The straitened economic circumstances in the North, coupled with uncertainties associated with the looming dynastic change of leadership in P'yongyang have led the North Koreans to modify their confrontational strategy toward the South, as well as toward the United States, Japan, and the United Nations. Tensions between North and South have decreased somewhat, though the actual military threat to the South has not changed significantly.

We expect that many of the North's military advantages over the South will erode throughout this decade, largely because of decreasing support from the North's traditional allies, coupled with its continuing economic problems:

-- North Korea's large inventory of weapons is becoming obsolete. The North's defense industry is based on 1960s technology and beset by quality problems. P'yongyang lacks the hard currency to purchase more advanced technology. We have seen no deliveries of major weapons from the Soviet Union or its successors since 1989. China cannot provide the types of weapons, such as modern aircraft or surface-to-air missile systems, that the Soviets supplied.

--- Fuel shortages -- principally a result of drastically reduced imports from the former Soviet Union -- are having a broad cumulative impact on all sectors, including the military.

Nevertheless, in the near term we could be entering a more dangerous period:

--- North Korean strategists could recommend an attack on the South while the North retains its substantial edge in numbers of men and weapons.

--- Difficulties in maintaining and modernizing P'yongyang's conventional forces could reinforce the North's determination to develop nuclear weapons and ballistic missiles.

That concludes my remarks in open session. I will have a little more to add about some of these issues when we resume in closed session.

0245

長 官 報 告 事 項

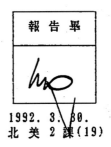

<u>題 目 : 하원군사위 청문회 CIA 국장 증언문</u>

> 지난 3. 27. 열린 하원 군사위원회 "지역위협 및 1990년대 국방대책" 제하의
> 청문회(공개회의)에서 밝힌 Gates CIA 국장의 증언문중 한국 관련 부분
> 요지를 아래 보고합니다.

1. 남북 협상 현황

  o 지난 12월 남북간 기본조약에 의거 JNCC 구성등 기본적 골격은 구성됨.

  o 핵사찰의 횟수, 사찰정도(thoroughness), 기본 규정등 핵관련 실질
    내용 도출에는 이견 상태

  o 주민 교류, 군사적 신뢰 구축 조치도 이견 노정

2. 북한의 위협에 대한 견해

  o 북한의 군사력 평가
    - 기습 공격에 적합한 대규모 지상군의 DMZ 부근 배치
      . 최근 동 병력의 기동성과 유연성(flexibility)이 증진됨
      . 동 병력은 한국에 대한 현존하는 심각한 위협 제기
    - 북한의 군사력 현황
      . 훈련 수준 저하로 인한 전투 준비 태세의 문제 존재
      . 방공, 병참의 취약성, 대외적 우방의 부재

- 1 -

0246

o 북한의 핵무기 개발 계획 관련 평가

  - 핵무기급 핵물질의 생산 시설 보유 노력 계속

    . 우라늄 광산 보유

    . 영변의 플루토늄 생산 가능한 원자로 2기 보유

      (1기는 4년전부터 가동중, 1기는 올해 가동 예정)

    . 핵재처리 시설 완공 단계

  - 핵시설 존재를 인정하지 않고 있어 북한의 의도에 의혹

    . 현재 진행중인 검증 절차와 체제에 관한 합의 결과에 따라 남북

      핵협정의 실효성이 판단될 것임.

    . 핵확산금지조약(NPT)에 따른 안전협정의 비준 여부 계속 주시 필요

  - 현재 북한의 핵개발 능력 보유 임박

    . 동 능력 보유시 동북아의 안보 위협 및 핵물질과 관련기술 수출에

      따른 핵확산 우려됨.

o 북한에 불리한 추세 및 금후 한반도 군사 상황 전망

  - 경제적 난국과 함께 지도자 계승에 따른 불확실성 상존

  - 북한의 대아국 군사적 우위는 90년대 말까지 점차 감소 예상

    . 방위 기술의 낙후, 구식 무기체제

    . 선진 무기 기술 도입 자금 부족, 연료의 부족

  - 단, 단기적으로 한반도 군사 상황이 위험한 시기에 진입할 가능성

    존재

    . 북한이 한국보다 병력과 군비의 우위가 있는 시기내 한국 공격 가능

    . 기존무기 체계 유지 및 현대화의 곤란을 보상하기 위한 북한의 핵무기,

      탄도 미사일 개발 추진 강화 가능성

- 끝 -

공   란

공 란

정리보존문서목록					
기록물종류	일반공문서철	등록번호	32694	등록일자	2009-02-26
분류번호	726.61	국가코드		보존기간	영구
명 칭	북한 핵문제, 1992. 전13권				
생 산 과	북미1과/북미2과	생산년도	1992~1992	담당그룹	
권 차 명	V.3 4-5월				
내용목차	* 4.28-5.4 카네기재단 시찰단 북한 방문 * 북한 핵관련 대책, 한.미국간 협의, 미국의 사찰과정 참여 요구 등				

0001

공　　　란

공 란

공　　　란

공   란

공 란

공   란

외 무 부

종 별 :

번 호 : USW-1689   일 시 : 92 0403 1956

수 신 : 장 관 (미일,미이,중동일,정특,국기,연일)

발 신 : 주 미 대사

제 목 : 볼튼 차관보 면담

2. 리비아 제재 결의안

- 본직이 리비아 제재 결의안이 성공적으로 통과된 것을 축하한데 대하여, BONTON 차관보는 중국이 찬성을 하도록 마지막 순간까지 노력하였으나 중국이 결국은 제 3 세계를 의식하여 기권을 하였다고 하면서, 그러나 PERM-5 기권은 찬성과 마찬가지라고 평가하고 있다고 하였음.

- 본직이 현재 리비아에는 아국 근로자가 5,000 명 이상 근무하고 있으며, 피해 추산액이 40 억불 이상에 달하고 있음을 설명하고, 앞으로 결의안을 이행해나가는 과정에서 근로자 보호문제등 아국이 당면할 수 있는 문제에 대하여 각별한 배려를 요청한데 대하여 BONTON 차관보는 잘알겠다고 하면서, 현재로서는 리비아가 4.12. 이전까지 의무사항을 이행하리라고 기대되지 않으므로 결국은 리비아에 대한 제재로 나아가게 될 것으로 본다고 전망하였음.

미주국 외정실	장관 분석관	차관 정와대	1차보 안기부	2차보	미주국	중아국	국기국	국기국

PAGE 1

4. 북한 인권문제

- 본직은 최근 북한 인권문제에 대한 국내외 관심이 고조되고 있다고 하면서, 우리로서는 인권문제로 북한을 궁지로 몰려는 것이 아니고, CSCE 과정에서 공산권의 인권문제 토의가 결국은 공산권의 인권상황 개선은 물론 정치적 자유화로도 연결된 경험도 있으므로, 북한 인권문제에 대한 국제사회의 인식을 제고시켜 나가고자 한다고 설명하였음.

- 이에대해 BOLTON 차관보는 미국으로서도 올바른 조치로 생각한다고 하면서, 우선은 ASIA WATCH, AMNESTY INTERNATIONAL 등 비정부기구 및 언론등을 통해북한 인권문제에 대한 국제사회의 인식을 제고시키는 것이 좋을 것으로 보며, UN 차원에서는 금년에는 결의안 통과등을 시도하기 보다는 북한내의 인권실태 파악을 위한 보고자(RAPPORTEUR) 임명등을 목표로 하는 방법도 있을 것으로 본다고 하였음.

- BOLTON 차관보는 과거 쿠바에 대해 유사한 조치가 취해졌을때 쿠바가 보고자 수용을 거부한 사례도 있음을 소개하고, 주유엔 미국대표부에도 이러한 사태 진전에 대비하도록 지시하겠다고 하면서 아측이 북한 인권문제에 대한 보도 광범위한 자료를 제공해 줄수 있을지에 대해 관심을 표시하였음.

끝.

공   란

공 란

공   란

공 란

북한 핵문제, 1992. 전13권 (V.3 4-5월) 399

공   란

공   란

공   란

공   란

공   란

공   란

공   란

공   란

공   란

외 무 부

종 별 :

번 호 : USW-1753

일 시 : 92 0407 1927

수 신 : 장 관 (미일,미이,아일,정특)

발 신 : 주 미 대사

제 목 : 부통령 안보보좌관 접촉

본직은 금 4.7 QUAYLE 부통령실 KARL JACKSON 안보보좌관과 오찬을 함께 하면서 주요 공통 관심사항에 관해 의견 교환한바, 요지 아래 보고함.

1. QUAYLE 부통령 방일

- JACKSON 안보보좌관은 5 월로 예정된 부통령 방일은 오끼나와 반환 20 주년 기념식 참석을 명분으로 추진되고 있으나 실제로는 최근 악화되어 온 미.일 관계를 개선시키기 위한 노력의 일환이라고 밝혔음. 특히 지난번 BUSH 대통령의 아주 순방시 통상문제에 지나친 비중을 둠으로써 여러가지 불피요한 잡음을 불러일으킨 점을 감안, 금번 부통령 방일에서는 안보.통상문제를 망라한 전반적인 양국 관계의 중요성을 부각시키는데 초점을 두고 있다고함.

- 부통령의 방일 기회에 다른나라를 방문하는 것도 검토되었으나 금번 여행시기 (5.12/13-16)는 분주한 선거운동 기간중에 유일하게 짬을 낼수 있는 시기라는 점에서 여타 우방국 방문은 고려할 수가 없는 상황이며, 이에따라 일본만 방문하고 다녀오는 일정으로 추진하고 있다고함.

- 이어서 JACKSON 보좌관은 QUAYLE 부통령으로서는 지난 89 년 방한이래 한국에 대한 관심이 매우 높아졌으므로 대통령 선거후 적절한 시기에 한국을 다시한번 방문하게 되기를 희망하고 있다고 부연함.

미주국 청와대	장관 안기부	차관	1차보	2차보	아주국	미주국	외정실	분석관

PAGE 1

 4. 양국의 선거정국

- JACKSON 보좌관은 공화당의 선거전략과 관련, 현재로서 QUAYLE 부통령은 선거운동 전면에 나서기 보다는 공화당의 지원조직을 관리해 나간다는데 역점을 두고 있다고 밝히면서, 아직까지는 외교문제가 선거운동의 쟁점으로 등장되고 있지 않으나 한국의 경우 어떤 문제든 양국간에 쟁점화 시키지 말고, 금융시장 자유화등 현안문제에 대하여 실질적인 조치를 취해나가는 것이 BUSH 대통령의 선거를 도와주는 결과가 될 것이라는 의견을 피력함.

- 본직은 지난번 국회의원 선거결과와 관련한 최근 정국동향을 설명하면서, 앞으로 여야 정치인들의 방미시 미행정부 요인 면담을 빈번히 요청해 올 것으로 예상된다고 한바, JACKSON 보좌관은 미행정부로서는 그와 같은 요청이 있는 경우 CASE BY CASE 로 처리할수 밖에 없겠으나 어떤 정파 지도자 (FACTIONAL LEADER)를 편파적으로 취급함으로서 다른나라의 국내정치에 관여한다는 인상을 주는것은 피한다는 것이 확고한 지침의 하나라고 언급하였음. 끝.

    (대사 현홍주-차관)

    예고: 92.12.31. 일반

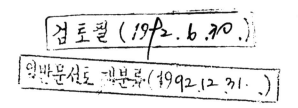

검토필 (1992. 6. 30.)

일반문서로 재분류 (1992. 12. 31.)

PAGE 2

0024

외 무 부

관리
번호 92-444

종 별 :

번 호 : USW-1792   일 시 : 92 0409 1649

수 신 : 장 관 (미일,미이,정특)

발 신 : 주 미 대 사

제 목 : 북한학자 참석 CSIS 학회

　　연: USW-1383, 1364

　　대: WUS-1600

　　대호 북한 외교부 고위관리 방미 관련 마이니찌 신문보도에 관하여 당관이 파악한
바를 아래 보고함.

　　1. "손낙운"의 신분

　　- 마이니찌 신문기사 내용중 "손낙운" 미일국장은 지난 3.16-18 간 당지 CSIS
세미나에 참석한 북한 대표단장 송락은과 동일 인물로 추정됨.

　　- CSIS 세미나를 주관한바 있는 GERITT GONG 박사와 접촉 확인한바에 의하면,
GONG 박사는 91.11. CSIS 방북시 평양에서 송락은과 만났으며, 당시 동인은 외교부와
평화군축연구소에 겸직 근무하고 있다고 밝힌바 있었으나 금번 방미시에는 1-2 개월전
부터는 평군축 부소장으로만 근무하고 있다고 말했다고 함.

　　2. 국무부의 비자발급

　　- 국무부 KARTMAN 한국과장은 상기보도 내용과 관련, 미측으로서는 송락은
일행에게 평군축과 CSIS 간의 학술교류 목적의 방미라는 점에서 비자발급 하였을뿐,
송락은 전력에 관하여는 고려한바 없다고 말하였음.

　　- 동 과장은 송락은 북한 외교부에서 다년간 근무하였다는 사실을 전해들은바
있다고 언급하였음.

　　3. 행정부, 의회인사 접촉시 특히 동향　　검토필 (1992. 6. 30.)

　　- 국무부 KARTMAN 한국과장, HASTINGS 북한담당관, 정보조사국 MERRILL 연구관 및
소수의 의원 보좌관등 일부 참석자들이 CSIS 리셉션 및 세미나 다과회에서 송락은
일행과 가벼운 인사교환 정도로 접촉한 사실은 있었으나, 특별한 의미를 둘만한
대화를 나눈 사실은 없다고함.

미주국 안기부	장관	차관	1차보	2차보	미주국	외정실	분석관	청와대

공문에 의거 재분류(19...)

0025

92.04.10　06:51

외신 2과　통제관 BZ

- MERRILL 연구관은 송락은의 영어구사 능력이 제한되어 있어 (청취 이해력은 좋은편) 말을 하기보다는 주로 듣는 편이었다고 언급함. 끝.
　　(대사 현홍주-국장)
　　예고: 92.12.31. 일반

외 무 부

종 별 :

번 호 : USW-1814　　　　　　　　　　일 시 : 92 0409 1935

수 신 : 장 관 (미일, 미이, 아일, 정특)

발 신 : 주 미 대사

제 목 : GREGG 주한 미대사 초청 간담회

　　GREGG 주한 미대사는 금 4.9. ASIA SOCIETY 주최 조찬 간담회에 초빙 연사로 참석, 한.미관계 및 남.북한 관계등에 관한 연설에 이어 질의.응답을 가진바, 요지 아래 보고함.(동 간담회에는 국무부 관계관, 학회인사등 100 여명이 참석한바, 당관에서는 김봉규공사등 관계직원 참석)

　　1. GREGG 대사 연설요지

　　- 독일 봉일직후 한국 국민들은 한때 봉일향수에 젖어 있었으나 이제는 봉일의 엄청난 경제적 댓가등을 감안 점진적인 봉일쪽으로 기울고 있음. 한편, 한국정부는 북방정책의 성공과 북한의 외교적 고립화등에 힘입어 북한과의 대화에 큰 자신감을 갖고 대처하고 있음.

　　- 한국의 민주화는 착실히 성숙되어 가고 있음.(광주사태 치유, 군부의 정치적 중립, 선거 스캔들 관련 안기부장 경질, 봉일국민당의 원내진출등 예시)

　　- 2 년전 부임이래 어떠한 단일문제 보다도 경제통상 문제에 많은 관심과 정력을 기울이고 있는바, 한국과의 경제관계에 있어서 난점은 기업간의 문제가 아니라 한국정부의 구태의연하고 선명치 않은 규정 적용에 있음.

　　- 한국은 늘 외세에 의한 침략의 희생자였는바, 북한의 위협을 극복한 다음의 위협은 일본이라고 인식하고 있음. 미국은 한국과 일본의 맹방으로서 양국이 국민감정을 해소하고 진정한 협력관계를 발전시켜 나가는데 협조해야 함.

　　- 미국인의 한국에 대한 인식은 매우 빈약하며 한국인의 미국에 대한 인식도 피상적인 경우가 많음. 미국인에 대한 인식제고를 위해 미대학내 한국학 보급을 위해 기금모금등 노력중에 있으며, 최근 한국문화재단이 미국 연구단체들의 한국연구 증진을 위해 지원 노력을 하고 있는 것은 양국민간의 이해와 인식제고를 위해 바람직한 현상임.

미주국 분석관	장관 정와대	차관 안기부	1차보	2차보	아주국	미주국	외연원	외정실

PAGE 1

0027

92.04.10　09:37

외신 2과 통제관 BX

2. 질의응답 요지

가. 남북한 관계및 북한 핵문제

- 남북한 관계는 남북한 기본조약 체결, 한반도 비핵화 선언 채택등 6개월전만해도 상상할수 없었던 만큼 진전을 보이고 있음. 남북 정상회담은 남북대화의 진척에 맞추어 신중히 추진되어야 한다는 여론에 따라 서두르지 않는다는 방침으로 선회하였음.

- 북한은 그동안 핵사찰 문제와 관련 지연작전을 펴왔는 바, 금일 최고인민회의에서 IAEA 안전협정을 비준한 것은 긍정적인 진전임. IAEA 에 의한 국제사찰과 더불어 남. 북 합의에 의한 상호사찰을 통해 IAEA 의 취약점을 보완해 나가야할 것임.

- 북한의 대량 살상무기 확산, 특히 북한이 초보적인 핵폭탄을 개발하여 제3 국에 판매할 가능성에 대한 우려가 미조야에 팽배해 있으나 과도하게 비관적으로 생각할 필요까지는(NOT TO BE OVERLY PESSIMISTIE) 없다고 봄. 북한내에서도 개방과 대외협력의 필요성을 인식하고 미.일과의 관계개선을 위해 핵문제의 해결이 불가피하다고 생각하는 사람들이 늘고 있는 징후가 보이고 있음.

나. 한. 미 통상관계

- 일부 한국 관료들은 경제문제의 해결을 위해 장기적, 근본적인 정책을 마련하기 보다 임시변통의 정책을 쓰는 경우가 종종 발견되는 바, 금년도 무역적자억제 목표달성을 위해 항공기 구매를 지연키로 했던 결정이 그대표적인 예임. 이러한 단견의 정책은 불필요한 통상마찰의 소지를 제공하는 것이며, 한국세관도불투명한 규정적용등 많은 문제점을 안고 있음.

- 여론조사에 의하면 많은 한국 국민들이 한. 미 경제. 통상 관계를 제로섬게임으로 인식하고, UR 관련 농산물 개방 요구를 미국의 한국에 대한 일방적인압력을 받아들이고 있는바, 이러한 인식의 전환을 위해 한. 미 양국의 노력이 요망됨. 끝.

(대사 현홍주-국장)

예고: 92.12.31. 까지

관리 번호	92-460

외 무 부

종 별 :

번 호 : USW-1839

일 시 : 92 0410 1858

수 신 : 장관(미일)동구일,정총)

발 신 : 주 미 대사

제 목 : 미의회 북한 핵관계 보고서 발간

대: WUS-1182

연: USW-1334(3.16)

1. 당관 박인국 서기관은 금 4.10 LARRY NIKSCH CRD(CONRESSIONAL RESEARCHSERVICE) 아주담당관을 면담하고 자신이 집필한 북한 핵무기 개발에 관한 CRS 보고서 4.8 자 개정판을 입수하였는 바 금번 개정판은 북한의 핵개발 현황, 북한의 핵개발 목적, 북한 핵문제를 위요한 미국의 정책 그리고 북한 핵개발 저지가 실패하였을 때의 제제 대안들에 관해 언급하고 있음. (사본 팩스편 송부)

2. NIKSCH 담당관은 금번 개정판 내용은 3.11 자 판과 동일하며 대호 KGB 극비문서 관련 내용만 추가 되었다고 언급하면서 CRS 내 러시아 전문가들은 "논거와 사실"지의 편집 관행상 오보를 했을 가능성이 없다는 결론을 내리고 동지 보도내용을 매우 심각하게 받아들이고 있다고 하면서 80 년대에 쏘-북한 관계의 특수성을 고려할 때 KGB 가 북한 권력층 내부 침부대가로 쏘련 핵기술 지원을 주도했을 가능성이 농후하다는 견해를 표명하면서 동지 보도 내용에 관한 추가 정보가 있는지를 문의하였음.

3. 상기 KGB 문서 보도관련 당관 보고와 추가 정보가 있으면 통보 바람.

첨부:USWF-Z231

(대사 현홍주-국장)

예고:일반 92.12.31.

검토필(1992. 6. 30.)

미주국	차관	1차보	구주국	외정실	분석관	청와대	안기부

0029

PAGE 1

92.04.11   10:13

외신 2과 통제관 BX

주 미 대 사 관

USW(F) : 2231   년월일 : 92.4.10   시간 : 18:58

수 신 : 장 관 (미일, 동구일, 정보)

발 신 : 주 미 대 사

제 목 : 첨부

보 안 통 제	ㅗ

(출처 :   )

외신 1과 뜸 제	

0030

Order Code IB91141

CRS Issue Brief

North Korea's
Nuclear Weapons Program

Updated April 8, 1992

by
Larry A. Niksch
Foreign Affairs and National Defense Division

Congressional Research Service • The Library of Congress

CONTENTS

0032

North Korea's Nuclear Weapons Program

SUMMARY

North Korea is constructing nuclear reactors and a plutonium reprocessing plant at a site called Yongbyon. According to some U.S. officials and other knowledgeable people, this will give North Korea the ability to manufacture atomic weapons, possibly as early as mid-1992. North Korea also is upgrading potential delivery systems, including SCUD missiles.

Pyongyang has used concern over the Yongbyon facility to pressure the United States to remove U.S. nuclear weapons alleged to be stationed in South Korea and probably the withdrawal of all U.S. forces in South Korea. North Korea, too, may view nuclear weapons as giving it greater deterrence against military attack and/or retaliation by the United States and South Korea. The regime may believe that nuclear arms would strengthen it internationally and at home, as currently it faces diplomatic isolation and the collapse of supportive communist regimes in the Soviet Union and Eastern Europe.

Apparently responding to the U.S. withdrawal of nuclear weapons from South Korea and other U.S. and South Korean policy inducements, North Korea signed agreements with South Korea and the International Atomic Energy Agency (IAEA) providing for inspections of North Korean facilities; but it is uncertain whether North Korea will permit these to be implemented in the near future.

A potential North Korean nuclear weapons program has major implications for U.S. policy in a number of areas. It could add to military instability in Korea, where the United States has about 40,000 troops stationed. South Korean reactions could threaten U.S.-South Korean policy coordination and political instability in the South. The issue has become a major factor in U.S.-Japan diplomatic cooperation and could become important in military cooperation. U.S. relations with Russia and with China increasingly would be affected by this issue. North Korean production of nuclear arms would damage U.S. nuclear nonproliferation policy.

The Bush Administration has set as an objective of U.S. policy the dismantling of the reprocessing plant at Yongbyon. It views the securing of international inspection of Yongbyon as a useful interim goal but not totally adequate, since North Korea could complete the reprocessing plant under an inspection regime. The Bush Administration has gained assistance from numerous governments in pressuring North Korea to allow inspection, and it has offered to improve relations with North Korea if Pyongyang complies.

If North Korea completes the Yongbyon complex, the U.S. and South Korean governments might consider more coercive options. A request for U.N. Security Council action likely would be the first step. An air strike or a naval blockade are possible measures, but either would risk the outbreak of a war. A military buildup in and around Korea would aim at containing a North Korean nuclear threat, but would represent an abandonment of the dismantling objective. Military options would raise the issue of Japanese and other allied support.

ISSUE DEFINITION

According to numerous press and journal articles (see **For Additional Reading**), U.S. intelligence estimates reportedly have concluded that a North Korean nuclear reactor and reprocessing facility presently under construction will give North Korea the ability to manufacture atomic weapons. This issue could have serious implications for the U.S. military/security role in Korea and Northeast Asia, and could threaten peace and stability there. It also could affect U.S. policy regarding the proliferation of nuclear weapons. A U.S. response could involve both diplomatic and military measures, involving not only North and South Korea, but also Japan, Russia, and China. Depending on how far the issue develops, Congress might be involved in at least four ways: (1) review of the findings of U.S. intelligence agencies; (2) oversight of the annual reports to Congress by the Bush Administration on the status of U.S. troops in South Korea; and (3) participation through hearings, floor debate, and legislation in consideration of U.S. policy responses.

BACKGROUND AND ANALYSIS

North Korea's apparent nuclear program is set against a security situation in the Korean peninsula that contains long-standing ideological and military tensions and dangers alongside significant political, diplomatic, and economic changes since 1987. The major elements include:

-- A high level of confrontation between North Korea and South Korea (Republic of Korea-R.O.K.): 1.1 million North Korean troops face 650,000 South Korean troops across the armistice line of 1953. North-South negotiators reached an agreement on reconciliation and cooperation in December 1991, but detailed accords still must be negotiated.

-- A deep ideological gap between a democratizing South Korea and a rigid, closed communist system in North Korea under Kim Il-sung, North Korea's President.

-- A "diplomatic revolution" in which North Korea's allies -- the Soviet Union and East European countries -- have established relations with South Korea, are building economic and other ties with it, and are reducing support for North Korea. China is moving in that direction, although more slowly. North Korea increasingly is isolated diplomatically and ideologically, and its economy is weakening. However, it continues to uphold its communist system.

-- North Korean initiative since 1990 aimed at normalizing relations with Japan, apparently to secure Japanese financial assistance. Negotiations between Japan and North Korea are ongoing.

-- Minimal contacts between the United States and North Korea: government-to-government discourse has been confined largely to sub-ambassadorial meetings between U.S. and North Korean officials in Beijing, China.

-- A U.S. military presence of over 40,000 troops in South Korea, scheduled to be cut to about 35,000 by the end of 1992 in the first stage of a plan to reduce the size of U.S. forces. Under its "neither confirm nor deny" policy, the U.S. Defense Department never has stated whether the United States has nuclear weapons in South Korea. However, numerous reports indicate that the United States withdrew nuclear weapons from South Korea in October-December 1991.

North Korea's Nuclear Program

Several U.S. and Japanese journals have published articles on the North Korean nuclear weapons program. The following description is based largely on the Japanese journal, *Seiron*, February 1991, and by Janes Intelligence Review, September 1991. U.S. and French reconnaissance satellites reportedly have taken numerous photographs of a North Korean nuclear facility located at Yongbyon, which is about 60 miles north of the North Korean capital of Pyongyang. The photographs have shown several structures that have led U.S. intelligence agencies and other experts to conclude that North Korea is developing a plant and equipment that could produce atomic bombs:

- A relatively small -- no more than 30 megawatt -- atomic reactor, constructed between 1980 and 1987: it reportedly is capable of expending enough uranium fuel to produce about 7 kilograms of plutonium annually -- enough for the manufacture of a single atomic bomb every one or two years.

- A larger (50-200 megawatts) atomic reactor under construction since 1984: when operational, it reportedly would be capable of producing enough spent fuel for 18 to 50 kilograms of plutonium annually -- enough for 2 to 5 atomic bombs.

- A building with the size and shape of a plutonium reprocessing plant: such a reprocessing plant would allow the North Koreans to separate nuclear weapons-grade Plutonium-239 from the reactors' spent uranium fuel rods. This separation process is crucial to the ability to produce atomic bombs.

Satellite photographs reportedly also show that the atomic reactors have no attached power lines, which they would have if used for electric power generation. There are no electric power generation plants in the vicinity of Yongbyon. Large numbers of military guards are at the site, and the area is ringed with anti-aircraft weapons. Professor Toshibumi Sakata of Japan's Tokai University's Information and Technology Center has studied Yongbyon since 1984. He has stated that the evidence is substantial that North Korea is constructing an atomic weapons facility.

Some experts and reports point to possibilities that North Korea also may have other, hidden nuclear weapons facilities, similar to the recently discovered Iraqi facilities. Bakchon, 60 miles north of Pyongyang, has been cited by Professor Sakata and others as one such site.

Persons interviewed for this study believe that North Korea has been constructing the two reactors and the apparent reprocessing plant with its own resources and technology. North Korea reportedly has about 3,000 scientists and research personnel devoted to the Yongbyon program. Many have studied nuclear technology (though not necessarily nuclear weapons production) in the Soviet Union and China and reportedly Pakistan. The training of nuclear scientists at North Korean universities reportedly is intense. North Korea has uranium deposits, estimated at 26 million tons. North Korea is believed to have one uranium producing mine. The North Korean reactors appear to be based on design and technology of the 1940s and early 1950s -- a type often found in developing countries.

In March 1992, the Russian newspaper *Arguments and Facts* quoted from a classified Soviet KGB report of Feb. 22, 1990, that the KGB had received information from "a reliable source" that "the first North Korean atomic explosive device has been completed. . . in the city of Yongbyon." The KGB undoubtedly had an extensive intelligence gathering operation in North Korea in the 1980s when military cooperation between the Soviet Union and North Korea was extensive. If the KGB report is accurate, North Korea has produced the basic components of an atomic bomb, especially the detonator which triggers a nuclear explosion; thus, it would need only reprocessed plutonium for a complete atomic bomb. U.S. officials stated in early 1992 that North Korea's plutonium reprocessing plant at Yongbyon was close to being operational and possibly could begin to produce fissionable material in the summer of 1992. These officials believe that, once operational, the reprocessing plant could produce enough weapons-grade plutonium for a bomb within a few months. Thus, if such a timetable proves correct, North Korea could have an atomic weapon by the end of 1992 or early in 1993.

International Assistance

Knowledgeable individuals believe that the Soviet Union has not assisted directly in the development of Yongbyon in the 1980s. The U.S.S.R. provided North Korea with a small research reactor in the 1960s, which also is at Yongbyon. However, North Korean nuclear scientists continued to receive training in the U.S.S.R. up to the demise of the Soviet Union in December 1991.

Several analysts interviewed said that there is no direct evidence that China is assisting North Korea in its nuclear weapons program. Non-government experts, however, have noted the reports that China was helping North Korea in the development of missiles. The publication *Nucleonics* (June 21, 1990) asserted that "Some sources believe the country [North Korea] is being assisted by China...." Another publication *Nuclear Fuel* (Oct. 2, 1989) cited U.S. officials as saying that the subject of China's nuclear cooperation with North Korea "has been raised" with the Chinese government and that there was "speculation" that China had provided technology for the North Korean reprocessing plant.

North Korea's Delivery Systems

The international concern over the Yongbyon facility has been exacerbated by North Korea's reported progress in developing and acquiring weapons systems capable of transporting nuclear warheads to targets in South Korea and Japan. North Korea presently produces a variation of the SCUD-B missile with an estimated range of nearly 200 miles. This would cover about two thirds of South Korean territory. According to an analysis of North Korea's missile program by Joseph Bermudez and Seth Carus in *Janes Soviet Intelligence Review*, April 1989, and subsequent U.S., British, and South

Korean press reports, North Korea also is developing a more advanced SCUD missile with a range of over 400 miles. Experts believe this missile will be deployed in 1992. This SCUD is thought to be more suited to carry a nuclear warhead than the SCUD-B; it would include all of South Korea in its range and could reach Japanese territory. In addition to the SCUDs, several aircraft in the North Korean arsenal probably could carry atomic bombs.

North Korean Objectives

North Korean Denials of Atomic Weapons Intentions

North Korea has denied in all of its statements that it intends to produce atomic weapons. North Korean spokesmen have described Yongbyon as a research facility. However, North Korea has left open the possibility it could begin nuclear weapons production. The Soviet newspaper *Komsomolskaya Pravda*, the official newspaper of the Soviet Communist Party youth organization, reported on Nov. 29, 1990, from Pyongyang that: "During his September talks with Eduard Shevardnadze, the D.P.R.K. foreign minister said that, in the event of diplomatic relations being established between Moscow and Seoul, the D.P.R.K. would consider itself not bound by the pledges not to create its own nuclear weapons." According to Japanese press reports based on Soviet sources, Foreign Minister Kim Yong-nam also handed Shevardnadze a memorandum, one clause of which stated that if Moscow established relations with South Korea, the North Korean-Soviet military alliance would lose validity and that "we will have no option but to take measures to produce ourselves those weapons that we have heretofore relied on from our alliance."

Focus on U.S. Alleged Nuclear Weapons

One North Korean objective in constructing an apparent nuclear-capable facility at Yongbyon appears to have been to create a bargaining chip to force the withdrawal of U.S. nuclear weapons from South Korea. The North Korean Vice Minister of Foreign Affairs stated in April 1991 that North Korea's decision to sign the Nuclear Non-Proliferation Treaty (NPT) in 1985 "was aimed at creating a condition for the withdrawal of U.S. nuclear arms in the South." Since North Korea signed the NPT, it has not fulfilled the treaty obligation to place its nuclear installations under inspection by the International Atomic Energy Agency (IAEA). The North Korean government has asserted that it will not allow IAEA inspection until the United States removes nuclear weapons from South Korea and ends the "nuclear threat" to North Korea.

Pyongyang has laid out these conditions in the form of a number of proposals for negotiations with the United States: bilateral talks with the United States; tripartite talks involving North Korea, South Korea, and the United States; and an international conference involving North Korea, South Korea, the United States, China, and the Soviet Union aimed at creating a nuclear-free zone for Korea. The North Korean government also has stated that the United States must provide a "legal written document" or "legal assurances" that it will not use nuclear weapons against North Korea or pose a "nuclear threat" to North Korea. North Korean proposals also have called for inspection of U.S. military bases in South Korea by a joint North Korean-South Korean team.

A Possible U.S. Troop Withdrawal

The pronouncements and policies of the Kim Il-sung regime suggest that it seeks broader objectives than the removal of U.S. nuclear weapons from South Korea. One is to turn any negotiation over nuclear weapons into a broader negotiation for the withdrawal of all U.S. troops from South Korea; or, as a step in this direction, expand a negotiation to discuss restrictions on U.S. military exercises and various types of U.S. weapons systems in South Korea.

North Korea's demand that the United States end the "nuclear threat" is aimed at a broad array of U.S. military activities in South Korea. North Korea applies the term "nuclear threat" to U.S.-South Korean military exercises, which it usually describes as "nuclear war exercises." North Korea has been vehement in denouncing as a nuclear war exercise the big U.S.-South Korean Team Spirit exercise held annually, and North Korea has used Team Spirit several times as a pretext for breaking off negotiations with South Korea. North Korea also has described U.S. combat aircraft stationed in South Korea as posing a nuclear threat.

North Korea has called for an end of the U.S. "nuclear umbrella" protection of South Korea, an end to U.S. military overflights and port calls of South Korea, termination of U.S. military exercises in which nuclear "equipment" is used, and a total U.S. troop withdrawal.

Stronger Deterrence Against the United States and South Korea

North Korea also may have other objectives related to military deterrence. The North Korean government has displayed a detailed awareness of the capabilities of U.S. military forces in and around Korea. U.S. and British press reports from Pyongyang and Beijing have asserted that the North Korean government was shocked at the effectiveness of the United States and the allies in crushing Iraq during the Persian Gulf war, and that it was reassessing its own military strategy. Such a reassessment could strengthen the arguments in Pyongyang for a nuclear weapons capability to strengthen deterrence against any U.S. and/or South Korean decision to take military measures against North Korea.

In the North Korean context, deterrence has meant dissuading Seoul and Washington from retaliating against North Korea for the repeated aggressive and terrorist acts committed by the North Korean government, especially in the 1980s: the blowing up of 17 cabinet and top advisory officials of the R.O.K. government in Rangoon, Burma (1983), a commando attack on a South Korean nuclear power plant (1983), and the blowing up of a South Korean airliner (1987). The R.O.K. government reportedly came close to ordering retaliation for the airliner bombing. High-ranking North Korean officials, who advocate and plan such acts, could argue that possession of an atomic deterrence would give North Korea the flexibility to continue such a confrontational strategy in the future.

Prevention of Diplomatic and Political Erosion

North Korea's recent diplomatic setbacks and its growing political isolation could be used by proponents of an atomic weapons capability to argue that this would compel other governments to give more attention to North Korea and its interests. North

CRS-5

0038

Korean statements to Soviet Foreign Minister Shevardnadze in September 1990, as described above, were an attempt to use the threat of nuclear weapons to influence the Soviet government on key policy issues affecting North Korea.

A nuclear weapons capability also could serve North Korea's policy of building relations with radical regimes like Iran, Syria, Libya, Cuba, (and possibly Iraq), including stepped-up sales of missiles and other arms to these states. Nuclear weapons technology could be a valuable commodity which Pyongyang could offer to these regimes (or other friendly countries) in exchange for economic and political support. A number of these governments reportedly are attempting to acquire nuclear weapons technology.

Dictatorial regimes often view advanced weapons systems as serving domestic political needs. North Korean leaders may believe that the status of a nuclear weapons power would provide the Kim Il-sung regime another pillar of strength and security at home, add to the mythology of Kim's invincibility, and help him ward off any domestic political challenges. The regime has demonstrated apprehension that the collapse of Eastern European and Soviet communist governments, political liberalization in the Soviet Union, and the 1989 pro-democracy movement in China could stimulate domestic opposition to Kim Il-sung and to Kim's plan to have his son, Kim Chong-il, succeed him. Government statements and other reports indicate that opposition exists.

Agreements with South Korea and the IAEA

On Jan. 31, 1992, North Korea signed an agreement with the International Atomic Energy Agency (IAEA) providing for IAEA inspection of nuclear facilities in North Korea. North Korea apparently decided to sign the accord in response to U.S. and South Korean moves since September 1991, including the withdrawal of U.S. nuclear weapons from South Korea and declarations by R.O.K. President Roh Tae-woo that there are no nuclear weapons on South Korean soil, that South Korea would not manufacture or possess nuclear weapons and would not build nuclear reprocessing plants, and that South Korea would agree to a system of mutual North-South inspections. Pressures from a worsening economy and China also may have been factors in the North Korean decision.

North Korea first signed an agreement with South Korea on Dec. 13, 1991, on reconciliation and cooperation, which contains a pledge of non-aggression and establishes committees to negotiate an opening of contacts, cooperation, and arms reduction. Then, on Dec. 31, 1991, it signed a Joint Declaration for a Nuclear-Free Korean Peninsula. North Korea and South Korea pledge not to possess, manufacture, or use nuclear weapons and not to possess reprocessing and uranium enrichment facilities. They agree to negotiate the establishment of a mutual nuclear inspection system.

Because of the reported U.S. intelligence estimates that Pyongyang's plutonium reprocessing plant will begin operating as early as mid-1992, key questions arising from these agreements are: (1) how quickly will North Korea ratify the IAEA agreement and submit to the IAEA a list of facilities for inspection; (2) how extensive the list will be and whether it will include all structures at Yongbyon and facilities at Bakchon; and (3) whether North Korea will negotiate seriously over a North-South inspection system and accept intrusive South Korean inspection of its facilities.

CRS-6

In signing the IAEA agreement, North Korean officials said that ratification by North Korea's parliament could take up to 12 months. One official said later that ratification was possible in April 1992. This raises a strong possibility that North Korea hopes to delay any IAEA inspection, since the parliament has no record of independence from President Kim Il-sung. In meetings with South Korean officials, the North Koreans have rejected South Korea's proposal for "pilot inspections" of facilities in April 1992 and have counterproposed negotiations over the specifics of implementation of the December 31 denuclearization agreement and joint action to secure an international guarantee for a non-nuclear Korea. North Korea also has begun to charge that Japan is plotting to produce nuclear weapons, using Japanese plutonium reprocessing plants — thus suggesting a possible new North Korean condition or demand. Kim Il-sung raised the Japanese reprocessing issue during the Feb. 18-21, 1992, North-South Prime Ministers' meetings. He also issued new demands for a total U.S. military withdrawal from South Korea.

It now seems that there will be no inspection until June 1992 at the earliest. Since the signing of the December 31 Joint Declaration, there has been no sign of activity at Yongbyon to indicate that a dismantling of the reprocessing plant has begun.

Implications for U.S. Policy

The apparent North Korean nuclear weapons program has numerous foreign policy and security implications for the United States. These unquestionably would grow even more complex if North Korea completes the Yongbyon facility over the next 2 years.

Military Implications

North Korea's possession of nuclear weapons would increase the danger that any new Korean war would turn into a nuclear conflict. It likely would affect the perceptions of North Korean and U.S. and South Korean military strategists regarding the status and composition of deterrence and military strategy options in various contingencies. A more unstable situation would develop if North Korean leaders concluded that nuclear weapons gave them more military options toward South Korea, or if South Korean leaders decided on drastic military countermeasures. Moreover, many experts believe that the situation in North Korea and between North Korea and South Korea will be especially unstable during the period of succession following Kim Il-sung's death (he will be 80 years old in April) and that North Korea's possession of nuclear weapons would increase the danger of conflict even further.

South Korean Reactions

South Korea's reactions to a North Korean atomic weapons capability could become a serious problem for the United States. Both governments see this as a security threat; but South Korea views the issue within the confines of North Korea-South Korea relations, whereas, the U.S. Government also perceives it as a threat to its global non-proliferation policy. The U.S. Administration in Washington would perceive U.S. interests to lie in influencing South Korea to coordinate policy with the United States and refrain from adopting diverse or unilateral policies. So far, Seoul and Washington have coordinated closely. However, several possible courses of action by South Korea could confront the United States with undesired situations.

Bush Administration officials and several executive branch specialists on Korea presently are concerned that the R.O.K. government may lower the priority it gives to the nuclear weapons issue in coming months, after reaching the agreement with North Korea on reconciliation and cooperation on Dec. 13, 1991. President Roh Tae-woo may wish to avoid a confrontation with North Korea over nuclear weapons in 1992 while he seeks to negotiate follow-up accords with Pyongyang (as provided for in the December 13 agreement) -- even if North Korea nears completion of the Yongbyon facility. Presidential and National Assembly elections in 1992 may add political incentives for Roh to avoid a confrontation.

Nevertheless, there is sentiment within the R.O.K. government, particularly within the army and the intelligence organs, for a tougher policy. Such a policy could include consideration of a preemptive military response. On Apr. 12, 1991, South Korea's Defense Minister, Lee Jong-koo, stated that South Korea might launch a commando attack on Yongbyon if North Korea continued with its construction there. The influential South Korean magazine, *Wolgan Choson*, reported in the March 1991 issue that South Korean defense planners were studying the option of an aerial strike at Yongbyon. South Korean government officials reportedly told U.S. Defense Secretary Cheney in November 1991 that they did not favor the direct use of force against North Korea, but such sentiment no doubt exists.

A growth of nuclear tensions on the Korean peninsula thus could also endanger political stability in South Korea and the more democratic political system that has emerged since the end of military-dominated government in 1987. The potential exists for discord between the government and army over the proper response to the North Korean nuclear program, especially if military measures are considered. The army dominated the South Korean government from 1961-1987.

Some observers and commentators have expressed concern that the R.O.K. government would consider its own nuclear weapons program in response to North Korea. South Korea currently has nine nuclear reactors for the production of nuclear power. South Korea stores spent uranium fuel from these reactors. It has no reprocessing plant, but is believed to be technically capable of constructing one. During the late 1970s, President Park Chung-hee had government agencies examine a nuclear weapons option in response to U.S. proposals for the withdrawal of American troops from Korea.

U.S.-Japan Relations

The Japanese government's policy towards the North Korean nuclear weapons program became a central issue in U.S.-Japan security relations when Japan and North Korea agreed in September 1990 to negotiate the normalization of relations. The Bush Administration urged the Japanese government to press the North Koreans on the nuclear arms question in the talks.

The Japanese government has set as a condition for normalization that North Korea allow IAEA inspection of the Yongbyon facility. At the end of 1991, Japanese officials began to assert that North Korea must dismantle the reprocessing plant. Some observers believe that Japanese pressure may be the most effective kind of outside influence because of North Korea's worsening economic conditions and its apparent desire to secure Japanese financial assistance. Thus, the United States will have a continuing interest in Japanese diplomacy remaining in parallel with U.S. strategy.

Moreover, if the North Korean nuclear program should lead to a deteriorating security situation on the Korean peninsula, U.S. views regarding Japan's security role in Korea could change. The Persian Gulf crisis demonstrated the willingness of the U.S. Government to press Japan to make a major financial commitment and take a military role in an emerging international security crisis. (See CRS Report 91-444 F, Japan's Response to the Persian Gulf Crisis: Implications for U.S.-Japan Relations). Such sentiment among U.S. policymakers and resultant pressure could be stronger in the case of Korea, given the general trend in American attitudes and the U.S. awareness of Japan's own interests in Korea.

If the United States were to pressure for Japanese military involvement in Korea, acute tensions would arise inside Japan and South Korea, whose peoples share animosities toward one another based on the history of Japanese invasions and occupations of Korea, including the harsh occupation from 1905 to 1945. It also would place severe strains on the Japanese government's adherence to the pacifist provisions of Japan's constitution.

U.S. Relations with the Russia and China

A continued North Korean nuclear weapons program would become more central to U.S. bilateral relations with Russia and China. The United States would seek greater Russian and Chinese support in the forms of direct bilateral pressures on North Korea through denials of aid, cooperation with the United States in the United Nations, and backing for U.S. initiatives. The collapse of the Soviet Union enhances the prospects of Russian support for the U.S. policy. China, however, could face increasingly difficult choices between backing a more assertive U.S. policy and retaining supportive ties to its long-standing ally, North Korea. Russia and China could be expected to react negatively toward any Japanese military involvement in Korea, which historically has been the focus of Russian-Japanese-Chinese rivalries in Northeast Asia.

Impact on U.S. Nonproliferation Policy

The U.S. Government would view the North Korean manufacture of an atomic weapon as a serious breach of the U.S.-led international effort to prevent the further proliferation of nuclear weapons. Because North Korea is a signatory of the NPT, its production of nuclear weapons could undermine international support for the treaty. This could be especially damaging since the treaty is due for an extension in 1995. South Korean and Japanese abilities to produce nuclear weapons could present a danger of escalating proliferation in response to the North Korean manufacture of an atomic bomb. U.S. officials and other American experts fear that North Korea might provide nuclear weapons technology to other radical states, thus further undermining the NPT and the nonproliferation policy.

CRS-9

Current U.S. Policy

The Bush Administration policy has two objectives: 1) inspection of the Yongbyon and other suspected facilities by the IAEA and South Korea and 2) a dismantling of the apparent North Korean reprocessing plant. Several U.S. officials, interviewed for this study, portrayed IAEA and South Korean inspection as useful interim measures that could limit (but not necessarily stop) production of nuclear weapons. The ultimate U.S. goal is a dismantling of the reprocessing plant, according to several statements by Pentagon officials.

U.S. officials and other experts outlined in interviews the weaknesses of the IAEA regime and inspection system, and the NPT regime with regard to a state like North Korea. Under IAEA, governments can limit the number and types of facilities to be inspected. Governments are permitted to construct nuclear reprocessing plants and produce atomic weapons-grade plutonium; IAEA inspectors only monitor the stored plutonium. Nevertheless, weapons-grade plutonium can be hidden, and some experts fear that North Korea might try to hide some portion of reprocessed plutonium from inspectors. North Korea has allowed IAEA inspection of the small Soviet-supplied reactor at Yongbyon but has severely restricted the inspectors, recently limiting them to nighttime inspections. Signatories of the NPT cannot use such plutonium to produce an actual atomic bomb, but the treaty has a provision allowing any signatory to withdraw 90 days after giving notice. In the past, North Korea has threatened to withdraw.

The Bush Administration's strategy so far contains two elements, which it seeks to integrate into a program of pressure on North Korea. The first is to offer North Korea inducements to give up its nuclear weapons program. These are intended to meet North Korea's most often stated condition for allowing IAEA inspection and take away Pyongyang's justification for its nuclear weapons policy. The United States and South Korea have announced and affected several key inducements since September 1991. The United States withdrew nuclear weapons from South Korea by December 1991, after President Bush decided to do so in October. President Roh, as stated previously, declared South Korea free of nuclear weapons, disavowed nuclear weapons and reprocessing facilities, and offered North Korea mutual inspections -- including inspection of U.S. military bases in South Korea. The United States and South Korea also suspended the Team Spirit military exercise scheduled for February 1992. The United States initiated a diplomatic meeting with North Korea at the United Nations in January 1992, the highest level of diplomatic contact yet between them. Earlier, the Bush Administration issued a "negative security guarantee" to North Korea: a general statement of U.S. policy that the United States would not use nuclear weapons against a non-nuclear power unless that country staged an armed attack against the United States or a U.S. ally and received support from a nuclear weapons state.

The Bush Administration intends these inducements to reinforce the second element of its strategy: a strong diplomatic campaign to encourage other governments to pressure North Korea to agree to IAEA and South Korean inspections and abandon its nuclear weapons program. The State Department has urged Japan, Russia, China, the Western European bloc, Australia, and other countries to pressure North Korea through bilateral talks and in international fora. U.S.-R.O.K. inducements are intended to gain greater Chinese and Russian cooperation by satisfying their desires that the United States make concessions and overtures to North Korea on this and other issues.

CRS-10

The Bush Administration no doubt hopes that these inducements will show governments and publics in allied countries that the United States is making significant efforts to resolve the issue peacefully.

U.S. Policy Prior to North Korean Completion of the Reprocessing Plant

In coming months, the United States will face three complicating factors if North Korea continues with its policy to develop a nuclear weapons capability. This will be the case despite and to a degree because of North Korea's agreements with South Korea and the IAEA. One is the need to produce results within the time period prior to North Korea's completion of the reprocessing plant — possibly as early as mid-1992. A second factor is the possibility that U.S. goals may diverge from those of other governments if North Korea allowed an IAEA inspection in June 1992. It is not certain whether Japan, Russia, China, and other countries would press North Korea to dismantle the reprocessing plant if Pyongyang allowed inspection. A third factor will be the emergence of clearer South Korean priorities on the nuclear weapons issue as North-South negotiations proceed.

Consequently, Bush Administration policy in the first half of 1992 likely will turn more towards pressure on North Korea if Pyongyang does not respond to U.S.-R.O.K. inducements by allowing comprehensive IAEA and South Korean inspections of Yongbyon (and possibly Bakchon). U.S. strategy probably contains or will contain some or all of the following elements:

(1) The Bush Administration is pressing North Korea to ratify immediately the IAEA agreement and agree to full-scale IAEA inspection of all facilities at Yongbyon. According to press reports, the Administration is pressing for inspections no later than June 1992.

(2) The Administration has urged Japan and other allies not to make concessions to North Korea (i.e., Japanese financial aid) even if North Korea allows inspections but, instead, to demand a dismantling of the Yongbyon reprocessing plant.

(3) If North Korea continues with the construction of the reprocessing plant, the Administration can be expected to publicize this and accuse North Korea of violating the provisions banning reprocessing facilities contained in the North Korea-South Korea Joint Declaration for a Nuclear-Free Korean Peninsula. The Administration likely will seek from inspectors verification of a reprocessing plant.

(4) The Administration no doubt will press South Korea to insist on an intrusive inspection system in the North-South negotiations over a mutual inspection agreement; and it undoubtedly will offer South Korea advanced U.S. equipment to conduct inspections. At the Prime Ministers' meeting, Feb. 18-21, 1992, South Korea pressed North Korea unsuccessfully to begin "pilot" inspections by April.

(5) The Administration has urged South Korea to make future negotiations with North Korea on aspects of the Dec. 13, 1991, agreement on reconciliation and cooperation dependent on North Korean agreement to comprehensive inspections.

Options Beyond Diplomacy

The context and agenda of U.S. policy will change if North Korea completes a nuclear reprocessing plant and begins to produce atomic weapons grade plutonium. The United States would face a setback to both its security policy in the Northwest Pacific and its nonproliferation policy. The U.S. Administration would face the choice of adopting stronger measures or modifying the goal of securing North Korean abandonment of the program.

Consideration of Coercive Measures. If diplomacy fails, the U.S. Government might consider stronger measures. Statements by R.O.K. and U.S. officials and recent collective moves against Iraq's nuclear weapons program indicate that at least 4 options likely could be considered:

-- U.N. Security Council action: There are indications that the Bush Administration and South Korea may take the issue to the Security Council in 1992. U.S. proposals could be in stages, calling initially for a Security Council directive to North Korea to allow IAEA inspection of any suspected nuclear weapons facilities. If North Korea refused, the United States could propose economic sanctions or a total economic embargo. China's position could be the main obstacle to Security Council approval of sanctions. Chinese and Russian adherence to an embargo would be crucial to its successful implementation. An economic embargo would signal to North Korea a nearly total isolation on the nuclear weapons issue. It would hurt further the already weakening North Korean economy. Thus, it might contribute to the reported unhappiness over economic policy among some members of the North Korean elite. There is no guarantee, however, that the North Korean government would comply with Security Council conditions. Pyongyang might look to exploit leaks in an embargo, possibly through continued dealings with fellow radical states. North Korea could blunt a U.S.-R.O.K. initiative in the U.N. by allowing a single IAEA inspection in June 1992.

-- A United Nations-authorized air and naval blockade to enforce a U.N.-directed economic embargo against North Korea: this would be similar to the measures against Iraq after the invasion of Kuwait. It could be imposed in reaction to significant leaks in an economic embargo. A blockade would put extreme pressure on North Korea. If China participated, it would prevent Pyongyang from exporting nuclear weapons materials to other radical states. It possibly would have to be a protracted effort over many months. A blockade also would carry the risk of North Korean military action. However, the involvement of the United Nations and support of other governments, especially China and Russia, might deter North Korea from retaliating militarily. The United States and South Korea would require support and/or involvement from Japan, other allies, China, and Russia to obtain U.N. Security Council approval and the full implementation of an air and naval blockade. Securing Chinese consent could be especially difficult.

-- G-7 Action: If securing Security Council action proved impossible or had to be postponed, the United States and South Korea could move through the G-7 group to secure U.S., Western European, and Japanese economic sanctions on North Korea. The G-7 countries also could seek the cooperation of Russia and

CRS-12

other potentially sympathetic governments. G-7 economic sanctions, backed by Russia, would penalize North Korea economically almost as much as a U.N.-imposed embargo. Japan would be the key to the effectiveness. The most effective sanctions (G-7 or U.N.) would require Japan to cut off the flow of money and capital from the pro-North Korean segment of the ethnic Korean community in Japan. This has been for years North Korea's chief source of foreign exchange. However, the Japanese government could face domestic turmoil instigated by ethnic Koreans. Imposing an embargo would be a politically difficult decision.

-   A surgical air strike aimed at destroying the Yongbyon facility and any other discovered in the future: South Korean and U.S. officials have spoken of this option. Air operations in the Persian Gulf war indicate that this likely would be effective in eliminating the reprocessing facility and the nuclear reactors at Yongbyon. However, it would not eliminate North Korea's nuclear weapons program if Pyongyang has other, more concealed facilities in other locations for producing nuclear weapons materials. An air strike would carry a high risk that North Korea would retaliate militarily against a selected target or targets in South Korea or, worse, that North Korea might launch an invasion of South Korea. If North Korea did not retaliate militarily, its record suggests that it might launch future terrorists acts against South Korea and the United States.

-   A buildup of U.S. conventional and nuclear forces in and around Korea but no direct military action against North Korea: this would represent a modification of the basic U.S. objective of preventing North Korea from fulfilling its nuclear weapons program. A new primary goal would be to contain and deter an expected nuclear armed North Korea. A force buildup also would be intended to reassure South Korea of U.S. resolve if the United States decided against direct military action against North Korea. In November 1991, Secretary Cheney announced that the United States would not withdraw troops from South Korea during the 1993-95 stage of a planned Western Pacific force reduction. (The United States is withdrawing about 13,000 troops from Korea and Japan in the 1991-1992 period.) A military buildup would add several billion dollars annually to the cost of U.S. military forces in the Western Pacific (about $16.4 million annually, including forces in Alaska, Hawaii, and Guam, according to an August 1991 General Accounting Office report).

FOR ADDITIONAL READING

Bermudez, Joseph A. North Korea's nuclear programme. Jane's intelligence review, September 1991: 404-411.

Mack, Andrew. North Korea and the bomb. Foreign policy, summer 1991: 87-104.

Spector, Leonard S. and Jacqueline R. Smith. North Korea: The next nuclear nightmare? Arms control today, March 1991: 8-13.

관리
번호 **92-
474**

외 무 부

종 별 : 지급

번 호 : USW-1888

수 신 : 장관 (미일, 미이)

발 신 : 주 미 대사

제 목 : 국무부 한국과 부과장 면담

일 시 : 92 0414 1942

당관 임성준 참사관은 금 4.14. 국무부 한국과 SCHMIEL 과장대리와 면담, 북한 핵문제등에 관하여 협의한바, 요지 아래 보고함.

1. 북한 핵시설

- 임참사관은 지난 4.9. 북한 최고인민회의에서 북한이 최초의 연구용 원자로 이외의 여타 핵시설의 존재를 인정한 이래, 4.11. 에는 원자력 공업부 간부가일본기자와의 회견에서 영변일대의 가동 또는 건설중인 원자로가 5 개라고 언급하는등 북한의 핵시설에 관하여 공개적인 입장을 취하고 있는 사실에 대하여 미측의 평가를 문의하면서 특히 현재까지 미측이 파악하고 있는 정보내용과의 상이점등이 검토되고 있는지 여부를 아울러 문의하였음.

- SCHMIEL 과장대리는 미측도 북한의 그와같은 동향을 흥미롭게 관찰하고 있다고 말하면서 현재 행정부내 관련부서에서 면밀한 검토가 진행중이라고 밝혔음.

2. 대북한 밀 수출관련 보도

- 임참사관은 4.15. 자 경향신문의 대북한 밀 극비 수출허가 보도와 관련, 보도 내용중 사실과 다른 내용이 많아 당관으로서는 당지 특파원들에게 사실관계를 적절히 설명해 줌으로써 더이상의 추측보도를 방지하고 있다고 설명하였음.

- SCHMIEL 과장대리는 상기 보도내용을 접하고 있지 않기 때문에 현재로서는 특별한 의견이 없으나 아측의 조치를 적절하게 생각한다는 의견을 표명하였음.끝.

(대사 현홍주-국장)

예고: 92.12.31. 일반

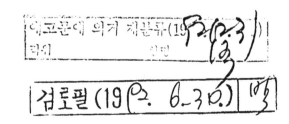

외교문서 의거 재분류(19)
원안   검토
검토필(19 . 6-30.)

미주국	차관	1차보		미주국		분석관	정와대	안기부

PAGE 1

92.04.15   09:43
외신 2과 통제관 BZ

공   란

공   란

공   란

공   란

공   란

공　　　란

공   란

공   란

종   별 :

번   호 : USW-1912   일   시 : 92 0415 1818

수   신 : 장관(미일,미이,정특)

발   신 : 주미대사

제   목 : 국무부 브리핑

　　금 4.15 국무부 정례브리핑시 언급된 미-북한관계 질문답변 내용을 하기 보고함.
(관련부분은 별전 USWF-2332 편 송부함)

　　. (질문) 금일 WASHINGTON TIMES 지에 게재된 인터뷰 기사에서 김일성이 미국과의
관계개선을 요청한 데 대한 논평은 ?

　　. (답변): TUIWILER 대변인)

　　- 특별히 논평할 것이 없음.

　　- 북한이 미국과의 관계개선을 위해 취해야 할 조치들은 재론할 것도 없으며,
미국의 정책은 변함이 없음.

　　- 동지 기사 내용만으로는 북한의 미국의 대한 태도에 진정한 변화가 있는지
판단키 어려움.

　　(대사 현홍주-국장)

미주국　　1차보　　미주국　　외정실　　분석관　　안기부

주 미 대 사 관

USW(F) : 2332 년월일 : 92. 4. 15 시간 : 1828

수 신 : 장 관 (미인, 미이, 정록)

발 신 : 주 미 대 시

제 목 : 천부문   (출처 : FNS)

보안통제	..

MS. TUTWILER: Mmm-hmm.

Q   Margaret, do you have any reaction to the interview in the Washington Times today by **Kim Il-Sung** in which he calls for better relations with the United States?

MS. TUTWILER: Not particularly. I can restate for you what it takes to have better relations with the United States -- our policy hasn't changed -- and we can't judge this morning if this is indeed a shift in North Korea's attitude towards the United States.

(2332 - 1 - 1)

외신 1과 통 제	

0057

외 무 부

종 별 :

번 호 : USW-1911   일   시 : 92 0415 1818

수 신 : 장 관 (미일,미이,정특)

발 신 : 주 미 대사

제 목 : 미-북한 관계

   금 4.15. 백악관 정례 브리핑시 언급된 미-북한관계 질문답변 내용을 하기 보고함.(관련부분은 별전 USW(F)-2333 편 송부함)
   - (질문) 금일 WASHINGTON TIMES 지에 게재된 김일성의 미-북한 관계 개선 요청에 대한 논평은 ?
   (답변)
   . 동 기사에 대해 논평할 것은 없음.
   . 미국은 다만 이미 합의된 핵사찰이 이루어지고, 핵무기 부재가 확인된후, 미-북한 관계가 개선될 것을 희망함.
   - (질문) 핵사찰 문제가 미-북한 수교의 마지막 장애물(THE LAST OBSTACLE) 인지 ?
   (답변)
   . 미국과 북한간의 이질성(DIFFERENCES) 은 오랜기간을 통해 형성된 것이며, 다양한 국면(ASPECTS) 을 지니고 있음.
   . 북한과의 수교를 고려하기 이전에 거쳐야할 중간 단계들(INTERIM STEPS) 이 있다고 생각함.
   - (질문) 김일성이 언급한 미국대사관 개설 희망, 김정일에 권력이양 완료등에 대한 반응은 ?
   (답변)
   . 특히 논평할 것이 없음.
   . 일반론적으로 (OVERALL) 미국이 북한과의 관계개선을 기대한다고 (LOOKING FOR) 말할수 있으나, 미국은 핵사찰이 당사국들이 이미 합의한바에 따라 이루어지기를 희망함. 끝.

미주국   1차보   미주국   외정실   분석관   정와대   안기부

                                                                      0058

PAGE 1   92.04.16   08:03 DQ
                                                      외신 1과 통제관

첨부: USW(F)-2333(2 매)

(대사 현홍주-국장)

USW(F) : **2333** 년월일 : 92.4.15 시간 : 18:18

수 신 : 장 관 (머일, 머이, 정특)

발 신 : 주 미 대 사

제 목 : 첨부물   (출처 : FNS)

보 안 통 제	..

THE WHITE HOUSE WASHINGTON, DC REGULAR BRIEFING
BRIEFER: MARLIN FITZWATER   WEDNESDAY, APRIL 15, 1992

    Q   Marlin, in **North Korea**, Kim Il Sung had a lengthy
interview with the Washington Times which appeared in this morning's
paper. And in which he says that the relations between (us are
becoming ?) better because North Korea has already abandoned its
nuclear program. And does the White House have any comment on this
interview?

    MR. FITZWATER: We don't have any comment on the interview.
You know the status of that in terms of the inspections to take
place, and we are hopeful that those inspections will take place and
will prove that both sides are indeed taking out their nuclear
weapons as promised and that we can have better relations with North
Korea.

(**2333** - 2 - 1)

외신 1과 통 제	.

0060

Q   Yeah, is the question of nuclear inspection the last obstacle to diplomatic relations with North Korea?

MR. FITZWATER: Well, we don't want to cite any one obstacle or a last piece. There are so many aspects of that situation and certainly -- but we have to watch the relationship. Our differences with North Korea are well-known and long, and there are a lot of various aspects. We'd have to consider it as we move forward. But I suspect there are interim steps before we get to that kind of recognition.

Q   One of the major components of that interview that seemed to be along the line that you -- your folks had talked about wanting, and one was the overture, to open an embassy specifically. The second was the declaration that he has already turned over the total power internally to his son, which goes beyond the previous military position. And I'm wondering, does this encourage you, are you discouraged, do you have no reaction as opposed to --

MR. FITZWATER: Well, yeah, I'm sorry I didn't read the interview this morning, for other reasons. But --

(Laughter.)

Q   He'd already crumpled the paper up. (Laughter.)

MR. FITZWATER: That's right. I'm surprised you had room for it today. (Laughter.)

I'll see if we can get any other response from the State Department. But I do want to say that overall that we are looking for better relations with North Korea. We are hoping these inspections work out, that all -- both sides live up their agreements. We certainly intend to. But I don't have specifics on the interview.

2333-2-2

0061

主要外信隨時報告

北 10만이상 살상용 核무기개발
릴리차관보 李基澤대표와 요담

外務部 情報狀況室
受信日時 92.4.16.08:20

(워싱턴=聯合) 洪相杓기자= 미국을 방문중인 민주당의 李基澤대표는 16일새벽(한국시간) 제임스 릴리 美국방부 국제안보담당차관보와 리처드 술로몬 국무부東亞.太담당차관보를 각각 만나 북한의 核사찰을 포함한 남북한문제와 韓美관계전반에 관해 의견을 나누었다.

이자리에서 릴리차관보는 "미국은 북한이 일시에 10만명이상을 살상할수 있는 核무기개발을 진행중인 것으로 파악하고 있다"고 밝히고 "특히 북한의 핵통제권이 金正日에게 넘어갈 경우 남한은 물론 일본등 아시아지역에 심각한 위협이 될 것"이라고 말한 것으로 한 배석자가 전했다.

릴리차관보는 북한이 오는 6월까지 핵사찰을 불응할 경우 군사제재를 가할 가능성에 관해 "美행정부는 對北군사제재에 관해 어떤 결론도 내린바 없다"고 밝히고 "군사적인 압력을 가해야 한다는 의견은 행정부의 공식 견해가 아니며 의회나 학계및 언론이 제기하고 있는 문제일뿐"이라고 말했다.

릴리차관보는 "북한이 核사찰문제에 관해 분명한 응답을 해올때까지 미국은 고위인사간 접촉을 자제하는 등 對北압력을 계속할 것"이라면서 "일본도 북한과의 수고교섭을 신중히 진행하고 한국도 경제협력, 교류등에 있어 북한을 고무시키는 행동을 삼가는 것이 바람직하다"고 말했다.

李대표는 또 이날오전 워싱턴소재 카네기재단이 주최한 세미나에도 참석, <차기 대통령선거의 전망>이라는 주제로 연설한뒤 참석자들과 질의응답을 벌였다. (끝)

(YONHAP) 920416 0759 KST

0062

공   란

공   란

공   란

공 란

9

외 무 부

관리
번호 92-482

종 별 : 지 급

번 호 : USW-1923

일 시 : 92 0415 2136

수 신 : 장 관 (미일(미이,정북,기정))

발 신 : 주 미 대사

제 목 : 미국의 대북한 조치

당관 임성준 참사관은 금 4.15. 국무부 SCHMIEL 과장대리와 면담, 대호 미국의 대북한 조치 여부등에 관하여 협의한바, 아래 요지 보고함.

1. 미.북 직통전화 개설 보도(대: WUS-1732)

- SCHMIEL 과장대리는 일본 마이니찌 신문보도는 전혀 사실 무근이며 미정부는 현단계에서 어떠한 종류이든간에 대북한 완화조치를 고려하고 있지 않다고 말하면서 동 보도는 대베트남 조치와 혼동한 것으로 본다는 의견을 보였음.

- 동 과장은 이어 미측이 아측과 충분히 협의한대로 북한이 성실하게 IAEA 핵사찰뿐 아니라 남북한 상호 사찰을 받게되면 그때가서야 미.북한 고위급 대화의 정례화가 이루어질 것이고, 그 이후 대북한 직접봉신 제한 철폐문제가 논의될것이라고 덧붙였음.

2. 미.북한 교류확대(대: WUS-1747)

검토필 (1992. 6. 30) 103

- 임참사관은 최근 미.북한 학술교류가 상당히 활발하게 이루어지면서, 그와같은 학술회의 참석을 이유로 한 북한 고위인사의 방미문제도 아울러 거론됨으로써, 북한의 IAEA 핵안전협정 비준을 계기로 마치 미행정부가 대북 유화조치를 취하고 있는 듯한 인상을 줄 우려가 있음을 지적, 이에대한 미측의 의견을 문의하였음.

- SCHMIEL 과장대리는 북한의 4.9. 비준과 관련하여 미국의 대북한 입장에 아무런 변화도 없다고 강조하고, 미.북한 학술교류는 북한체제를 개방으로 유도한다는 차원에서 문제삼고 있지 않으며 북한측 참석인사에 대한 비자발급은 계속사안에 따라 CASE BY CASE 로 운영하고 있다고 밝혔음. 동인은 상기 관련, 북한 유엔대표부 허종에 대한 여행허가도 지난번 LA 재외동포 주관 흥행사업 참석은 불허했으나, 대학주최 학술회의 참석이라면 신축성 있게 대처할 것임을 시사하였음.

3. 대북한 수출허가

미주국	차관	1차보	2차보	미주국	외정실	분석관	정와대	안기부

0067

- 상기 면담시 동석한 HASTINGS 북한 담당관은 아국언론의 미국 밀 대북한 수출허가 보도문제와 관련, 당관이 당지 아국특파원에 대하여 잘못 보도된 내용을 바로 잡아주는등 신속하게 대처한 것에 사의를 표하면서 본건의 보다 상세한 내용을 알려주고 싶어도 미측의 영업비밀 보호규정 때문에 한계가 있음을 아측이 이해해 주기를 바란다고 말하였음.

- 동 담당관은 최근(북한의 4.9. 핵안전협정 비준 이전이라고만 언급)에도 수백만불 상당의 면(COTTON)에 대한 대북수출 허가 신청이 있어 현재 행정부내 관련부서에서 검토중에 있다는 사실을 알려줌.

- 임참사관은 미국의 대북한 수출문제에 관하여는 추후 아측입장을 표명하겠으나 아측과 긴밀히 사전 협조해 나가는 것이 매우 중요함을 강조하여 두었음. 끝.

(대사 현홍주-국장)

예고: 92.12.31. 일반

외 무 부

종 별 : 긴 급

번 호 : USW-1924   일 시 : 92 0415 2137

수 신 : 장 관 (미일,미이,정특)

발 신 : 주 미 대사

제 목 : W.T. 지 김일성 인터뷰 기사

연: USW-1912

표제관련, 금 4.15. 국무부 동아태국 대변인실에서 발표한 논평 내용을 하기 보고 함.

- 동 기사 내용대로 북한의 미국에 대한 태도에 변화가 생긴 것으로도 볼수 있겠으며, 미국은 이것이 북한의 최소한 제반문제들을 논의할용의 (WILLINGNESS) 를 보인 것으로도 볼수 있다고 생각함.

- 미국은 북한 핵개발 문제에 우려를 표시해왔으며, 미-북한 관계의 실질적 진전 (SUBSTANTIAL MOVEMENTS) 이전에 북한이 그들의 약속을 이행해야 함을 강조하고자함.

- 미국은 북한의 IAEA 협정비준을 환영한바 있으며, 북한이 철저하고 신속하게 핵 시설들을 신고하고 사찰을 받을 것을 촉구함.

- 미국은 또한 IAEA 사찰과 병행하는 남북한간의 상호사찰 REGIME 협상이 이루어져서, 한반도 핵확산의 위험을 불식시킬수 있는보장 (ASSURANCE) 이 제공되기를 촉구함.

- 미-북한 관계개선 이전에 북한은 핵문제를 포함한 일련의 문제들 (A NUMBEROF ISSUES) 에대한 미국의 우려를 불식시켜야 함. 동 문제들은(1) 남북관계 진전, (2) 테러리즘, (3) 미군유해송환, (4) 북한 미사일 및 제조기술 수출문제,(5) 북한내인권 문제를 포함하는 것임.끝.

(대사 현홍주-국장)

미주국   1차보   미주국   외정실   분석관   청와대   안기부   장관 차관

PAGE 1

공 란

공   란

외 무 부

종 별 :

번 호 : USW-1934   일 시 : 92 0416 1748

수 신 : 장 관 (미이,미일,정특,정안,기정)

발 신 : 주 미 대사

제 목 : 북한 핵 비데오

　　1. 금 4.16. 국방부 정례 브리핑시 북한이 핵시설 비데오를 공개한 것과
관련,하기와 같은 질의.응답이 있었음.

　　(질의)

　　- 북한이 공개한 핵시설 관련 비데오에 대해 평가가 있는지 ?

　　(답변)

　　- 아직 보지는 못하였으나, 일반적으로 할수 있는 평가는 북한은 IAEA 핵안전
협정에 따른 사찰을 받아 들일 의무가 있다는 것임.

　　(질의)

　　- 북한이 사찰을 받아들일 것으로 보는지 ?

　　(답변)

　　- 사찰을 받아봐야 확실히 알수 있을 것임.

　　2. 질의.응답 전문을 FAX 송부함.

　　첨부: USW(F)-2348 편).끝.

　　(대사 현홍주-국장)

미주국	1차보	미주국	외정실	외정실	분석관	정와대	안기부

USW(F) : 2348 년월일 : 92. 4. 16 시간 : 0248

수 신 : 장 관 (메,메일, 30특. 302. 이정) 보 안 / 통 제

발 신 : 주 미 대 사

제 목 : USW- 1934 의 격부물   (출처 : 2NS)

DEFENSE DEPARTMENT REGULAR BRIEFING   BRIEFER: PETE WILLIAMS
12:05 P.M (EDT)   THURSDAY, APRIL 16, 1992

    Q   New subject? North Korea. Has the Pentagon had a chance to look at this videotape that the North Koreans have released showing their **nuclear facilities**, and if so, what does the Pentagon see in that videotape?

    MR. WILLIAMS: I don't know yet. I don't know if we've seen it or not. Let me check on it. I think, obviously, as instructive as a videotape produced by a foreign government might be, nonetheless, we continue to maintain that Iraq -- or North Korea has obligations under the International Atomic Energy Agency safeguards, which they themselves have signed up to, that they haven't yet complied with to allow robust international inspections. I will nontheless look into the question of whether we've seen the tape and what we make of it.

    Q   Is there now a belief that they are going to allow these inspections? Or do we still sort of view this as a -- another version of cheat and retreat?

    MR. WILLIAMS: I don't -- I think we'll believe it when we see it.

(2348 - 1-1)   외신 1과 / 평 제

0073

공   란

공   란

공   란

공   란

공   란

공   란

공   란

공   란

외 무 부

종 별 :

번 호 : USW-1996

일 시 : 92 0420 1753

수 신 : 장 관(북미 1과장)

발 신 : 주 미 대사 (안호영)

제 목 : 솔로몬 차관보 회견

1. 4.17. 일본 요미우리 신문에 보도된 솔로몬차관보 회견내용중 미-북한 관계 부분 TEXT를 국무부에서 입수, 팩스 송부함. (USW(F)-2452)

2. 상기 TEXT 에 따르면 솔로몬 차관보는'북한이 IAEA 및 남한과의 제협정들에 따른 철저한 사찰을 통하여 핵개발 계획 부재 및 한반도내 핵 군비경쟁 부재를 확인시킨 후에야 비로서 미국은 (1) 북한과의 대화수준을 격상시키고, (2) 미-북한간 다른 잇슈들을 해결하며,(3) 양국관계를 개선하기 위해 노력할 태세를 갖게 될 것이다'라고언급함.끝.

미주국

주 미 대 사 관

USW(F) : 2452   년월일 : 92.4.20. 시간 : 17:50
수 신 : 장 관 (배신 김명복 2광님)   보안통제 4
발 신 : 주미대사
제 목 : USW-1996 의 첨부물   (출처 : DOS)

prefer that such facilities are not destroyed, as, after all,
this is a Korean achievement? And in a reunified Korea,
nuclear capability might well be something that the present
South Korean government would like to possess rather than
destroy. Therefore, is the US imposing its view on this matter
-- (inaudible) -- North as well as South?
DR. SOLOMON: Well, first of all, the North Koreans tell us,
they tell the world, that they do not have a nuclear weapons
program, that they do not have a reprocessing facility that
could extract from irradiated fuel the plutonium needed to make
weapons. And in recent days they have identified publicly that
they do have certain reactors that they say are related to
development of nuclear power.
As far as the South Korean government is concerned, all I can
tell you is that President Roh Tae Woo, at his own volition,
has put forward some very farsighted proposals that have now
led to certain agreement with the North that the Korean
Peninsula should be free of nuclear weapons and free of a
reprocessing capability.
We applaud this development because we think the prospect of
nuclear proliferation on the Peninsula would be highly
destabilizing. It would create the prospect of an arms race
and it would create threats to other states in the region.
There is unanimity of view, frankly, with Japan, with Russia,
with China, that a nuclear arms race on the Peninsula would be
very destabilizing to the entire region. So for that reason,
this is not a matter of the United States imposing its will;
it's a matter of, I think, some farsighted leaders realizing
that a nuclear arms race in the Peninsula serves no one's
purpose.

(2452-3-1)   외신 1과 통제

0083

And for our part, we have encouraged reconciliation between
North and South through the dialogue that began several years
ago. (And we have indicated our willingness, if these various
agreements with the International Atomic Energy Agency and
between North and South Korea are fully implemented through
inspections that confirm that there is no nuclear weapons
program or nuclear arms race developing on the Peninsula, that
in that context we would then be prepared to raise the level of
our dialogue with North Korea, address some of the other issues
we have between us, and try to improve our relations.)
I think far from twisting anybody's arm, we have been pleased
that North Korea has responded positively in recent months. I
think no one on our side would have predicted we would have
seen the progress in terms of the various agreements that were
reached, first between the North and South Koreans at the end
of last year, and now North Korea signing and ratifying the
IAEA inspection regime, beginning to implement the agreements
with the South in terms of control of the nuclear issue. So we
think all parties see their interests served by this positive
development. We encourage it.

There is still a great deal of suspicion between the two
Koreas, and the burden of the past in terms of our past
confrontation with North Korea is something that still has to
be worked on. But we believe there's been positive
development, and we want to encourage it. And our only hope is
that the implementation of these agreements will be realized in
the next month or two or three. And we have been pleased in
recent days that we've seen statements by Mr. Kim Il Sung and
Mr. Hong Si-hak, even more recently by Kim Il Sung, that they
intend to honor these various agreements, implement the things
that they have signed, and build that confidence.
Q: Dr. Solomon, sticking on the question of security, the
United States already has established bilateral ties with
several countries in this region. Do you envisage a situation
in the future where there would be a multilateral security
system?
DR. SOLOMON: That's a very interesting question. There has
been some discussion of that. As you know, over the past year
and a half, some people were talking about taking the European
experience through the so-called CSCE, the Conference on
Security & Cooperation in Europe, and somehow applying that to
Asia. The informal debate on that question did not seem to
lead to a consensus that there should be a multilateral
security structure in East Asia. The region is very large.
The only reason you had the successful security structures in
Europe is that there was a very clearly defined threat, a very
clear demarcation line across which armies confronted one
another. You have not had that kind of a situation in the
Asia-Pacific region, which, apart from its huge geographical
scope, has lacked the sense of a common threat. So, if you
like, psychologically and in terms of the structure of the
region's security needs, it wasn't the basis for the
multilateral security structure.

2452-3-2

0084

What we have seen is that within the context of the ASEAN post-ministerial dialogue, there has been discussion of creation of more of a dialogue about security issues. And we have indicated that we are receptive to discussing security concerns in the ASEAN post-ministerial framework. Whether out of that would come from multilateral structure for security, it seems to me, is really in question. I still don't see the impulse for it, the rationale for it. I think the countries of the region are fortunate now to have a peaceful environment where they can focus on their economic development. And so I myself would doubt that we have the basis for a multilateral security framework. But circumstances change, and maybe over some years, with some discussion, there might be a new development.
We feel that, again, APEC is addressing the real security concerns of the region which are related to the vitality of the economy of the region, maintaining rates of economic growth

2452-3-3

0085

공   란

공   란

공   란

공   란

공   란

공   란

공   란

공   란

공   란

공   란

공 란

공   란

캔터 美정무차관 11일께 한국방문

(워싱턴=聯合) 박정찬특파원=아놀드 캔터 美국무부 정무담당차관이 오는 11일께 한국을 방문, 북한의 핵문제등 현안에 관해 논의할 것으로 23일 알려졌다.

美국무부는 캔터 차관이 오는 5일부터 23일까지 中國, 태국, 한국, 日本, 독일을 차례로 방문하고 오는 23일 귀국할 것이라고 말했으나 자세한 일정은 밝히지않았다.

캔터차관은 오는 11일을 전후해 2박3일간 서울에 머무르면서 국제원자력기구(IAEA)의 對북한 핵사찰등 핵문제를 중심으로 관심 현안을 한국 관리들과 논의할 것으로 알려졌으며 이번 방문이 북한의 핵시설 신고를 몇일 앞두고 이루어 진다는 점에서 주목을 받고 있다.

국무부의 한 관리는 캔터차관이 한국정부측과 핵문제를 비롯, 광범위한 현안을 다루게 될 것이라고 말했다.(끝)

(YONHAP) 920424 0750 KST

0098

외 무 부

종   별 :

번   호 : USW-2122

일   시 : 92 0427 2105

수   신 : 장 관 (미일, 미아, 정총)

발   신 : 주 미 대사

제   목 : 신시내티 세계문제협의회 학술회의

1. 오하이오주 신시내티 세계문제협의회(WORLD AFFAIRS COUNCIL)는 4.24. 동 협의회의 제 38 차 연차회의로서 "THE ASIA-PACIFIC BASIN: A NEW WORLD CENTER" 제하의 세미나를 개최하였음.

2. 동 세미나에는 SOLOMON 차관보, PAAL NSC 아주선임보좌관, MICHAEL DEWAR 국제전략문제연구소(IISS) 부소장, HARRY HARDING 브루킹스 연구소 연구원, 당관 임성준 참사관등이 참석하여 토론을 가졌는바, SOLOMON 차관보 연설내용및 토론회 주요 내용을 하기 보고함.

가. SOLOMON 차관보 연설내용

- "지리경제학(GEOECONOMICS)시대의 미국과 아시아. 태평양" 제하의 연설에서 SOLOMON 차관보는 냉전후 시대변화를 개관하면서 바야흐로 세계는 무역, 재정, 기술의 흐름이 한나라의 힘과 새시대의 정치모습을 형성해 나가는 지경학적(GEOECONOMICS) 시대에 접어들었다고 전제하고, 동 관점에서 볼때 작년 미국과의 교역액이 3 천 1 백억에 다다른 아시아-태평양 지역의 중요성은 매우 크다고 말함.

- 그러나 동 차관보는 일본. 한국을 포함한 아시아 신흥개발국의 경제적 성공은 2 차대전후 자국의 이익만을 추구하지 않고 이들 국가들의 자립을 도운 미국 외교정책이 큰 역할을 했다고 하면서, 미국과 경쟁관계에 접어든 이들 아. 태국가들은 APEC 과 같은 범태평양적(TRANS-PACIFIC) 포럼을 통해 시장경제 저해요소 제거및 자유주의 무역확대에 힘써야 할때라고 언급함.

- 결론적으로 동 차관보는 동아시아가 경쟁의 상대로 부상하면서, 미국으로서는 대외적으로 시장확보를 위한 자유주의 무역을 고수하고, 대내적으로는 저축.투자증대, 생산성 증대등의 과업을 안게되었다고 하면서, 미국의 대아시아 정치, 군사관계도 경제관계를 제대로 정립할때 안정될수 있을 것이라고 말하고, 미국이 금세기전에

미주국	장관	차관	1차보	2차보	미주국	외연원	외정실	분석관
정와대	안기부							

0099

PAGE 1

92.04.28   11:09

외신 2과 통제관 BX

주장하던 "OPEN DOOR" 정책의 필요성이 오늘날에도 제기된다고 강조함.

나. 북한 핵문제

- SOLOMON 차관보는 북한 핵개발 시도가 북한의 대중동 미사일 수출과 더불어 동북아 안보의 가장 큰 위협이 되고 있다고 하면서, 미국은 이에 대처키 위해한, 미간 긴밀한 협조체제를 바탕으로 영국, 불란서, 러시아등 국제사회의 CONSENSUS 를 형성해 나가고 있다고 밝힘.

- 이어 동 차관보는 북한이 지난 6 년간 지연해오던 IAEA 안전협정을 최근 서명, 비준했으나, 중요한 것은 실제로 핵사찰을 받는데 있다고 하고, 북한이 IAEA 사찰 수용의사는 보이면서도 한반도 비핵협정에 따른 남북 동시사찰에는 소극적 태도를 보이는 것에 우려가 되며, 6 월까지는 북한의 의도가 들어날 것인 만큼 그때까지 대북 압력을 계속해 나가야 할 것이라고 강조함.

다. 아시아 다자안보 협력

- DEWAR IISS 부소장은 아시아가 유럽의 NATO-WTO 양대체제와는 달리 양자동맹 체제에 의한 안보를 유지해 온 것은 사실이나, 이제 유럽의 CSCE 와 같은 다자적 안보협의체를 도입할 필요성이 제기되고 있다고 주장함. 또한 그는 일본이 경제력에 버금가는 국제적 책임을 져야 하며, 미-일 관계를 축으로 반드시 군사적 역할은 아니더라도 UN 평화유지 활동등을 통해 적극적 역할을 수행하는 것이 바람직하다고 강조함.

- SOLOMON 차관보는 아시아는 유럽과는 안보환경이 달라 양자관계를 통해 원만한 안보협력 체제를 이루어 왔다고 하고, 따라서 당분간 다자간 안보협력 체제의 조속 실현은 힘들 것이라고 전망함. 동 차관보는 ASEAN 확대 외상회의 및 APEC 을 통해 다자간 대화(COLLECTIVE DIALOGUE)는 가능할지 몰라도, 안보에 관한 역내 공통의 AGENDA 를 정하기는 힘들 것이라고 부언함.

라. 북한의 장래

- HARDING 연구원은 북한이 현재 경제 침체, 김일성 부자 세습문제등으로 많은 어려움에 봉착하고 있다고 하면서, 중국, 북한, 베트남 정도가 아직도 공산주의를 고수하고 있으나, 공산주의는 몰락하게 될 것이며, 따라서 북한체제도 결국 붕괴하게 될 것이라고 강조함.

3. 상기 솔로몬 차관보 연설문을 별첨 FAX 송부함. 끝.

첨부: USW(F)-2629(9 매). 끝.

PAGE 2

0100

(대사 현홍주-국장)
예고: 92.12.31. 일반

주 미 대 사 관

USW(F) : 2628   년월일 : 92.4.27   시간 : 21:05

수 신 : 장 관 (미일, 미이, 정총)

발 신 : 주미대사

제 목 : 첨부물   (출처 :   )

(2628 - 9 - 1)

외신1과
통제

0102

CINCINNATI COUNCIL ON WORLD AFFAIRS

"THE U.S. AND THE ASIA-PACIFIC IN AN ERA OF GEOECONOMICS"

A PRESENTATION BY

RICHARD H. SOLOMON

ASSISTANT SECRETARY OF STATE
FOR EAST ASIAN AND PACIFIC AFFAIRS

APRIL 24, 1992

THE ASIA-PACIFIC REGION IN A NEW ERA

YOUR DELIBERATIONS TODAY HAVE HIGHLIGHTED ALL THE
REASONS WHY THE ASIA-PACIFIC REGION IS EMERGING AS A
GLOBAL POWER CENTER. AND THERE IS NO QUESTION THAT
AMERICA'S FUTURE IS CLOSELY LINKED TO THE NATIONS OF THE
PACIFIC BASIN. THE ISSUE WE MUST ASSESS AS WE CHART A
COURSE TO THE COMING CENTURY IS WHAT SORT OF POST-COLD WAR
WORLD ARE WE ENTERING: WHAT SHAPE WILL ITS ECONOMIC,
POLITICAL, AND SECURITY INSTITUTIONS TAKE -- AND HOW WILL
THE NATIONS OF THE ASIA-PACIFIC BE STRUCTURED WITHIN IT.

LET'S LOOK AT THE WORLD WE ARE ENTERING, ONE SHAPED BY
THE INFORMATION REVOLUTION AND FILLED WITH SOME
INTRIGUIING CONTRADICTIONS:

O IN OUR 'GLOBAL VILLAGE', INSTANTANEOUS FLOWS OF
COMMUNICATION AND CAPITAL ARE ERODING NATIONAL
BOUNDARIES, COMPRESSING INTERNATIONAL DEALINGS IN TIME
AND SPACE.

O THE NATION-STATE IS BEING PULLED APART -- BY THE
SUPER-NATIONAL FORCES OF ECONOMIC INTEGRATION FROM
ABOVE, BY THE DEMANDS OF POLITICAL AND ENTREPRENEURIAL
DECENTRALIZATION FROM BELOW, AND BY THE REQUIREMENTS
OF COALITION POLITICS IN AN EVER-MORE INTERDEPENDENT
WORLD.

26P-P-3

0104

O ANCIENT POLITICAL FEUDS AND ETHNIC RIVALRIES ARE
BEING REPLAYED IN THE DECENTRALIZED POLITICAL
ENVIRONMENT OF THE POST-COLD WAR WORLD, BUT THIS TIME
WITH THE POWER OF MODERN WEAPONRY.

O TODAY, THE COMPONENT ELEMENTS OF NATIONAL SECURITY
ARE BEING REASSESSED TO INCLUDE ECONOMIC VITALITY AND
TRANSNATIONAL THREATS — THREATS TO THE ENVIRONMENT,
TO PUBLIC HEALTH AS IN THE AIDS EPIDEMIC, THE GLOBAL
THREAT OF ILLICIT NARCOTICS TRAFFICKING, AND REFUGEE
FLOWS.

O YET AS WE LEARNED IN LAST YEAR'S GULF CRISIS,
MILITARY CHALLENGES TO OUR SECURITY ENDURE, IN THE
PROLIFERATION OF MISSILES AND WEAPONS OF MASS
DESTRUCTION TO REGIONAL POWERS WHO SEEK GREAT POWER
STATUS IN HIGH-TECH ARMS.

FOR ALL THIS DRAMATIC CHANGE, HOWEVER, THE
MULTILATERAL INSTITUTIONS REQUIRED TO MANAGE THE EMERGING
WORLD OF THE 21ST CENTURY, TO GIVE IT ORDER, REMAIN TO BE
ESTABLISHED, OR TO EVOLVE AS EXISTING INTERNATIONAL
INSTITUTIONS ADAPT TO NEW REALITIES.

YET AMIDST ALL THE UNCERTAINTY AND TURBULENCE THAT
CHARACTERIZES THIS PERIOD OF HISTORIC TRANSITION, ONE
FUNDAMENTAL TREND IS CLEAR: WE ARE ENTERING THE AGE OF

0105

GEOECONOMICS, WITH FLOWS OF TRADE, FINANCE AND TECHNOLOGY
SHAPING THE POWER REALITIES AND THE POLITICS OF A NEW ERA.

IMPACT ON ASIA

IT IS IN THIS BROAD CONTEXT THAT WE MUST VIEW THE
ASIA-PACIFIC REGION. EAST ASIA HAS BEEN THE PACE-SETTER
IN THE GLOBAL TREND TOWARD THE ASCENDANCY OF ECONOMIC
POWER. IT IS STUNNING TO RECALL THAT ONLY TWO OR THREE
DECADES AGO, EAST ASIA WAS ENGULFED IN WAR AND GREAT POWER
CONFRONTATION, BURDENED BY GRINDING POVERTY AND CHALLENGED
BY INSURGENT COMMUNIST MOVEMENTS. OUR TRADE WITH THE
ENTIRE REGION UNTIL THE LATE 1960S WAS LESS THAN THAT WITH
LATIN AMERICA!

WE NOW TAKE THE FAMILIAR ASIAN SUCCESS STORY FOR
GRANTED: JAPAN HAS BECOME AN ECONOMIC SUPERPOWER; THE FOUR
TIGERS OF SOUTH KOREA, TAIWAN, HONG KONG, AND SINGAPORE
MAY SOON BE JOINED BY A DRAGON, AS SOUTHERN CHINA GROWS AT
DOUBLE DIGIT RATES; AND THAILAND, MALAYSIA, AND INDONESIA
SEEM DESTINED TO BE TIGERS IN THE 21ST CENTURY. TOGETHER
THE ECONOMIES OF EAST ASIA ACCOUNT FOR ABOUT ONE-QUARTER
OF WORLD GNP -- ROUGHLY THE SAME SIZE AS OUR OWN.

U.S. TWO-WAY TRADE ACROSS THE PACIFIC LAST YEAR
EXCEEDED $310 BILLION -- ALMOST FIFTY PERCENT GREATER THAN
OUR TRADE WITH WESTERN EUROPE. TODAY WE EXPORT MORE TO
MALAYSIA THAN TO ALL THE REPUBLICS OF THE FORMER SOVIET
UNION; MORE TO JAPAN THAN FRANCE AND GERMANY COMBINED;

0106

MORE TO SINGAPORE THAN TO ITALY.

NO DOUBT MUCH OF ASIA'S SUCCESS IS THE RESULT OF THE
HARD WORK AND DISCIPLINE OF ITS PEOPLES, AND THE ECONOMIC
POLICIES OF THEIR LEADERS. BUT THESE ACHIEVEMENTS HAVE
BEEN FACILITATED BY THE WORLD AMERICAN FOREIGN POLICY SET
OUT TO CREATE IN THE FIRST YEARS AFTER WORLD WAR II.

AT THE BEGINNING OF THE COLD WAR, WE ENOURAGED
DEFEATED FORMER ENEMIES LIKE JAPAN, AND IMPOVERISHED
ALLIES LIKE KOREA, TO PURSUE ECONOMIC DEVELOPMENT THROUGH
EXPORT-LED GROWTH. WE PROVIDED THEM READY ACCESS TO OUR
MARKETS EVEN THOUGH THEIR OWN MARKETS WERE HIGHLY
PROTECTED. AND OUR FORWARD-DEPLOYED MILITARY FORCES
GUARANTEED SECURITY IN THE REGION.

WHILE NATIONAL SECURITY CONCERNS WERE AN IMPORTANT
FACTOR IN OUR STRATEGY, WE DID NOT ACT OUT OF ECONOMIC
ALTRUISM. TRADE IS NOT A ZERO-SUM GAME; PROSPERITY HAS A
MULTIPLIER EFFECT AS GROWING ALLIES PROVIDE EXPANDING
MARKETS. LET ME CITE JUST ONE STATISTIC IN THIS REGARD:
OVER THE PAST FOUR DECADES, U.S. EXPORTS WORLDWIDE HAVE
GROWN BY SOME 4000 PERCENT, FROM $10.3 BILLION IN 1950 TO
OVER $400 BILLION BY 1991 -- A SIXFOLD INCREASE AS A
PERCENTAGE OF OUR GNP. AND SINCE 1986, 25% OF NEW JOB
CREATION IN THE U.S. HAS COME FROM THE GROWTH OF EXPORTS.
TODAY, OUR EXPORTS ACROSS THE PACIFIC -- $130 BILLION IN
1991 -- ACCOUNT FOR SOME 2.6 MILLION JOBS!

0107

BUT OUR ALLIES AND FRIENDS IN ASIA HAVE NOW BECOME
ROBUST COMPETITORS; THEIR SUCCESS ALLOWS US TO FORGE MORE
BALANCED PARTNERSHIPS --- SHARING ECONOMIC, POLITICAL AND
DEFENSE RESPONSIBILITIES ACCORDINGLY. YET MANY OF OUR
RELATIONSHIPS IN THE REGION ARE BESET WITH TRADE TENSIONS
AS ECONOMIC ISSUES MOVE CENTERSTAGE. THE ASYMMETRY IN THE
EASY ACCESS WHICH OUR ASIAN TRADING PARTNERS HAVE TO OUR
MARKETS, WITH OUR DIFFICULTIES IN GAINING ACCESS TO
THEIRS, MUST BE REMEDIED.

APEC: COHESION IN THE PACIFIC COMMUNITY

OUR CHALLENGE IS TO SHAPE THE POST-COLD WAR
INTERNATIONAL SYSTEM SO THAT IT IS EQUITABLE, STABLE AND
ENSURES WIDESPREAD PROSPERITY WHILE SERVING OUR INTERESTS
AS WELL AS THE INTERESTS OF OUR FRIENDS AND ALLIES. OUR
GAMEPLAN IS TO FORGE MORE EQUAL POLITICAL, DEFENSE --- AS
WELL ECONOMIC --- PARTNERSHIPS. THIS REQUIRES RESHAPING
BILATERAL RELATIONS AS WELL AS GLOBAL AND REGIONAL
INSTITUTIONS. AND THAT IS WHAT WE ARE DOING.

A PRIME EXAMPLE IS APEC --- THE ASIA-PACIFIC ECONOMIC
COOPERATION PROCESS. APEC IS OUR PREFERENCE FOR THE
FUTURE ARCHITECTURE OF THE ASIA-PACIFIC REGION. APEC WAS
FORMED LESS THAN THREE YEARS AGO, AND IT IS RAPIDLY
BECOMING THE INSTITUTIONAL VEHICLE OF OUR ECONOMIC
ENGAGEMENT IN THE REGION. APEC'S FIFTEEN MEMBERS TOGETHER
HAVE A GNP OF OVER $10 TRILLION, INCLUDING THE MOST
DYNAMIC ECONOMIES IN THE WORLD.

0108.

APEC IS DESIGNED AS A TRANS-PACIFIC FORUM THAT CAN
HELP REDUCE IMPEDIMENTS TO MARKET-ORIENTED GROWTH, PROMOTE
GLOBAL AND REGIONAL TRADE LIBERALIZATION, AND STIMULATE
DEVELOPMENT OF THE INFRASTRUCTURE -- TELECOMMUNICATIONS
NETWORKS, AIR AND SEA TRANSPORTATION CAPACITY -- THAT WILL
ENCOURAGE GREATER REGIONAL INTEGRATION AND GROWTH
THROUGHOUT THE PACIFIC BASIN. APEC HOLDS THE PROMISE OF
FOSTERING A TRUE SENSE OF ASIA-PACIFIC COMMUNITY.

TO BE SURE, MILITARY POWER REMAINS A SIGNIFICANT
COMPONENT OF NATIONAL STRENGTH -- AS WE SAW LAST YEAR IN
THE GULF. BUT TODAY, TECHNOLOGICAL AND COMMERCIAL
CAPABILITIES MORE THAN MILITARY STRENGTH ARE THE DEFINING
ELEMENTS OF NATIONAL POWER AND INFLUENCE.

CONCLUSION

IN A SENSE, THE CHALLENGE OF THE EMERGING ERA IS FAR
MORE COMPLEX THAN THAT OF THE COLD WAR YEARS. THEN THE
ENEMY WAS CLEAR, THE THREAT VISIBLE AND OFTEN OMINOUS.
NOW THERE IS NO UNIVERSAL "ENEMY," THE THREAT IS DIFFUSE,
LESS MILITARY IN CHARACTER -- AND OFTEN, IT IS IN OUR OWN
DEFICIENCIES.

FOR THE UNITED STATES, EAST ASIA HAS BECOME A SYMBOL
OF THE CHALLENGE OF COMPETITIVENESS. THIS CHALLENGE HAS
TWO DIMENSIONS: THE EXTERNAL -- SUSTAINING OPEN MARKETS
FOR OUR GOODS, AND ELIMINATING BARRIERS IN TRADITIONAL AND

0109

EMERGING SECTORS; AND THE INTERNAL -- THAT OF ATTAINING
ADEQUATE DOMESTIC SAVINGS AND INVESTMENT RATES, BOOSTING
EDUCATIONAL SKILLS, INCREASING PRODUCTIVITY AND
COMMERCIALIZING NEW TECHNOLOGIES.

TO BE SURE, THE CHALLENGES AHEAD FOR OUR RELATIONS
WITH ASIA ARE POLITICAL AND MILITARY AS WELL AS ECONOMIC.
BUT IF WE MEET THE CHALLENGE OF COMPETITIVENESS, OUR
LEADERSHIP AND SECURITY ROLE IN THE REGION WILL BE
WELL-GROUNDED.

THIS IS THE MEANING OF THE AGE OF GEOECONOMICS. IF WE
GET THE ECONOMICS RIGHT -- DOMESTICALLY, BILATERALLY,
REGIONALLY, AND GLOBALLY -- WE WILL SUCCEED IN LAYING THE
BASIS FOR A STABLE AND SECURE PACIFIC COMMUNITY.

OUR TREMENDOUS STAKE IN THE MOST ECONOMICALLY DYNAMIC
REGION OF THE WORLD, OUR HOPE TO SEE THE CONTINUING SPREAD
OF DEMOCRACY AND RESPECT FOR HUMAN RIGHTS, AND THE
ENDURING IMPORTANCE OF OUR SECURITY PRESENCE, PROVIDE
POWERFUL ARGUMENTS FOR SUSTAINING AMERICA'S ENGAGEMENT IN
EAST ASIA AND THE PACIFIC.

AS A MARITIME TRADING POWER, OUR GOALS OF COMMERCIAL
ACCESS, FREEDOM OF NAVIGATION, AND FORESTALLING DOMINATION
OF THE REGION BY ANY HEGEMON HAVE NOT CHANGED SINCE THE
DAYS A CENTURY AGO OF THE "OPEN DOOR." THEY ARE NO LESS
COMPELLING NOW.

0110

외 무 부

종 별 :

번 호 : SGW-0203   일 시 : 92 0429 1520

수 신 : 장 관(아동,미일,미이)

발 신 : 주 싱가포르 대사

제 목 : CHENEY 미국방장관 방싱

연: SGW-0176

1. 연호 CHENEY 미국방장관은 4.27.-29.간 당지를 방문,고촉봉수상,리관유 선임장관,YEO NING HONG 국방장관,WONG KAN SENG 외무장관과 면담함.

2. CHENEY 장관은 상기 면담후 가진 기자회견에서 아래 요지로 언급하였음.

가. 미국은 전세계적으로 군사력의 신속 배치능력이 향상되고 있으므로 미국의 해외기지 유지 필요성은 점차 감소되고 있음.

나. 대신 미국은 동맹및 우방국의 군사시설 이용및 합동훈련 여건을 개선시키고자 노력중임.

다. 미국과 싱가폴간의 군함기항및 수리,공군훈련등 군사협력 합의는 싱가폴내 군사시설의 활용에 관한것으로서 결코 군사기지를 제공한다는 것은 아님. 또한 미국은 현 미.싱간 군사시설 활용협정에 만족하고 있으며, 동 협정내용을 확대시킬 계획은 없음.

3. CHENEY 장관 방문결과에 관해 추가사항은 파악되는대로 보고하겠음. 끝.

(대사 한창식-국장)

예고:92.12.31.까지

아주국	차관	1차보	미주국	미주국	외정실	분석관	정와대	안기부

외 무 부

110-760 서울 종로구 세종로 77번지 / (02) 720-2321 / (02) 720-2686

문서번호 미일 0160-726

시행일자 1992. 4. 28.

수 신 수신처 참조

참 조

선결			지시		
접수	일자시간		결재		
	번호		공람		
처리과					
담당자	4/29 신				

제 목 미국의 대북한정책 지침

일반 □류 (1992.12.31)

　　　최근 미 행정부가 작성한 미국의 대북한정책 지침을 별첨 송부하니

업무에 참고하시기 바랍니다.

검토필 (1992.6.30)

첨 부 : 관련 장관보고사항 및 미국의 대북한정책 지침 사본 각 1부. 끝.

예 고 : 1992.12.31.일반

수 신 처 : 아주국장, 구주국장, 중동아프리카국장, 국제기구국장

미 주 국 장

0112

O   IN RECENT WEEKS, NORTH KOREA HAS BEEN ACTIVELY SEEKING
EXPANDED DIPLOMATIC AND ECONOMIC CONTACT WITH MANY
COUNTRIES. NORTH KOREA HAS ARGUED THAT:

-- IT IS TRYING TO EXPAND DIPLOMATIC AND OTHER CONTACTS;

-- AS A NEW (SEPTEMBER 1991) MEMBER OF THE UN, IT IS
APPROPRIATE AND DESIRABLE TO ESTABLISH TIES WITH FELLOW UN
MEMBERS;

-- IT HAS MET AT A HIGH LEVEL WITH U.S. OFFICIALS, IS
CONDUCTING NORMALIZATION TALKS WITH JAPAN, AND IS ENGAGED
IN A SUBSTANTIVE DIALOGUE WITH SOUTH KOREA WHICH HAS
PRODUCED SUBSTANTIVE AGREEMENTS.

-- IT IS EXPLORING THE DEVELOPMENT OF COMMERCIAL
RELATIONS WITH OTHER NATIONS, AND WELCOMES COOPERATIVE
MULTILATERAL PROJECTS SUCH AS THE TUMEN REGIONAL
DEVELOPMENT PROJECT;

O   WITH THE ENTRY INTO FORCE APRIL 10 OF ITS IAEA
SAFEGUARDS AGREEMENT, THIS EFFORT IS LIKELY TO INTENSIFY.

O   WE WELCOME NORTH KOREAN STEPS TO MEET THE BROADLY
VOICED CONCERNS OF THE INTERNATIONAL COMMUNITY.

O   HOWEVER, NORTH KOREA MUST TURN ITS WORDS INTO DEEDS IN
THE CRITICAL AREAS RELATING TO ITS NUCLEAR PROGRAM AND ITS
MISSILE PROLIFERATION PRACTICES.

-- NUCLEAR PROLIFERATION ON THE KOREAN PENINSULA IS A
GRAVE POTENTIAL THREAT TO THE REGION AND WOULD UNDERMINE
THE NUCLEAR NON-PROLIFERATION TREATY REGIME GLOBALLY.

-- NORTH KOREA EMBARKED ON AN EXTENSIVE SECRET NUCLEAR
PROGRAM OVER A DECADE AGO. SINCE 1987 IT HAS OPERATED AN
UNSAFEGUARDED REACTOR WELL-SUITED FOR PRODUCING PLUTONIUM.

-- NORTH KOREA ACCEDED TO THE NUCLEAR NON-PROLIFERATION
TREATY (NPT) IN 1985, AND IN JANUARY OF THIS YEAR, AFTER A
DELAY OF SIX YEARS, FINALLY SIGNED ITS SAFEGUARDS
AGREEMENT. ON APRIL 10, THE AGREEMENT WAS BROUGHT INTO
FORCE. NORTH KOREA HAS INDICATED IT WILL ACCEPT
INSPECTIONS BY JUNE. WE HOPE THEY MAINTAIN THIS SCHEDULE.

--THE DPRK AND ROK ISSUED A JOINT DECLARATION ON
DECEMBER 31, 1991, COMMITTING THEMSELVES TO BANNING
NUCLEAR WEAPONS AND TO NOT ENGAGE IN NUCLEAR REPROCESSING

0113

OR ENRICHMENT. NEGOTIATIONS ON A BILATERAL INSPECTION
REGIME TO MONITOR COMPLIANCE WITH THESE COMMITMENTS HAVE
JUST BEGUN.

O   HOWEVER, SIGNING NUCLEAR INSPECTION AGREEMENTS IS ONLY
THE FIRST STEP. THE TOUCHSTONE FOR IMPROVING DIPLOMATIC
AND OTHER RELATIONS WITH NORTH KOREA SHOULD BE THE ACTUAL
IMPLEMENTATION OF EFFECTIVE AND CREDIBLE INSPECTIONS IN
NORTH KOREA UNDER BOTH THE IAEA AGREEMENT AND THE
BILATERAL INSPECTION REGIME.

--WE MET WITH THE NORTH KOREANS ON A ONE-TIME BASIS TO
EXPLAIN AUTHORITATIVELY OUR POLICY THAT RELATIONS CAN
IMPROVE ONLY WHEN NORTH KOREA HAS MADE REAL PROGRESS ON A
WIDE VARIETY OF ISSUES, AND ESPECIALLY THE NUCLEAR ISSUE.

-- THE U.S. AND OTHERS HAVE TOLD NORTH KOREA IT CANNOT
EXPECT TO BEGIN EXPANDING CONTACTS OR IMPROVING RELATIONS
UNTIL IT HAS FULLY IMPLEMENTED ITS IAEA SAFEGUARDS
AGREEMENT AND ITS NON-NUCLEAR AGREEMENT WITH THE REPUBLIC
OF KOREA, RECEIVED INSPECTIONS UNDER BOTH THE IAEA
SAFEGUARDS AGREEMENT AND THE BILATERAL AGREEMENT, AND THUS
REMOVED INTERNATIONAL SUSPICIONS ABOUT ITS NUCLEAR PROGRAM.

O   WE HAVE ALSO TOLD NORTH KOREA THAT ITS EXPORT OF
MISSILES AND MISSILE TECHNOLOGY TO THE MIDDLE EAST
CONTRIBUTE TO INSTABILITY AND COMPLICATE THE VERY
DIFFICULT PROCESS OF NEGOTIATING PEACE IN THAT REGION. WE
HAVE ASKED NORTH KOREA TO REFRAIN FROM SUCH EXPORTS.

O   WE BELIEVE IT WOULD BE HELPFUL FOR YOUR GOVERNMENT TO
SEEK OPPORTUNITIES TO MAKE CLEAR TO NORTH KOREA THE
IMPORTANCE OF FULLY FOLLOWING THROUGH ON ITS COMMITMENTS
UNDER BOTH THE NPT AND ITS BILATERAL AGREEMENT WITH THE
ROK AND ACCEPT INSPECTIONS. IT WOULD ALSO BE HELPFUL TO
ASK FOR NORTH KOREAN RESTRAINT ON MISSILE AND MISSILE
TECHNOLOGY EXPORTS.

O • IT IS ESPECIALLY IMPORTANT TO MAKE THIS POINT IF NORTH
KOREA HAS APPROACHED YOU ABOUT ESTABLISHING, UPGRADING, OR
EXPANDING DIPLOMATIC OR ECONOMIC TIES.

O   THE DPRK SHOULD BE WILLING TO HELP ALLEVIATE
INTERNATIONAL CONCERNS BY COOPERATING FULLY WITH IAEA
INSPECTIONS AND BILATERAL INSPECTIONS.

O   IN ANOTHER AREA, THE DPRK HAS ATTEMPTED TO CALL INTO
QUESTION THE CONTINUED VIABILITY OF THE CEASE-FIRE AND
SECURITY ARRANGEMENTS IMPLEMENTED UNDER THE ARMISTICE
AGREEMENT OF 1953. IN PARTICULAR, IT HAS CITED ITS UN

0114

MEMBERSHIP AND NON-AGGRESSION AGREEMENT WITH THE ROK AS
EVIDENCE THAT THE ARMISTICE ARRANGEMENTS ARE NO LONGER
RELEVANT AND/OR HAVE BEEN SUPERSEDED.

O   THE ARMISTICE AGREEMENT STATES THAT IT SHALL "REMAIN
IN EFFECT UNTIL EXPRESSLY SUPERSEDED EITHER BY MUTUALLY
ACCEPTABLE AMENDMENTS AND ADDITIONS OR BY PROVISION IN AN
APPROPRIATE AGREEMENT FOR A PEACEFUL SETTLEMENT AT A
POLITICAL LEVEL BETWEEN BOTH SIDES."

O   IT IS CLEAR THEREFORE THAT THE UNILATERAL ACTION OF
ONE PARTY CANNOT ABROGATE THE ARMISTICE ARRANGEMENTS.

O   WE HOPE YOU WILL MAKE CLEAR TO THE DPRK THE IMPORTANCE
OF MAINTAINING THE ARMISTICE AGREEMENT AND ITS
ARRANGEMENTS UNTIL NORTH AND SOUTH KOREA CAN AGREE ON
SPECIFIC STEPS WHICH WILL BE THE BASIS FOR A PERMANENT
PEACE ARRANGEMENT.

O   AT THAT POINT ALL THE PARTIES TO THE ARMISTICE
AGREEMENT, INCLUDING THE U.S., WILL BE READY TO CONSIDER
STEPS TO END THE ARMISTICE ARRANGEMENTS.
IF ASKED ABOUT RECENT REPORTS OF U.S. SALE OF GRAIN TO
NORTH KOREA:

O   AS PART OF ITS POLICY INITIATIVE TOWARD NORTH KOREA IN
1988, THE U.S. BEGAN TO APPROVE THE SALE ON HUMANITARIAN
GROUNDS OF ITEMS TO MEET BASIC HUMAN NEEDS, SUCH AS FOOD,
MEDICINE, AND MEDICAL EQUIPMENT. THESE VERY MODEST FOOD
SALES, TOTALLING LESS THAN 15 MILLION DOLLARS SINCE 1988,
ARE FULLY CONSISTENT WITH THE POLICY OF PERMITTING THE
SALE OF GOODS ON A HUMANITARIAN BASIS.

0115

공   란

공　　　란

공   란

외 무 부

관리번호 82-556

종 별 : 지 급

번 호 : USW-2179

일 시 : 92 0429 2333

수 신 : 장 관 (정총, 미일)

발 신 : 주 미 대사

제 목 : 정책기획협의회

연: USW-2154

1. 금 4.29. 개최된 한. 미 및 한. 일 정책기획협의회 결과를 미.일측 언급요지를 중심으로 아래 보고함.

　가. 한. 미 정책기획 협의회

　0 시간 및 장소: 09:00-12:30 국무부 회의실

　0 참석자

　- 우리측 : 이승곤 외정실장외 본부대표 3 명, 임참사관외 대사관직원 2 명(총 7 명)

　- 미측 : STREMLAU 정책기획실 부실장, MANNING 동아태 차관보보좌관, KARTMAN 한국과장, CARLIN 정보조사국 동북아과장등 7 명

검토필 (19)2. 6. 30 이내료

　0 주요 협의내용

　- 정책기획협의회가 현안해결 보다는 중.단기 정책과제에 관한 의견교환과 협의에 중점을 두는 포럼이라는데에 공감

외정실	장관	차관	1차보	아주국	미주국	분석관	정와대	안기부

0119

PAGE 1

92.04.30　13:47

외신 2과　통제관 AN

(CIS)

- 대 CIS 지원에 있어 한국은 기술지원등 경제발전 경험의 공유를 통해 SOFTWARE 분야에서 중요한 기여를 할 수 있다고 평가하고 한국의 적극적 역할 희망

- 최근 세계은행 및 IMF 가 재정지원에 있어 군사비 지출현황 평가등 정치적 기준을 적용키로 결정하는등 긍정적 역할을 하고 있으나, 세계은행과 IMF 가 미 외교정책의 수단으로서 활용되고 있다는 비난은 사실과 다름.

- (한.러 관계에 관해) 최근 쿠나제 러시아 외무차관 방미시 북한을 아주 싫어하는 것으로 파악된바, 이점을 한국측이 러시아의 대북한 관계등에 있어 활용할 수 있을 것이라는 의견 표시

- 쿠나제 차관은 미.일 안보협력 관계가 러시아의 이익에 부합한다고 발언하고, 엘친대통령은 1.24. 연설시 군비축소 필요성을 강조하는등 외무부등은 과거와 다른 정책을 추구하고 있으나, 군부에서는 아태지역 집단안보 구상의 필요성을 강조하는등 종래 소련과 같은 입장을 취함으로써, 러시아 정부내 정책보조가일치하지 않는다는데 주목하고 신중히 지켜 보아야 한다는데 의견 일치

(한. 미 관계)

- 최근 한. 미 관계에서 경제적 요인의 중요성이 증대하였으나 양국간의 경제적 상호 의존성이 통상마찰보다 훨씬 깊고 중요함을 지적하고 이러한 시각에서통상현안을 슬기롭게 해결해야 한다는데 의견 일치

- TRANS-PACIFIC 관계의 중요성과 미국의 동아시아에서의 경제적 PRESENCE 유지 필요성에 공감하고, APEC 같은 기구가 이같은 목적에 부합하며 EAEC 와 같이 태평양 양안을 분리시키는 구상은 바람직하지 않다는데 의견 일치

- 우리측은, 한. 미 관계의 장기적 발전을 위해 인적교류, 학술.문화교류등GRASSROOTS 차원의 교류증대의 중요성을 강조하고, 이와관련 신설된 KOREA FOUNDATION 의 역할 설명

나. 한. 일 정책기획협의회

0 시간 및 장소 : 15:00-18:00 협의(RITZ-CARLTON 호텔 별실) 및 19:30-21:30 업무만찬

0 참석자

PAGE 2

0120

- 우리측 : 한. 미 협의회시와 동일

- 일측 : 스즈끼 정보조사국장, 다카하시 정책기획과장등 7 명

0 주요 토의내용

- 동북아정세, 한반도정세 및 동남아 특히 캄보디아 PKO 에의 일본참여 문제, 아.
태 안보협의, 아. 태 경제 협력등에 대해 중점 협의

(동북아 정세)

- 중국과 러시아 모두 당분간 국내문제에 몰두하여야 할 형편이기 때문에 적극적인
아. 태 외교를 전개할 형편이 되지 못하며, 특히 러시아의경우 아무런 대아시아
정책을 갖고 있지 못한 것으로 보임. 그러나 중장기적으로 러시아가 중국보다
주변국가에 대하여 위협요소가 될 가능성이 더큼 (일측은 북방영토문제로인하여
러시아의 위협정도를 예측하는데 많은 영향을 받고 있는 것으로 보임)

- 중국의 경우 외형적으로는 공산주의 정권이나 중국의 역사와 현실을 감안할때
미.중간의 관계에서와는 달리 일.중간에는 이념이 갈등요인으로 작용할 가능성은 크지
않음.

- 중국의 경우 개방과 개혁정책이 사회적 혼란없이 계속되도록 주변국가가
지원하는 것이 지역정세 안정을 위하여 도움이 됨.

(일본의 PKO 참여)

- 일본 자위대의 UN 산하 PKO 참여는 걸프전시와 같은 다국적군 참여와는
구별되어야 하며, 언론에 보도된 것과는 달리 중국 강택민 총리는 4 월 방일시 이점에
대하여는 이해를 표시하였음.

- 중국측은 종래 경제력이 곧 정치적 역할과 이어 군사력으로 이어진다고 주장하면서 경제적 역할이외의 일본의 역할에 부정적이었으나, 최근 일본의 정치적 역할까지는 허용할수 있다는 입장변화를 보이고 있음.

- 일본의 PKO 참여와 일본의 과거사를 인정, 청산하지 않고 정치 군사력을 증강하는 문제점을 연관 의견 교환

(아.태 집단안보)

- 아.태 지역 집단안보 구상과 관련 일체의 집단안보 구상 논의를 자동적으로 거부할 필요는 없음. 현단계에서의 논의는 기존 양자간의 안보체제들을 대체하는 것이 아니라 강화하는데 목적을 두어야함. CSCE 형태의 구상이 아.태지역에서는 적절한 것이 아니며 아세안 PMC 같은 기존 포럼을 우선 활용해 볼수도 있음. 그러나 아세안 PMC 활용을 당분간 일본이 공식 거론하지는 않을 것임.

(태평양 협력)

- 동아시아에 있어서 미국은 안보면에서 뿐 아니라 경제면에서도 필요 불가결한 존재임. 이런 측면에서 EAEC 와 같이 미국을 배제한 협의체 구성은 비현실적임. 그러나, 순수 민간차원에서 EAEC 논의나 모임 참석은 무방하다고 생각함.

2. 이실장 일행은 4.30-5.1 간 한.미.일 3자 정책기획협의회에 참가할 예정임.끝.

(대사 현홍주 - 차관)

예고: 92.12.31. 일반

공   란

공   란

공 란

공   란

공 란

IAEA 핵사찰 제도

1. IAEA 핵안전조치 절차
   o 제1단계 : NPT 가입 → 핵안전협정(안) 교섭 → IAEA 승인 → 협정서명 →
                비준 → 협정발효(이상 NPT 가입후 18개월이내에 필요한 조치)
   o 제2단계 : 사찰대상보고(협정발효후 30일이내) → IAEA의 임시사찰 →
                기존핵시설 설계정보제출 → IAEA의 설계정보확인 →
                「보조약정서 작성 .발효(협정발효후 90일이내)
   o 제3단계 : 일반사찰

2. 사찰내용 및 종류
   가. 사찰내용
   o IAEA 사찰관이 핵시설을 직접방문, 현장확인 및 서류검증을 통해 핵물질의
      군사적 전용여부 검증
   나. 사찰종류
   o 임시사찰(ad hoc) : 사찰 대상보고서에 포함된 정보의 검증, 핵물질의 국내
                         반입, 국외 반출시 핵물질의 동일성, 핵물질량 검증
   o 일반사찰(routine) : IAEA 보고사항과 현존 핵물질의 일치성 여부 현장확인
   o 특별사찰(Special) : 특별보고서에 포함된 정보의 검증 및 IAEA의 기존사찰
                         이 불충분한 경우 실시
   * 임시 및 일반사찰은 IAEA 사찰관 도착 최소 일주일전까지 당사국에 사찰
      일시통보
   * 특별사찰은 IAEA와 당사국간 "협의후" 사찰실시가능

3. 사찰제도의 문제점
   o 사찰대상의 제한
      - IAEA에 신고한 시설만 사찰가능
   o 특별사찰실시의 어려움
      - IAEA와 당사국간 합의시만 수행가능
   o 정보수집기능 부재
      - IAEA내 정보수집 관련 별도 조직 부재

0128

4. IAEA 안전조치 강화내용

  * '92.2월 IAEA 이사회시 권고안 채택, 9월 총회시 승인예정

  ㅇ 특별사찰 실시범위 확대
    - "신고된" 핵물질 → "모든" 핵물질
    - 사찰대상제한 → "어떠한 대상에도 접근"

  ㅇ 설계정보조기 제출 합의
    - 핵물질이 시설에 들어가기 6개월전 신고 → 핵시설 건설 시작할때로 강화
    * 현재 건설중으로 추정되는 북한의 핵재처리시설도 신고대상에 포함됨.

0129

외 무 부

종 별 : 지 급

번 호 : USW-2205 일 시 : 92 0501 1105

수 신 : 장관(미일, 미의) 사본:외교안보수석, 의전수석

발 신 : 주 미 대사

제 목 : KANTER 차관 초청 만찬

1. 본직은 5.13-15 간 방한하는 KANTER 국무부 정무차관 내외를 위해 4.30 관저 만찬을 개최하고 한반도 정세일반 및 향후 전망에 관한 의견교환 기회를 가졌는바, 동 만찬에는 RALPH CLOUGH SAIS 교수, GERRIT GONG CSIS 아시아 연구부장등 최근 북한을 방문한 인사이외에 STEPHEN ROSENFELD W.P. 지 논설위원 및 LILLEY 전 주한대사 부인이 참석하였음.

2. 동 만찬은 KANTER 차관이 취임이래 최초로 아시아 4 개국 순방(중국, 한국, 태국, 일본)의 일환으로 방한함에 즈음, 아국 주변상황에 대한 설명 및 의견교환을 목적으로 한 것이며, CLOUGH 교수 및 GONG 부장은 북한 방문시 받은 인상, 북한 핵문제에 대한 견해, 향후 통일전망 시나리오 등에 관해 언급하고, ROSENFELD 논설위원은 미국언론계가 보는 핵문제 및 한반도 전반에 관한 견해를 피력하였으며, LILLEY 부인은 서울올림픽등 한국의 발전상, 주한. 주중대사 시절 경험담등을 화제로 얘기 하였음.

검토필 (1) 92. 6. 30 인

3. KANTER 차관은 이번 아시아 순방, 특히 한국을 처음 방문하는 것에 많은기대를 갖고 있다고 하면서, 금번 방문을 통해 많은 것을 배우게 되길 바란다고 하고, (1)북한 핵문제에 대한 우리정부 방침, 동 문제 심각성에 대한 지도층의 인식 및 일반국민 여론 (2) 통일에 대한 우리국민 여론 (3) 북한의 변화가능성에 대한 시나리오 (4) 아국 국회의원, 대통령 선거등 국내 정치일정이 남북관계 및 대외정책 수행에 미칠 영향 (5) 한. 미, 한. 일, 미.일 관계 발전 및 금후전망등에 대해 관심을 표명함.

4. 상기 KANTER 차관의 관심사항에 대해 본직은 하기 요지로 설명함.

. 핵문제의 심각성에 대해서는 우리 지도층, 국민모두가 인식하고 있고, 한.미 양국이 그간 협의해 온 바에 따라 북한에 대한 회유, 압력의 강온양면 전략을 계속해

미주국 안기부	장관	차관	1차보	의전장	미주국	분석관	청와대	청와대

PAGE 1

92.05.02 01:37

외신 2과 통제관 EC

0130

나갈 것이며, 동 문제에 대한 정부내 혼선이 있는 듯한 일부 언론보도가 있었으나 우리정부의 정책은 확고함.

. 통일에 대한 여망은 우리 지도층, 국민 모두 높은것이 사실이나, 통일문제가 막연한 장래문제가 아니라 현실문제로 대두됨에 따른 대응방안, 통일비용등현실적 문제를 걱정하는 단계에 와 있으며, 비록 시간이 소요될 것이나 우리 주도하에 민주주의 체제하의 통일이 이루어지리라는 것에 대한 확신이 점차 높아지고 있음.

. 북한의 변화가능성에 대하여는 여러 시나리오가 있으나 우리정부로서는 북한의 갑작스러운 몰락 보다는 서서한 변화과정을 거쳐 통일로 연결되기를 희망하고 있음.

. 북한의 눈에는 최근 국내 정치일정 진행이 우리사회의 불안요인으로 비칠수 있겠으나 오히려 이와는 반대로 우리가 민주주의를 보다 성숙화 시켜 나감에 따라 장기적 정치안정을 이룩하게 될 것이고, 이를 바탕으로 그동안 성과를 이룩해온 제 6 공화국의 북방정책 및 대북정책은 국민적 지지에 힘입어 앞으로도 계속 유지될 것이며, 반드시 성공을 거두게 될 것임.

. 현재 한. 미 간에 핵문제등 안보문제, 통상문제, 기타문제등에 관하여 완벽한 협의가 이루어지고 있음을 만족스럽게 생각하며, 최근 심화되고 있는 미.일간 감정대립, 한. 일간 분위기 경색등의 문제해결을 위해 공동노력을 기울려야할것으로 생각함.

. 또한 본직은 다자안보 협의체 구상에 관한 우리정부의 견해를 재차 설명함.

5. KANTER 차관 방한 관련, 청와대 예방등 현재 확정된 체한 일정을 회시바람.

(대사 현홍주-장관)

예고: 일반 92.12.31.

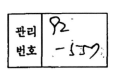

외 무 부

종 별 :

번 호 : USW-2236   일 시 : 92 0501 2319

수 신 : 장관 (정총,아일,미일)

발 신 : 주 미국 대사

제 목 : 정책기획협의회

연: USW-2179

1. 4.30-5.1 간 미국무부 회의실에서 개최된 한.미.일 제 2 차 정책기획협의회 결과를 미.일측 언급요지를 중심을 아래 보고함.

가. 참석자

- 우리측: 이승곤 외정실장등 7 명

- 미측: STREMLAU 정책기획실 부실장, MANNING 동아태 차관보 보좌관

KARTMAN 한국과장, CARLIN 정보사국 동북아과장

PRZYSTUP 국방부 차관 보좌관등 8 명

- 일측: 스즈끼 정보조사국장등 7 명(양자협의시와 동일)

나. 주요 협의내용

- 외교정책에 영향을 미치는 국내적 요인, 소연방 해체후 북태평양 안보, 대량파괴무기 역내확산(북한 핵문제 포함), CIS 지원, 집단개입(COLLECTIVE ENGAGEMENT)등에 대해 중점 협의

(북태평양 안보)

검토필 ('O~6. 30에 인

- 역내 다자안보 구상과 관련 미측(특히 국방부)은 현단계에서는 한. 미, 한. 일등 양자 안보동맹 관계가 역내 안보질서의 출발점이자 종착점이라는 입장을 명백히함. 이에대해 일측은 탈냉전시대의 위험관리(RISK MANAGEMENT)를 위해 다자안보 틀의 장기적 유용성이 인정된다고 하면서, 다만 현단계에서는 다자안보 모색할 의사는 없음을 표명

- 중국의 역할관련, 미측은 중국이 과거 냉전시대의 세력균형적 고정관념에사로잡혀 새로운 국제질서하에서의 바람직한 역할을 수행하지 못하고 있다고 지적하고, 이에따라 미.중 관계가 전반적으로 좋지 못한 상태에 있으나,

외정실	장관	차관	1차보	아주국	미주국	분석관	청와대	안기부

0132

미측으로서는 MFN 등 중국의 개혁, 개방을 촉진시키는 분야와 캄보디아, 리비아 사태, 미사일 수출봉제등 중국의 협조가 필요한 분야에 있어서는 선별적으로 양국간 협력관계를 증진시켜 나갈 것이라고 언급

　- 일측은 중국이 대일관계에 있어 매우 우호적인 태도를 보이고 있으며, 미.중 관계가 어려워질수록 중국으로서는 일본을 자기편에 끌어 넣으려 할 것이므로 대일 협력증진을 위해 적극적 자세를 취할 가능성이 있다고 전망

　- 최근 중국 전인대에서의 첨각열도 관련 영해법 제정에 대해 일측은 당초 중국에 강력한 항의를 제기했으나, 추후 조사결과 동 법령 제정이 중국의 법제도 현대화 작업의 일환으로 추진된 것일 뿐이라는 것이 판명됨에 따라 더 이상의 항의를 할 계획이 없다고 언급

　- 동북아는 동남아와는 상호 구별되는 안보 역학이 적용되는 지역이라는데 의견 일치

　(외교정책에 영향을 미치는 국내적 요인)

　- 부쉬 대통령과 클린턴 후보의 국제관은 기본적으로 진보적인 국제주의(LIBERAL INTERNATIONALISM)이며 양인이 공히 기존체제(ESTABLISHMENT) 인사들이므로 대외정책에 관한한 공통점이 많음. 일부에서 우려하는 고립주의 회귀등 미 외교정책의 큰 변화는 없을 것으로 전망

　- 일본 참의원 선거(7.26)시 자민당 의석(현재 148 석)이 다소 줄어들 것으로 보이며, 만약 선거에 회부되는 74 석중 최소한 58 석을 확보하지 못할 경우 공명당, 민사당과 연합해도 과반수를 점하지 못하므로 PKO 법안 통과등에 문제가될 것임.

　- 일본은 국제환경의 변화와 함께 안보정책에 대한 새로운 국민적 합의 형성 필요등 변화가 일어나고 있으나, 일본이 이에 능동적으로 대응하지 못하고 있다고 하면서, 농촌지역의 선거구 공동화(ROTTEN CONSTITUENCY)등 정치체제의 낙후성, 현상유지에는 강점이 있으나 변화에 적응치 못하는 관료체제의 경직성, 미.일 관계의 변화(대외정책 결정에 있어 미국의 리더쉽에 순응하는 종래의 방식을 더 이상 국내적으로 받아들이기 어렵게 됨)등 이유로 외교정책에 있어 일본의리더쉽은 전후 가장 취약한 상황에 있다고 설명

공   란

(CIS 지원)

- 일측은 일 북부지역과 러시아 극동지역간 민간경협 가능성은 증대되고 있으나, 러시아가 유럽에 치중하고 명확한 대아시아 정책을 밝히지 않고 있어(북방영토 문제 해결에 성의를 보이지 않는 점 암시) 일 정부로서는 대러시아 대규모 원조에 적극적으로 임할 입장이 아니라고 언급

. 최근 언론에 보도된 일본의 사할린 석유, 개스 개발사업 참여 관련, 민간부문의 진출은 가능하나 정부차원의 지원(수출입은행 차관공여, 재정보증등)은 하지 않을 것이라는 입장 표명

- 일측은 이어 CIS 구성국중 중앙아시아 국가에 대한 원조를 증가하고자 하나 러시아에 대하여 차별대우 내지 내분조장의 인상을 주기는 원치 않는다고 설명

- 한. 미 양측은 러시아의 개혁, 개방 촉진을 위해 현시점에서의 원조가 필요하다는 점에 공감하고, 특히 한국의 경우에는 대북한 관계에서 러시아의 협조를 확보하는 고려가 필요하여 일본과는 다소 입장이 다를수 밖에 없다는데 인식 일치, 일측도 이해 표명

- 미측은 러시아가 미.러간 동반자 관계를 추구하고자 하며, 북한문제등에 대한 명확한 입장 표명등을 통하여 동반자로서의 스스로의 가치를 증명하고자 노력하는 듯한 인상을 받았다고 설명

(집단 개입)

- 한. 일 양측은 걸프전, 대 CIS 인도적 지원등에서 나타났듯이 탈냉전시대의 국제협력 메카니즘으로 집단개입의 유용성이 어느정도 인정되나, 참여국 범위 결정, 관련국간 협의, 의견조정등 면에서 보완해야 할 점이 적지 않음을 지적함. 이에대해 미측은 전적인 동감을 표시하면서도, 때로 시간을 놓치지 않고 결론을 도출해야 하는 상황에 처하기 때문에 어려움이 있다고 설명하면서, 집단개입 개념이 아직도 초기 발전단계에 있다고 설명

(APEC)

- (KEATING 호주수상의 APEC 정상회담 구상에 대해) 3 자는 공히 장래의 필요성은 인정되나, 현단계에서는 목적, 실효성등 어려움이 많다는 입장 표명, 부시 대통령과

PAGE 4

0135

키팅 수상 사이에 사전 협의가 있었다는 언론보도에 대하여, 미측은 호주측의 입장을 듣는 정도였다고 설명하면서 미측으로서는 아세안의 찬성 여부를 주시하겠다고 함.

　(차기회의 개최)

　- 한. 미.일은 아. 태지역 안보의 기축을 이루는 미.일 동맹, 한. 미 동맹을 구성하는 3 자가 모두 모인 3 자 협의회의 큰 유용성에 대해 의견을 같이 하고, 차기 회의는 93 년도 봄에 순서에 따라 일본에서 개최키로 하고, 구체적 일자는 추후 협의, 결정키로 합의

　2. 이실장 일행은 예정대로 5.3. 당지 출발, 귀국 예정임.끝.

　(대사 현홍주-장관)

　예고: 92.12.31. 일반

외 무 부

종 별 :

번 호 : USW-2264

일 시 : 92 0504 2126

수 신 : 장 관 (미이,미일,정특,국기,기정)

발 신 : 주 미 대 사

제 목 : 북한 관계 지침

연: USW-2178

1. 국무부 한국과 SCHMIEL 부과장은 금 5.4. 당관 안호영 서기관과의 업무협의시 국무부는 연호 4 항과 마찬가지로 워싱턴 및 각국 수도에서 표제 지침에 따라 상호 사찰에 대한 인식을 제고시키고 이에대한 지지를 확대하기 위한 노력을 계속하고 있으며, 이러한 노력의 일환으로 ANDERSON 부차관보가 금일 주미 영국대사관 (MEYER) 공사와 협의하였다고 알려왔음.

2. SCHMIEL 부과장은 ANDERSON 부차관보가 상기 면담을 끝내고 영국이 동 문제와 관련 한국정부로 부터 충분한 입장전달을 받지 못한 것으로 감지되었다고평가하였다고 전언하면서, 한국이 연호 3 항 리스본에서 개최되는 EC 정무국장회의에 대비하여 구주각국과 접촉할 계획이 있는지를 문의하였음. (ANDERSON 부차관보는 당지를 방문한 이승곤 외정실장과의 5.1. 면담시 미국의 DEMARCHE 에미온적이었던 국가로 연호 4 항 프랑스 이외에 이태리 및 스페인을 거명한바 있었음)

3. 평가및 건의

가. 미측의 연호 DEMARCHE 와 관련, 솔로몬 차관보의 불란서 정무차관보앞 서한 발송, ANDERSON 부차관보의 주미 영국대사관 접촉을 갖고 아측에 대하여 EC정무국장 회의의 기회를 이용하도록 수차에 걸쳐서 권고하고 있는 것은 한. 미.일간에는 충분한 의견 교환과 공동입장 정립이 이루어지고 있으나, 최근 IAEA 에 대한 북한태도 및 이에대한 국제사회의 반응과 관련, 자칫 EC 의 협조기반이 약화될 우려가 있다고 판단하여 이를 방지하기 위한 노력인 것으로 평가됨.

나. 최근 미측과의 접촉을 통하여 느껴지는 것은 미측이 상호 사찰의 관철을 위해 상기와 같은 노력을 경주하고 있으나, 아국의 노력이 이에 상응하지 못하는 것 아닌가 하는 의혹도 갖고 있는 것으로 감지되는바, 아국이 상호사찰의 관철을 위해 한.

미주국 안기부	장관	차관	1차보	미주국	국기국	외정실	분석관	청와대

0137

PAGE 1

미.일은 물론 EC 각국에 대해서도 충분한 외교적 노력을 경주하고 있음을 과시할수 있는 분명한 조치를 취하여 두는 것이 동문제에 대한 한. 미협조체제 유지를 위해 긴요할 것으로 사료됨.

　　다. 금후 미측과의 업무협의시 참고코자 하니 상기 2 항과 관련 참고사항 있으면 회시바람. 끝.

　　　（대사 현홍주-국장）

　　　예고: 92.12.31. 일반

일반문서로 재분류(1992. 12. 31 .)

검토필 (1992. 6. 20.)

주 미 대 사 관

USW(F) : 2784 년월일 : 92. 5. 4 시간 : 18:14

수 신 : 장 관 (메미, 메닌, 지특, 국기)

발 신 : 주 미 대 사

제 목 : 북한核보리 추무부 브리핑   (출처 : 가AS)

보 안
통 제

STATE DEPARTMENT REGULAR BRIEFING   BRIEFER: MARGARET TUTWILER
MONDAY, MAY 4, 1992

Q   On the subject of North Korea, have you seen a list of
nuclear facilities offered by the North Koreans, and do you find it
sufficient?

MS. TUTWILER: Not yet. It's my understanding that they are
presenting their initial inventory list earlier today in Vienna. We
expect the IAEA to announce the list of facilities and types of
material on the North Korean inventory list. And until we've been
able to examine this information, we would prefer not to comment.

Q   Back to North Korean nuclear matters please?

MS. TUTWILER: Yes?

Q   Are you going to keep full support for the IAEA decision,
which might be made during the -- in the course of the investigation
process, regardless of the result? I mean, whether the IAEA
declared that they were satisfactory or dissatisfactory?

MS. TUTWILER: Well, that's too hypothetical for me. I can't
prejudge for you, when you say will we give our full support
depending on what the decision is of the IAEA, or the
recommendations. No, I just can't do that for you in a vacuum.

Q   Until now you have said that the United States fully
supports --

MS. TUTWILER: We do.

Q   -- the IAEA. So in the future also will you in the
process of investigations, you are prepared to give full -- full
support for --

(2784- 1-1)

외신 1과
통 제

0139

MS. TUTWILER: Will we continue, generically speaking, our full support of the IAEA? Yes, we do, concerning the North Korean situation, absolutely.

Q   Regardless of the result?

MS. TUTWILER: I'm not going to do the regardless of the result. That's the part of your question that's just totally speculative for me.

2784 -2-2

0140

공   란

공 란

```
GLGL
oO181 ASI/AFP-AB49-----
r i SKorea-NKorea-nuclear 1 · 05-06 0271
North Korea vows to stick to nuclear inspection timetable
```

SEOUL, May 6 (AFP) - <u>North Korea agreed Wednesday to draft a nuclear</u> <u>inspection timetable with the South by the end of this month that would allow</u> <u>Seoul to begin inspecting its nuclear sites by mid-June.</u>

Choi U-Jin, a senior member of the North Korean delegation to this week's high-level talks, told a press conference that the two sides "must finish their negotiations over joint inspections by the end of May as already agreed.

He said he hoped the two sides could finish their working-level talks on the details of an inspection regime and begin inspections 20 days later, as previously agreed.

Earlier, South Korean Prime Minister Chung Won-Shik, in his keynote address on the first day of talks, had accused the North of stalling on establishing a mutual inspection regime by the agreed May 19 deadline.

"As long as doubts and suspicion remain over the nuclear issue, it will not be possible to usher in an era of genuine reconciliation and cooperation between the South and the North," Chung said.

The two sides formally launched a nuclear ban accord, along with a separate inter-Korean reconciliation agreement, during the sixth round of prime ministerial talks in February.

But implementation of the accords has bogged down at working level talks in the truce village of Panmunjom.

The North is suspected of being close to developing a crude nuclear device, and Seoul and its Western allies have been pressuring it to allow inspections of its facilities to verify that they are for peaceful purposes.

North Korean Prime Minister Yon Hyong-Muk bristled at the pressure in his keynote address, saying the South was "interfering" in Pyongyang's separate agreement to allow International Atomic Energy Agency (IAEA) inspections of its nuclear facilities.

Pyongyang, he was, was "now working smoothly with the IAEA for receiving nuclear inspections without any problems."

The communist North on Monday presented the Vienna-based IAEA with an inventory of its nuclear facilities and materials, paving the way for IAEA inspections of its facilities in June.

The IAEA said Tuesday that the North had revealed the existence of 12 previously unknown nuclear facilities in its inventory, at least one of which the IAEA said could be used for military purposes.

South Korean spokesman Lee Dong-Bok reaffirmed the South's position in a press conference here, saying, "If the nuclear issue is not solved, overall South-North ties will certainly be affected."

He added that IAEA and inter-Korean mutual inspections must be carried out "by an appropriate time."
bw-ckp/src

AFP 060856 GMT MAY 92

10

0143

北韓 방사능연구소는 재처리 시설·
WP紙, 北핵시설 신고 전문가 분석결과

　　(워싱턴=聯合) 박정찬특파원=美國의 핵전문가들은 북한이 4일 제출한 핵 명세서에 포함시킨 寧邊 방사능 연구소가 핵연료 재처리 시설을 의미하는 것으로 평가하고 있다고 워싱턴 포스트가 6일 보도했다.

　　북한이 국제원자력기구(IAEA)에 제출한 핵 명세서 가운데 3개의 원자로는 美정보기관에 알려진 시설이었으나 "우라늄과 플루토늄의 분리 연구를 위한 방사능 연구소"라고 신고된 것은 놀라운 것이라고 이 신문은 보도했다.

　　전문가들은 북한이 그 연구소의 목적이라고 밝힌 특징은 그동안 핵무기 생산과 관련해 세계적인 우려를 야기한 핵연료 재처리 시설과 거의 일치하는 것으로 간주하고 있다고 이 신문은 보도했다.

　　무기통제협회(ACA)소속 핵 전문가인 존 윌프스탈씨는 "이것이 美 정보기관이 얘기하던 재처리 시설일 가능성이 높다"고 말한 것으로 이 신문은 전했다.

　　북한의 핵 신고로 IAEA는 핵사찰을 서두를 것이며 북한측이 소량의 플루토늄을 생산했다고 밝힌 것은 핵 사찰을 그만큼 더 중요하게 만들고 있다고 이 신문은 강조했다.

　　이 신문은 북한측이 생산된 플루토늄 양이 극히 소량이라고 말하고 있으나 전문가들은 핵 폭탄 하나를 만드는데 8-16 파운드의 플루토늄만 요구된다고 밝히고 있다고 덧붙였다.(끝)

공 란

공   란

공   란

외 무 부

종 별 :

번 호 : USW-2307

일 시 : 92 0506 1900

수 신 : 장 관(미9,미일,정특,국기,기정) 사본:국방부장관

발 신 : 주 미 대사

제 목 : 북한 핵 리스트 논평

1. 국무부는 북한이 IAEA 에 최초 보고서를 제출한 것과 관련 하기 요지의 PRESS GUIDANCE 을 준비하였다고 알려왔음.

가. (질문)

- 북한이 제출한 보고서의 내용은 ?

(답변)

- 그 내용은 공개하지 않았으나, IAEA 에 의하면 그 내용이 방대 (EXTENSIVE) 하다고 하는바, 우리는 이를 환영 (WELCOME) 하며, 동 보고서 제출이 조속히 이루어진 것도 바람직 (ENCOURAGING)한 것임.

나. (질문)

- 북한 보고서에는 재처리 시설도 포함되어 있는지 ?

(답변)

- 북한 보고서의 성실성을 확인하는데는 상당히 시간이 소요되고 몇차례의 사찰이 필요할 것으로 봄.

- 북한이 '방사능 화학연구소'라고 제출한 것이 재처리 시설일 수도 있으나, 발표된 내용만으로는 불명확 (INADEQUATE) 함.

다. (질문)

- 목적이 무엇이던 사용된 핵연료에서 플루토니움을 추출하는 것은 재처리임. IAEA 가 금번 사찰을 통해 이를 확인해야 할 것임.

- 남.북한은 91.12. 비핵화 공동선언을 통해서 재처리를 포기한바, 남.북한간에 협의중인 사찰제도를 가능한대로 철저 (COMPREHENSIVE) 하게하는 것이 매우 중요함.

라. (질문)

- 첫번째 사찰은 언제 실시되는지 ?

미주국	1차보	미주국	국기국	외정실	분석관	청와대	안기부	국방부

92.05.07 10.21 0148

외신 1과 통제관 ✓

(답변)

- IAEA 사무국은 6월 이사회전에 최초 사찰이 실시될 것이라고 하였음.

- BLIX 사무총장도 내주중 북한을 방문할것이나, 이는 사찰이 아님을 분명히 해야함.

2. 상기 PRESS GUIDANCE 별도 FAX 송부함.끝.

첨부: USW(F)-2846.

(대사 현홍주-국장)

주 미 대 사 관

USW(F) : 2846   년월일 : 92.5.6.   시간 : 19:00

수 신 : 장 관 (머., 머민, 20북, 3이, 기라)

발 신 : 주미대사   (사부, 리명박, 강브)

제 목 : 현부물 (USW-22.7-1)   (출처 : DOS)

보통 / 안제

(2846 - 3 - 1)

외신 1과 통제

0150

NORTH KOREA: PROVIDES SAFEGUARDS DATA TO IAEA

Q: WHAT INFORMATION DID THE DPRK PROVIDE TO THE IAEA?

A: -- ACCORDING TO THE IAEA'S PRESS RELEASE, THE DPRK HAS
SUBMITTED ITS INITIAL INVENTORY AND THE DESIGN INFORMATION.

-- ALTHOUGH THE DETAILS OF THE INFORMATION PROVIDED,
BEYOND THAT CONTAINED IN THE IAEA PRESS RELEASE, ARE HELD

IN CONFIDENCE BY THE AGENCY, IAEA'S PRESS RELEASE
INDICATED IT HAD RECEIVED AN EXTENSIVE INITITAL REPORT,
WHICH WE OF COURSE WELCOME. THE PROMPTNESS OF THIS REPORT
IS ALSO ENCOURAGING.

-- UNDER THE TERMS OF ITS SAFEGUARDS AGREEMENT, THE DPRK
IS REQUIRED TO PROVIDE TO THE IAEA BY MAY 30 A COMPLETE
INVENTORY OF ALL NUCLEAR MATERIAL IN ALL OF ITS NUCLEAR
ACTIVITIES, ALONG WITH A LIST OF THE FACILITIES CONTAINING
NUCLEAR MATERIAL.

-- THE DPRK IS ALSO REQUIRED TO PROVIDE DESIGN INFORMATION
ON ALL EXISTING FACILITIES SO THAT ARRANGEMENTS FOR
SAFEGUARDING THE FACILITIES CAN BE FINALIZED BY JULY 9.
DESIGN INFORMATION ON NEW FACILITIES IS REQUIRED AS EARLY
AS POSSIBLE BEFORE THE INTRODUCTION OF NUCLEAR MATERIAL.

Q: DID THE LIST NORTH KOREA PROVIDED INCLUDE ALL SITES?
IN PARTICULAR, DID IT INCLUDE THE REPROCESSING PLANT?

A: -- THE COMPLETENESS OF THE LIST PROVIDED TO THE IAEA
WILL BE FOR THE IAEA TO DETERMINE. BECAUSE NORTH KOREAN
FACILITIES HAVE BEEN OPERATING WITHOUT SAFEGUARDS FOR
SEVERAL YEARS, THIS WILL BE A DIFFICULT TASK.

-- WE HOPE NORTH KOREA WILL COOPERATE FULLY WITH IAEA
EFFORTS TO VERIFY THE DECLARATION'S COMPLETENESS. THIS
WILL LIKELY TAKE SOME TIME AND SEVERAL INSPECTION VISITS.

-- IT IS POSSIBLE THAT WHAT THE DPRK DESCRIBES AS A
"RADIOCHEMICAL LABORATORY" IS WHAT HAS BEEN IDENTIFIED AS
A LIKELY REPROCESSING PLANT, ALTHOUGH THE NORTH KOREAN
DESCRIPTION WOULD SEEM TO BE AT BEST AN INADEQUATE
CHARACTERIZATION OF THE FACILITY.

Q: CAN YOU COMMENT ON THE REPORTS OF PLUTONIUM
PRODUCTION? ARE THERE ANY RESTRICTIONS ON REPROCESSING
ACTIVITIES IN THE DPRK?

A: -- WE KNOW ONLY THAT A NORTH KOREAN OFFICIAL HAS STATED
THAT A VERY SMALL QUANTITY OF PLUTONIUM HAS BEEN
SEPARATED. PROCESSING OF SPENT FUEL TO RECOVER PLUTONIUM
IS REPROCESSING, REGARDLESS OF ITS PURPOSE. IT WILL BE
IMPORTANT THAT IAEA IN ITS UPCOMING INSPECTIONS, DETERMINE
THE QUANTITY OF THE PLUTONIUM PRODUCTION AND ANY
CONTINUING CAPABILITY FOR SEPARATING PLUTONIUM.

-- REPROCESSING IS PRECLUDED BY THE NON-NUCLEAR

2846-3-2

0151

DECLARATION OF DECEMBER 31, 1991 BETWEEN NORTH AND SOUTH
KOREA. IT WILL THUS BE EXTREMELY IMPORTANT THAT THE
BILATERAL INSPECTION REGIME BEING NEGOTIATED BETWEEN THE
NORTH AND SOUTH BE AS COMPREHENSIVE AS POSSIBLE.

Q: WHEN IS THE FIRST INSPECTION?

A: -- THE IAEA SECRETARIAT HAS SAID THAT THE FIRST
INSPECTION WILL TAKE PLACE BEFORE THE NEXT IAEA BOARD OF
GOVERNORS MEETING IN MID-JUNE.

-- WE LOOK FORWARD TO THE DIRECTOR GENERAL'S REPORT OF
PROGRESS ON IMPLEMENTATION AT THAT BOARD MEETING.

-- THE DIRECTOR GENERAL WILL ALSO BE VISITING NORTH KOREA
NEXT WEEK. HOWEVER, THAT VISIT IS NOT/NOT AND SHOULD NOT
BE CHARACTERIZED AS AN INSPECTION AND CANNOT BE EXPECTED
TO CLARIFY THE TECHNICAL ASPECTS OF DPRK COMPLIANCE WITH
ITS SAFEGUARDS OBLIGATIONS.

END TEXT. YY

2446-3-3

0152

공   란

공   란

공   란

공　　　란

공   란

공 란

공   란

공   란

공 란

북미2 72

外務部 情報狀況室
受信日時　92. 5 . 7 . 09:40

美, 북한 플루토늄 생산에 주목

　　(워싱턴=聯合) 박정찬특파원=美국무부는 6일 북한이 극소량의 플루토늄을 분리했다고 밝힌데 대해 "그 용도에 관계없이 핵폐기물로 플루토늄을 생산하는 것은 재처리"라고 말하고 "앞으로 핵사찰시 IAEA(국제원자력기구)가 플루토늄 생산량과 앞으로의 생산능력을 측정하는 것이 중요할 것"이라고 말했다.

　　국무부의 한 대변인은 이날 북한의 핵 명세서 제출조치와 빠른 제출시기에 대해 환영하며 "고무적"이라고 말하고 북한측이 최근 밝힌 플루토늄 생산 확인에 대해 이같이 논평했다.

　　이 대변인은 지난해말 남북한간의 비핵화선언에 따라 핵재처리는 금지돼 있다고 상기시키고 "따라서 남북한간의 상호사찰 규정이 가능한한 포괄적인 내용이 되는 것이 매우 중요하다"고 강조했다.

　　이 대변인은 또 북한의 명세서 가운데 영변의 "방사능 연구소" 시설에 언급, "이 시설에 대한 북한측의 설명이 불충분한 것으로 보이지만 북한이 방사능연구소라고 묘사한 것은 재처리 공장일 것이라고 추측해온 시설일 가능성이 있다"고 논평했다.

　　미국내 일부 핵 전문가들은 북한측이 "우라늄과 플루토늄의 분리 연구를 위한 방사능 연구소"라고 제시한 영변 핵시설이 핵연료 재처리 시설일 것이라고 주장하고 있으며 워싱턴 외교 관측통들은 "이 시설의 정체가 무엇인지 좀 더 두고봐야 할 것"이라고 말하고 있다.(끝)

0162

92. 5. 7 (목)
16:30 pierce
1등서기관이 건네줌

O   IN RECENT WEEKS, NORTH KOREA HAS BEEN ACTIVELY SEEKING
EXPANDED DIPLOMATIC AND ECONOMIC CONTACT WITH MANY
COUNTRIES. NORTH KOREA HAS ARGUED THAT:

-- IT IS TRYING TO EXPAND DIPLOMATIC AND OTHER CONTACTS;

-- AS A NEW (SEPTEMBER 1991) MEMBER OF THE UN, IT IS
APPROPRIATE AND DESIRABLE TO ESTABLISH TIES WITH FELLOW UN
MEMBERS;

-- IT HAS MET AT A HIGH LEVEL WITH U.S. OFFICIALS, IS
CONDUCTING NORMALIZATION TALKS WITH JAPAN, AND IS ENGAGED
IN A SUBSTANTIVE DIALOGUE WITH SOUTH KOREA WHICH HAS
PRODUCED SUBSTANTIVE AGREEMENTS.

-- IT IS EXPLORING THE DEVELOPMENT OF COMMERCIAL
RELATIONS WITH OTHER NATIONS, AND WELCOMES COOPERATIVE
MULTILATERAL PROJECTS SUCH AS THE TUMEN REGIONAL
DEVELOPMENT PROJECT;

O   WITH THE ENTRY INTO FORCE APRIL 10 OF ITS IAEA
SAFEGUARDS AGREEMENT, THIS EFFORT IS LIKELY TO INTENSIFY.

O   WE WELCOME NORTH KOREAN STEPS TO MEET THE BROADLY
VOICED CONCERNS OF THE INTERNATIONAL COMMUNITY.

O   HOWEVER, NORTH KOREA MUST TURN ITS WORDS INTO DEEDS IN
THE CRITICAL AREAS RELATING TO ITS NUCLEAR PROGRAM AND ITS
MISSILE PROLIFERATION PRACTICES.

-- NUCLEAR PROLIFERATION ON THE KOREAN PENINSULA IS A
GRAVE POTENTIAL THREAT TO THE REGION AND WOULD UNDERMINE
THE NUCLEAR NON-PROLIFERATION TREATY REGIME GLOBALLY.

-- NORTH KOREA EMBARKED ON AN EXTENSIVE SECRET NUCLEAR
PROGRAM OVER A DECADE AGO. SINCE 1987 IT HAS OPERATED AN
UNSAFEGUARDED REACTOR WELL-SUITED FOR PRODUCING PLUTONIUM.

-- NORTH KOREA ACCEDED TO THE NUCLEAR NON-PROLIFERATION
TREATY (NPT) IN 1985, AND IN JANUARY OF THIS YEAR, AFTER A
DELAY OF SIX YEARS, FINALLY SIGNED ITS SAFEGUARDS
AGREEMENT. ON APRIL 10, THE AGREEMENT WAS BROUGHT INTO
FORCE. NORTH KOREA HAS INDICATED IT WILL ACCEPT
INSPECTIONS BY JUNE. WE HOPE THEY MAINTAIN THIS SCHEDULE.

--THE DPRK AND ROK ISSUED A JOINT DECLARATION ON
DECEMBER 31, 1991, COMMITTING THEMSELVES TO BANNING
NUCLEAR WEAPONS AND TO NOT ENGAGE IN NUCLEAR REPROCESSING

0163

OR ENRICHMENT. NEGOTIATIONS ON A BILATERAL INSPECTION
REGIME TO MONITOR COMPLIANCE WITH THESE COMMITMENTS HAVE
JUST BEGUN.

O   HOWEVER, SIGNING NUCLEAR INSPECTION AGREEMENTS IS ONLY
THE FIRST STEP. THE TOUCHSTONE FOR IMPROVING DIPLOMATIC
AND OTHER RELATIONS WITH NORTH KOREA SHOULD BE THE ACTUAL
IMPLEMENTATION OF EFFECTIVE AND CREDIBLE INSPECTIONS IN
NORTH KOREA UNDER BOTH THE IAEA AGREEMENT AND THE
BILATERAL INSPECTION REGIME.

--WE MET WITH THE NORTH KOREANS ON A ONE-TIME BASIS TO
EXPLAIN AUTHORITATIVELY OUR POLICY THAT RELATIONS CAN
IMPROVE ONLY WHEN NORTH KOREA HAS MADE REAL PROGRESS ON A
WIDE VARIETY OF ISSUES, AND ESPECIALLY THE NUCLEAR ISSUE.

-- THE U.S. AND OTHERS HAVE TOLD NORTH KOREA IT CANNOT
EXPECT TO BEGIN EXPANDING CONTACTS OR IMPROVING RELATIONS
UNTIL IT HAS FULLY IMPLEMENTED ITS IAEA SAFEGUARDS
AGREEMENT AND ITS NON-NUCLEAR AGREEMENT WITH THE REPUBLIC
OF KOREA, RECEIVED INSPECTIONS UNDER BOTH THE IAEA
SAFEGUARDS AGREEMENT AND THE BILATERAL AGREEMENT, AND THUS
REMOVED INTERNATIONAL SUSPICIONS ABOUT ITS NUCLEAR PROGRAM.

O   WE HAVE ALSO TOLD NORTH KOREA THAT ITS EXPORT OF
MISSILES AND MISSILE TECHNOLOGY TO THE MIDDLE EAST
CONTRIBUTE TO INSTABILITY AND COMPLICATE THE VERY
DIFFICULT PROCESS OF NEGOTIATING PEACE IN THAT REGION. WE
HAVE ASKED NORTH KOREA TO REFRAIN FROM SUCH EXPORTS.

O   WE BELIEVE IT WOULD BE HELPFUL FOR YOUR GOVERNMENT TO
SEEK OPPORTUNITIES TO MAKE CLEAR TO NORTH KOREA THE
IMPORTANCE OF FULLY FOLLOWING THROUGH ON ITS COMMITMENTS
UNDER BOTH THE NPT AND ITS BILATERAL AGREEMENT WITH THE
ROK AND ACCEPT INSPECTIONS. IT WOULD ALSO BE HELPFUL TO
ASK FOR NORTH KOREAN RESTRAINT ON MISSILE AND MISSILE
TECHNOLOGY EXPORTS.

O   IT IS ESPECIALLY IMPORTANT TO MAKE THIS POINT IF NORTH
KOREA HAS APPROACHED YOU ABOUT ESTABLISHING, UPGRADING, OR
EXPANDING DIPLOMATIC OR ECONOMIC TIES.

O   THE DPRK SHOULD BE WILLING TO HELP ALLEVIATE
INTERNATIONAL CONCERNS BY COOPERATING FULLY WITH IAEA
INSPECTIONS AND BILATERAL INSPECTIONS.

O   IN ANOTHER AREA, THE DPRK HAS ATTEMPTED TO CALL INTO
QUESTION THE CONTINUED VIABILITY OF THE CEASE-FIRE AND
SECURITY ARRANGEMENTS IMPLEMENTED UNDER THE ARMISTICE
AGREEMENT OF 1953. IN PARTICULAR, IT HAS CITED ITS UN

0164

MEMBERSHIP AND NON-AGGRESSION ·AGREEMENT WITH THE ROK AS
EVIDENCE THAT THE ARMISTICE ARRANGEMENTS ARE NO LONGER
RELEVANT AND/OR HAVE BEEN SUPERSEDED.

O   THE ARMISTICE AGREEMENT STATES THAT IT SHALL ·"REMAIN
IN EFFECT UNTIL EXPRESSLY SUPERSEDED EITHER BY MUTUALLY
ACCEPTABLE AMENDMENTS AND ADDITIONS OR BY PROVISION IN AN
APPROPRIATE AGREEMENT FOR A PEACEFUL SETTLEMENT AT A
POLITICAL LEVEL BETWEEN BOTH SIDES."

O   IT IS CLEAR THEREFORE THAT THE UNILATERAL ACTION OF
ONE PARTY CANNOT ABROGATE THE ARMISTICE ARRANGEMENTS.

O   WE HOPE YOU WILL MAKE CLEAR TO THE DPRK THE IMPORTANCE
OF MAINTAINING THE ARMISTICE AGREEMENT AND ITS
ARRANGEMENTS UNTIL NORTH AND SOUTH KOREA CAN AGREE ON
SPECIFIC STEPS WHICH WILL BE THE BASIS FOR A PERMANENT
PEACE ARRANGEMENT.

O   AT THAT POINT ALL THE PARTIES TO THE ARMISTICE
AGREEMENT, INCLUDING THE U.S., WILL BE READY TO CONSIDER
STEPS TO END THE ARMISTICE ARRANGEMENTS.
IF ASKED ABOUT RECENT REPORTS OF U.S. SALE OF GRAIN TO
NORTH KOREA:

O   AS PART OF ITS POLICY INITIATIVE TOWARD NORTH KOREA IN
1988, THE U.S. BEGAN TO APPROVE THE SALE ON HUMANITARIAN
GROUNDS OF ITEMS TO MEET BASIC HUMAN NEEDS, SUCH AS FOOD,
MEDICINE, AND MEDICAL EQUIPMENT. THESE VERY MODEST FOOD
SALES, TOTALLING LESS THAN 15 MILLION DOLLARS SINCE 1988,
ARE FULLY CONSISTENT WITH THE POLICY OF PERMITTING THE
SALE OF GOODS ON A HUMANITARIAN BASIS.·

0165

공   란

공   란

공 란

공   란

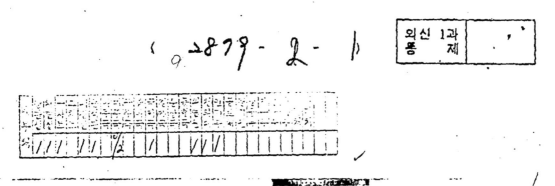
72

USW(F) : 2879 년월일 : 92. 5. 7 시간 : 17:35
수 신 : 장 관 (이메신, 정특, 축기, 기평)
발 신 : 주미대사
제 목 : 北韓 IAEA 報告에 영한 國務部 許價(출처 : 7 N.S.)

STATE DEPARTMENT REGULAR BRIEFING BRIEFER: MARGARET TUTWILER
THURSDAY, MAY 7, 1992

Q   On another subject, could you -- recently you or Richard
or maybe both, when asked about the North Korean nuclear program,
have said that you wanted to see what the report was to the

International Atomic Energy Agency. This has now been --- they've
issued press releases on it and I presume -- in fact I'm pretty sure
by now the US government has taken a fairly good look at what they
submitted -- do you now have some response as to what the US thinks
of what the North Koreans have presented?

MS. TUTWILER: I don't have a US response. I have US views of
the IAEA press release of the other day. As you know, the rules are
that the IAEA issues to everyone through a press release. They do
not deal directly with governments. So our experts I'm sure will be
continuing to review this. But I don't have anything other than our
initial response to that press release, and I believe it was -- two
days ago?

Q   Did you ever make this response?

MS. TUTWILER: I thought we'd done all this. We didn't?

Q   I think you said you didn't have enough information.

MS. TUTWILER: Oh.

As you know, that they have submitted their initial inventory
and design information. Although the details of the information
provided beyond that contained in the IAEA press release are held in
confidence by the agency, IAEA's press release indicated it had
received an extensive initial report which we of course welcome.
The promptness of the report is also encouraging.

(2879 - 2 - 1)

외신 1과
통 제

0170

Under the terms of its safeguards agreement, the DPRK is required to provide to the IAEA by May 30th a complete inventory of all nuclear material in all of its nuclear activities (may mean facilities), along with a list of the facilities containing nuclear materials. The DPRK is also required to provide design information on all existing facilities so that arrangements for safeguarding the facilities can be finalized by July 9. Design information on new facilities is required as early as possible before the introduction of nuclear material.

Does that help you?

Q   Do you see anything encouraging in a pattern of this and the agreement signed between North and South Korea? Is there some changing pattern of behavior that you see in the case of North Korea?

MS. TUTWILER: I don't think, Jim, that I'm in a position today to take a guess at that for you. We obviously have all seen changes over the last 18 months in various patterns of behavior. But I'd rather, if you don't mind, defer and let someone who is an expert in this area give you a more analytical analysis of their interpretation of what's going on.

Q   On that point, the US government -- certainly, Mr. Gates and I believe Secretary Baker -- have made a good deal of the belief that the North Koreans are bulding a reprocessing plant, making it possible for them to produce plutonium. One of the things mentioned in the press release and in the North Korean submissions is indeed a plant, or a "laboratory" as they call it, to separate out uranium into plutonium. You probably can't do it now, but could someone either verbally or on paper give us some idea of what the US government thinks of the North Korean report that they indeed do have a facility which, at least on an experimental basis, is doing this, and whether inspection of that facility would alleviate the US concern about it?

MS. TUTWILER: Mmm-hmm. What I'd rather do -- I have something here on a reprocessing plant, but I'd rather get you a fuller answer that more directly asks what you're answering, if that's okay.

217? -2-2

0171

공   란

공   란

공 란

공 란

공 란

공   란

공   란

공   란

공 란

공   란

공   란

| 관리
번호 | 92-
252 |

외 무 부

종 별 :

번 호 : USW-2369

일 시 : 92 0508 1754

수 신 : 장관 (미일,미이)

발 신 : 주미국 대사

제 목 : NSC 아주담당관 방한

　　1. 5.12-16 간 예정된 QUAYLE 부통령 방일을 수행하는 TORKEL PATTERSON NSC 아주담당관은 방일후 5.18-20 간 방한 계획임을 당관에 알려왔음.

　　2. PATTERSON 담당관은 금번 방한을 통해 외무부, 청와대등 관계기관 인사들과 면담, 양국간 현안문제를 협의하기를 희망하고 있는바, 동 담당관이 NSC 에서 한국과 일본을 전담하고 있으며, 당관과도 긴밀한 협조체제를 유지하고 있음을 감안, 적절한 일정을 주선해 줄것을 건의함. 끝.

　　(대사 현홍주-국장)

　　예고: 92.12.31. 일반 　검토됨 (1 92 6. 3?) 인

　　　　　예고문에 의거 재분류(1 92 12 31)
　　　　　직위　　　　성명

미주국　　1차보　　미주국

PAGE 1

0183

92.05.09　08:14

외신 2과　통제관 BS

북한 핵문제, 1992. 전13권 (V.3 4-5월)　569

공   란

공 란

공   란

(캔터 미국무차관 방한)

10항 하단 예상 질문

핵문제와 관련 북한의 최초보고서상 기재된 목록과 미국이 보유하고 있는

정보 내용과 차이가 있는지?

특히 핵재처리 시설이 포함되지 않는데 대한 미측 평가는?

ㅇ 미국은 북한이 최초보고서를 시일내 제출한 것을 환영하고 북한의 동 태도를 일단
  긍정적인(encouraging) 것으로 평가

ㅇ 북한의 성실한 보고 여부 및 북한의 핵 재처리 시설 보유 여부를 포함한 핵 개발
  능력에 대한 평가는 5월말 또는 6월초로 예정된 IAEA 임시사찰 결과를 지켜보는
  것이 좋겠음.

〈참고자료〉

ㅇ 5.15 IAEA는 Hans Blix 사무총장의 방북결과를 Press Release로 배포하였는 바,
  그 내용은 다음과 같음
  - 블릭스 사무총장은 영변 핵연구센터 소재 "방사능 화학 연구소" 등 3개 핵시설과
    태천에 건설중인 원자력발전소, 박천 및 평산소재 우라늄 정련 생산시설을 방문
  - 북한측은 우라늄 회수 및 플루토늄 추출을 위한 핵연료 재처리 능력을 개발,
    실험중임을 인정

0187

- 북한측은 수주내 방북 예정인 IAEA 사찰단이 희망할 경우 모든 핵시설(IAEA
  제출 핵 보고서 포함 여부 불문)에 대한 방문 허용 약속

o 북한이 핵 재처리 시설을 보유하고 있다면 이는 "한반도의 비핵화 선언" 제3조
  "남과 북은 핵 재처리 시설과 우라늄 농축시설을 보유하지 아니한다"라는 규정에
  정면으로 위배되는 것으로서, 문제삼지 않을 수 없음.
  (IAEA로서는 북한이 평화적 목적으로 사용하는 것을 확인할 수 있는 한 핵 재처리
  시설 보유와 플루토늄 추출 등에 대하여 제지하는 권한이 없음)

0188

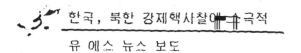

3. 한국, 북한 강제핵사찰에 소극적
유 에스 뉴스 보도

북미2과 김
—US News
기사 확인

(위싱턴=聯合) 박정찬특파원=한국정부는 북한의 金日成을 코너로 밀어붙이기를 원치 않고 있으며 美國이 비밀핵시설을 발견하는데 필수적이라고 간주하는 강제핵사찰을 북한에 강요하는 것을 달갑지 않게 여기고 있다고 13일 발매된 美 시사주간지 유 에스 뉴스 앤드 월드 리포트 최신호가 주장했다.

이 주간지는 북한이 핵안전협정을 비준함으로써 영변에 있는 핵재처리 궁장을 사찰대상에 포함시킬것인지 여부와 국제사찰 전문가의 入北이 언제 이루어지느냐가 북한의 진실성을 시험하는 관심사항으로 남게 되었다고 말했다.

이주간지는 그러나 美행정부가 북한을 제2의 이라크로 간주하고 곧 사찰을 받지 않으면 제재를 가하려는데 비해 한국정부는 북한의 의도를 의심하면서도 金日成을 코너로 몰아부치기를 원치않고 있다고 보도했다.

이 주간지는 "우리는 김일성이 사담 후세인과 같은 인물임을 알고 있지만 그렇게 말하고 싶지는 않다. 우리는 그의 체면을 세워줄 필요가 있다"고 말한 한 한국문석가의 발언을 인용했다.

"남한은 미국이 북한의 비밀핵시설을 발견하거나 적어도 핵폭탄개발계획을 지연시키는데 필수적이라고 간주하는 강제사찰을 추진하는 것을 달갑지 않게 여기고 있다"고 이 잡지는 주장하고 남북상호사찰 규정에 관해서도 한국측이 보다 유연한 자세를 취하고 있음을 시사했다. (끝)

4. 핵비준 따른 美-북한 접촉격상 부인
터트와일러 국무부 대변인 브리핑서

(위싱턴=聯合) 박정찬특파원= 마거릿 터트와일러 미국 국무부 대변인은 13일 북한의 핵안전협정 비준에 따른 美-북한간 관계격상 가능성에 대해 "나는 누가 관계격상을 얘기하는 것을 들어본 적이 없다"고 말했다.

터트와일러 대변인은 이날 정례 브리핑에서 이같이 밝히고 "우리는 북경에서 회담을 갖고 있으며 최근 뉴욕에서 국무부 차관이 매우 궁개적인 회담을 가진 적이 있었다"고 밝혔다.

한편 터트와일러 대변인은 日本의 플루토늄 도입계획과 관련, 日本이 미국과의 협정에 따라 첫 도입본을 프랑스로부터 선적해 올 준비를 하고 있다고 말하고 "미국은 이 계획에 만족하고 있으며 완전한 이행을 위해 일본과 협조를 계속 할 것"이라

0189

공   란

공　　　란

공   란

공   란

공   란

공   란

공   란

공　　　란

공   란

공 란

공   란

공 란

공   란

공   란

공   란

공   란

공   란

공　　　　란

공   란

공   란

공 란

공   란

공   란

공   란

공   란

공   란

공   란

공   란

공   란

공   란

관리
번호 92 -646

외 무 부

종 별 :

번 호 : USW-2562   일 시 : 92 0519 1914

수 신 : 장관 (미이)

발 신 : 주 미 대사

제 목 : 남.북 핵사찰

검토필(19 92. 6. 30.) 103

　　1. 국무부 KARTMAN 과장은 금 5.19. 당관 임성준 참사관에게 당지 FBIS 를 통해 입수된 5.18. 자 중앙일보는 '한국정부가 특별사찰의 관철을 조건으로 소규모의 재처리및 농축시설을 허용할 것을 검토중'이라는 요지로 보도하였다고 알리면서 사실관계 확인을 요청하여 왔는바, 회시바람.

　　2. 상기 보도내용 FAX 송부함. 끝.

　　첨부: USW(F)-3219

　　(대사 현홍주-국장)

　　예고: 92.12.31. 일반

예고문에 의거 재분류(19   .)
직위   성명

미주국	장관	차관	1차보	외정실	분석관	청와대	안기부

0220

PAGE 1

92.05.20   09:08

외신 2과 통제관 BX

주 미 대 사 관

USF(F) : 3219   년월일 : 92. 6. 19   시간 : 19:14

수 신 : 장 관 (미이)

발 신 : 주 미 대 사

제 목 : 정박문

보안통제	

(출처 :   )

(3219 - 2 - 1)

외신1과통제	

0221

ROK: ALTERED STANCE ON NORTH NUCLEAR LABORATORIES CONSIDERED
SK19051332SZ SEOUL CHUNGANG ILBO IN KOREAN 18 MAY 92 P 2

[Un<TEXT>]
[TEXT] THE GOVERNMENT IS CONSIDERING THE EXCLUSION OF
REPROCESSING LABORATORIES AND URANIUM ENRICHMENT FACILITIES, WHICH
FALL BELOW A CERTAIN LEVEL, FROM PROHIBITED FACILITIES AS SPECIFIED
IN THE JOINT DECLARATION ON DENUCLEARIZATION OF THE KOREAN
PENINSULA. THEY WILL EXCLUDE THESE LABORATORIES IF NORTH KOREA
INCLUDES THE TERM "SPECIAL INSPECTION" IN MUTUAL NUCLEAR INSPECTION
REGULATIONS BETWEEN THE NORTH AND THE SOUTH.
    THE GOVERNMENT WILL CONSULT RELEVANT MINISTRIES AND THE UNITED
STATES ON AN ACCEPTABLE SAFETY RANGE OF REPROCESSING FACILITIES AND
URANIUM ENRICHMENT FACILITIES.
    ASSERTING THAT THE GOVERNMENT POSITION HAS NOT BEEN FINALIZED AND
THAT THERE ARE CONTRADICTORY ARGUMENTS AMONG GOVERNMENT
ORGANIZATIONS, A RELEVANT GOVERNMENT OFFICIAL ON 18 MAY SAID: IT IS
POSSIBLE THAT A CERTAIN REPROCESSING FACILITY CANNOT PRODUCE EVEN A
SINGLE NUCLEAR CORE WITH EXTRACTED PLUTONIUM FOR MORE THAN 100
YEARS. THEREFORE, IF THE NUCLEAR INSPECTION IS THOROUGHLY CARRIED
OUT, THE POSSESSION OF SUCH REPROCESSING FACILITIES MAY AS WELL BE
ALLOWED.
    HE ALSO SAID: THE REPROCESSING CAPACITY OF "RADIOCHEMICAL
LABORATORIES" UNDER NORTH KOREAN CONTROL SHOULD BE CONFIRMED THROUGH
FIRST-HAND INSPECTION BY THE INTERNATIONAL ATOMIC ENERGY AGENCY
IIAEA] AND US. HE AVOIDED MENTIONING WHETHER THE REPROCESSING
FACILITIES, WHICH NORTH KOREA HAS, CAN BE CLASSIFIED AS ACCEPTABLE.
TO DEFINE THE ALLOWABLE CAPACITY OF REPROCESSING FACILITIES, A
SEPARATE NORTH-SOUTH AGREEMENT SHOULD BE ADOPTED AND A PRECONDITION
IS REQUIRED IN ORDER TO CONSOLIDATE A GUARANTEE THAT THIS TECHNOLOGY
NOT BE USED FOR MANUFACTURING WEAPONS. THE FORCIBLE INSPECTION
CALLED "SPECIAL INSPECTION" SHOULD BE INCLUDED IN INSPECTION
REGULATIONS WITHOUT FAIL.
    IN AN INTERVIEW WITH ROK REPORTERS IN BEIJING ON 17 MAY, NORTH
AMBASSADOR YI SAM-NO ARGUED THAT SINCE NORTH KOREA'S "RADIOCHEMICAL
LABORATORY" WILL SERVE AS A LABORATORY FOR PEACEFUL PURPOSES, IT CAN
NOT BE SCRAPPED, RAISING DOUBTS CONCERNING FORCIBLE REALIZATION OF
THE JOINT DECLARATION ON DENUCLEARIZATION. GOVERNMENT ACTION ON
THIS ISSUE WILL BE CAREFULLY MONITORED.
    ANOTHER RELEVENT OFFICIAL SAID: ALTHOUGH ITS CAPACITY IS
CLASSIFIED AS ONLY A LABORATORY, ALLOWING THE EXISTENCE OF THE
REPROCESSING FACILITY WILL RESULT IN A DE FACTO INVALIDATION OF
ARTICLE 3 OF THE "JOINT DECLARATION ON DENUCLEARIZATION ON THE
KOREAN PENINSULA," THREATENING THE DENUCLEARIZATION DECLARATION. HE
ADDED THAT HE OPPOSES ALLOWING THE LABORATORY AS DOES THE UNITED
STATES.
19 MAY 1417Z AMC
NNNN

3-19-2-2

0222

분류번호	보존기간

발 신 전 보

번 호 : WUS-2393   920520 1928 DG 종별 : 지급

수 신 : 주 미 대사. 총영사

발 신 : 장 관 (미이)

제 목 : 남북 핵사찰

검토필(1992. 6. 30.) [서명]

대 : USW-2562

1. 대호 5. 18자 중앙일보 기사는 사실 무근이며, 정부 차원에서 동 기사
   내용과 같은 방침이 검토된 일이 전혀 없음을 미측에 설명 바람.

2. 동 기사 게재후, 여타 국내 언론사에도 동 기사 내용이 사실 무근임을
   설명한 바 있으며, 타신문사에서는 이를 보도하지않음.

3. 금 5. 20. 주한미대사관 Pierce 서기관도 동건 문의해온 바, 이호진
   북미2과장은 상기와 같이 설명하였으며, 동인은 충분한 이해를 표시
   하였음을 참고바람.   끝.

(미주국장 정태익)

예고 : 92. 12. 31. 일반   예고문에 의거 재분류(19 92.12.31)
직위   성명 [서명]

[서명]

보 안 통 제	[서명]

앙 고 재	92 년 5 월 21 일	북 미 2 과	기안자 성명 [서명]	과 장 [서명]	국 장 [서명]	차 관	장 관 [서명]	외신과통제

0223

공 란

공   란

공   란

공   란

공   란

主要外信隨時報告

체니, 北韓 核禁 약속 아직 신뢰 못해

(워싱턴=聯合) 李文鎭특파원= 딕 체니 美 국방장관은 20일 북한이 더 이상 적극적으로 核무기개발을 추구하지 않는다고 믿게 되기까지에는 아직도 많은 단계가 남아 있다고 말했다.

그는 이날 워싱턴의 내셔널 프레스클럽 초청 오찬연설회에서 북한의 核문제와 관련, 최근 몇달동안 남북대화를 통해 이루어진 진전에 만족한다고 지적한후 그러나 아직도 문제가 남아 있다며 이같이 말하고 核무기로 무장된 북한이야말로 아시아지역에 주둔하는 미군과 美우방들에 대한 중대한 위협이라고 주장했다.

그는 美군사력의 아시아 계속 주둔을 희망한다고 밝히고 예컨데 일본이 학교·주택·기지건설 등 상당부분의 비용을 부담하기 때문에 항공모함 전단을 샌디에고에 주둔시키는 것보다 일본의 요코스카에 주둔시키는 것이 훨씬 경제적이라고 말했다.

그는 미군이 이 지역에서 철수하면 힘의 진공상태가 조성되고 조만간 다른 누가 그 공백을 메꿀 것이라고 말하고 그것은 결코 미국의 이익이 아니며 불안을 조성하는 요인이 될 것이라고 주장했다. (끝)

솔라즈, 북한核 지하잠적 가능성 지적

(워싱턴=聯合) 박정찬특파원=스티븐 솔라즈 美하원 외무위원회 아시아 태평양 소위 위원장은 20일 北韓의 핵사찰과 관련 "북한은 대규모 땅굴 공사를 잘하는 나라로서 핵무기가 지하에 들어갔을 가능성이 있다"고 지적했다.

솔라즈 위원장은 따라서 국제원자력기구(IAEA)는 북한핵에 대해 적극적이고 철저한 사찰을 실시하여 이라크에서 실추된 명예를 회복해야 한다고 주장했다.

솔라즈 위원장은 이날 美헤리티지 재단이 주최한 北韓 인권문제 세미나에 참석, 이같이 주장하고 "북한의 핵무장은 핵 전쟁과 핵확산 위험을 증대시킬 뿐 아니라 북한에게 자신감을 줌으로써 재래식 전쟁도발의 가능성도 높일 것"이라고 말했다.

그는 미국은 앞으로 강온 양면정책을 통해 핵문제의 만족한 해결이 유도될 때까지 유엔 安保理의 강제 재재조치를 포함, 철저하게 대처해 나가야 한다고 덧붙였다. (끝)

0229

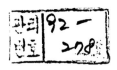

8 / 14	長 官 報 告 事 項	報告畢

1992. 5. 21.
美 洲 局
北 美 1 課(53)

題目 : 美 白堊館 NSC Patterson 補佐官 面談 結果

美 白堊館 NSC Patterson 補佐官(韓.日 擔當)은 5.20. 美洲局長을 面談하였는 바, 同 補佐官 說明 要旨 다음 報告드립니다.

검토필(19P2. 6. 3 0.) 103

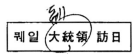
퀘일 (大統領) 訪日

(槪　　要)

o 퀘일 대통령은 향후 미국의 계속 발전과 번영을 위해서는 일본과의 협력이 필수적이라는 신념으로 미.일관계 증진을 강조
  - 미.일의 GNP는 전 세계 GNP의 40% 점유

o 일본측은 오키나와 반환 20주년과 관련, 러시아가 북방영토를 반환치 않고 있는점을 강하게 비판하고 미국의 협조를 요청

(韓半島 問題)

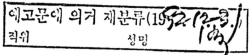
대고문대 의거 재분류(1952.12.3 .)
직위　　　　성명

o 퀘일 부통령은 미야자와 수상, 와다나베 외상외에 카네마루와도 면담한 바, 가네마루 면담시에는 일체 한반도 문제는 거론치 않았으며, 가네마루를 방미 초청함.
  - 가네마루 방미시 북한 문제는 거론치 않기로 사전 약속
    * 가네마루 6. 12. - 13. 방미 예정

0230

o   와다나베 외상은 북한정세에 관해 논의하면서 일본의 대북한 인식은 미국의
     인식과 차이점이 없다고 설명함.

     -   여타 정치인.언론인과의 면담에서도 대부분 일.북한 조기수교 필요성을
         제기치 않음.

美 國內情勢

o   현재 대통령 후보중 대외정책뿐 아니라 대내정책도 균형있게 추진할 수 있는
     후보는 부쉬대통령 뿐 임.

     -   클린턴과 페로의 약점은 계속 부각될 전망

o   대외정책 분야에 비해 대내정책이 효율적으로 추진되지 않고 있는 것은 미국의
     헌법과 국내제도 때문임.

     -   국내의 다양한 기관.조직.정치세력에 대한 대통령 통제 개념 부재

o   부쉬대통령은 재선시, 국내정치제도 개혁에 착수할 예정

     -   의원의 임기제한, 의회의 상임위 축소 및 행정부내의 카운터파트격 조직
         폐쇄등 (의회-행정부간 이익 유착 고리 차단)

o   부쉬대통령이 캘리포니아등 대형주와 남부에서 패배할 경우 50% 과반수 획득
     불가 가능성도 가상적이긴 하나, 불배제

     -   동 경우 의회에서 대통령 선출 (클린턴 당선 가능성)

0231

o 동 보좌관은 아국의 국내정세, 북한 핵문제, 통상.재정정책에 대해 관심을
  표한 바, 아측은 우리입장에 따라 적의 설명

  - 동 보좌관은 아국의 선거등 정치일정의 진행과는 별도로 남.북관계등 대외
    분야의 정책이 차분히 진행되고 있는 점 평가
    · 금융시장개방이 아국의 선진국 진입에 필수적이며, 한.미정상간 합의가
      하부에 충분히 전달되지 않은 느낌이라고 언급

o 부쉬대통령은 11월 선거 이전까지 G - 7 참석, 일부 구주국 방문외에는 별반
  해외일정은 계획치 않고 선거전에 전념 예정

                                                    - 끝 -

예　고　:　1992.12.31.일반

0232

연합 H1-239 S01 정치(258)

"북한 핵개발 경계해야"-2

　　玄대사는 북한의 核문제는 국지적 또는 지역적 현안이 아니라 냉전이후 세계평화를 위협하는 대량살상무기의 확산을 금지한다는 관점에서 파악돼야 한다면서 "남북상호사찰이 이뤄져야 美.日의 對北관계개선이 실현될 수 있다는 점을 북측에 분명히 인식시킬 필요가 있다"고 말했다.

　　玄대사는 자신의 일시귀국이 한반도와 주변 4강에 의한 <2+4회담>과 관련이 있다는 일부 보도는 "전혀 사실무근"이라면서 "한반도 문제는 우리가 주도적으로 해결해야 한다는 입장을 이미 美國정부에 설명한 바 있으며 美國도 이를 지지하고 있다"고 말했다.(끝)

0233

"北韓 核개발 경계해야"-1

玄대사 특별사찰필요성 강조

　　(서울=聯合) 玄鴻柱駐美대사는 26일 "北韓의 核문제가 완전히 해결되기 위해서
는 국제원자력기구(IAEA)의 사찰과 함께 한반도 비핵화궁동선언에 의한 南北상호사
찰이 반드시 이뤄져야 한다"면서 "IAEA의 사찰제도를 보완하기 위해 남북상호사찰에
특별사찰이 포함돼야 할 것"이라고 말했다.

　　북한의 핵문제를 비롯한 韓.美관계 전반에 관해 본국정부와의 협의차 일시귀국
중인 玄대사는 이날오전 외무부에서 기자들과 만난 자리에서 "核문제의 해결없이는
南北관계의 진전이 이뤄지기 어려우며 미국과 일본의 對北관계도 개선될 수 없다는
것이 우리 정부의 일관된 정책기조"라며 이같이 밝혔다.

　　玄대사는 특히 북한의 플루토늄 추출문제와 관련, "북한이 실험실에서 추출한
극소량의 플루토늄으로 무기를 제조하기에는 미약하다고 일부 언론에서 보도하고 있
으나 이는 잘못된 것"이라고 지적하면서 "2차대전시 맨해턴 프로젝트에 의해 경험했
던것 처럼 실험실 추출은 곧바로 核무기생산으로 연결될 수 있는 것"이라고 북한의
핵무기 개발가능성에 우려를 표명했다.(계속)

0234

駐美대사 돌연귀국, 盧대통령 独対

북한核관련 특별 보고

美「사찰거부 대책」 전한듯

玄鴻柱 駐美대사가 23일 北核포기 압력에 대한 美돌연 귀국, 25일 청와대에서 盧泰愚대통령과 独対, 某種의 특별보고를 한것으로 알려졌다.

玄대사의 이번 귀국은 지난주 초 李相玉외무장관을 통해 청와대에 특별보고를 신청함으로써 이루어졌다.

정부의 한 소식통은 이 귀국이 北核포기 압력에 대한 美정부는 최근 北韓 核문제를 비롯한 한반도 안보문제는 중장기적인 외교정책, 그리고 이에 대한 美정부의 구상들을 설명드렸다고만 밝혔다.

정부의 한 소식통은 이와 관련「美국은 현재 北韓의 軍사기지 공개 기피로 南北 상호사찰이 조기에 실시되지 않고 있는 상황에 대해 심각한 우려를 가지고 있다」고 전제,「美정부는 최근 北韓 核문제를 한국측의 반발로 무산된「2+4」회담 제의가 참석하는 베이커 美국무장관의주변 열강이 참여하는 多者간 협의체에서 궁극적으로 해결·보장돼야 한다는 구상을 외교경로를 통해 국가들에도 전달한 것으로 안다」며, 玄대사의특별보고가 이와 무관하지 않은 것으로 관측했다.

또 다른 소식통은「지난해말 美·日·中·러시아 등이 核협상을 국제적으로 지원하기 위한 多者안보협력체구축 주장이 南北韓의 核협상을 중심으로 한바 있음에도 최근 美국무부를 중심으로 南北韓의 核군축을 국제적으로지원하기 위한 多者안보협력체 구축 주장이 다시 제기되고 있다」며 玄대사의 돌연 귀국에 우려의 뜻을 표시했다.

대해 구체적인 설명없이 실시되지 않고 있는 상황외무당국자들은 이에 대해, 玄대사 자신은 独対했으며,

〈조　선〉 5. 26

0235

외 무 부

원 본

종 별 :

번 호 : USW-2699   일 시 : 92 0527 1837

수 신 : 장 관(미이),미일,국기.정안) 사본:주미대사

발 신 : 주 미 대 사

제 목 : 북한핵 관계 세미나

1. 당지 조지타운 대학이 주관하는 한반도 문제세미나 (RETHINKING THE KOREAN PENINSULA : ARMS CONTROL,NUCLEAR ISSUES, ECONOMIC REFORMATION) 가 5.26-27 양일간 죠 지타운 대학에서 개최되고 있음.

2. 동 세미나는 금 5.27 북한 핵문제에 대해 토의한 바, 동 내용을 하기 요지 보고함.

가. 윤정석 중앙대 교수

. (1) 한국 국내에서는 남.북한 관계가 잘진전되고 있는 데 미국이 핵문제를 불필요하게 과도하게 추구함으로써 남.북한 관계에 장애가 초래되는 것이 아닌지, (2)핵문제에 집착하는것은 북한에게 정치적 이득 (POLITICAL LEVERAGE)을 주게 되는 것 아닌지 하는 시각이 있으며, (3)김태호 같은 이는 재처리 포기를 핵 정책의 실패라고 주장하고 있음.

나. LEONOARD SPECTER (카네기 재단 연구원)

. IAEA 는 이락사찰을 경험으로 SPECIAL INSPECTION을 실시하려고 노력하고 있음.

. 그러나 IAEA SPECIAL INSPECTION 은 문제가 많음.

1) 거증책임(CAUSE) 이 IAEA 에 있음.

2) 회원국을 설득해야 하는 정치적 어려움(POLITICAL THRESHOLD)

3) SPECIAL INSPECTION 실시 결정과 시행기간에 시차가 너무 크므로 은폐가능

- 비자획득, 여행등

4) 피사찰국의 거부 가능성

. 따라서 남.북한 당사자간의 상호사찰이 무엇보다도 중요함.

. 남.북간의 사찰은 거증책임이 없고, 제도화되어 있으며, 사찰통보와 실시사이의 시차가 적으므로 훨씬 유효한 사찰이 되 수 있음. (NO-CAUSE,ANNUAL, SHORT-NOTICE

미주국   1차보   미주국   국기국   외정실   분석관   미주국

0236

PAGE 1   92.05.28   09:08 WG

외신 1과 통제관 ✓

INSPECTION)

. 불시사찰은 남한뿐 아니라 북한에게도 핵무기부재의 확신 (ASSURANCE) 을 줄수 있음.

. 군사기지 개방은 군사시설에 대한 부명성 (TRANSPARENCY) 을 제고시킴으로 써 남.북한간의 신뢰구축에도 기여할 수 있음.

다. 당관 안호영 서기관

. 북한은 IAEA 사찰에는 비교적 적극적으로 호응하고 있으나, 남.북한 상호사찰에서는 부정적태도로 이로간하고 있음.

. 따라서 나.북한 상호사찰은 난항을 거듭하고있으나, 냉전후기의 국제질서 변화, 동북아의역학구조 변화, 남.북한 관계의 진전현황등을 볼 때 결국은 핵문제도 해결 될것임.

. 국내.외에서는 한국이 핵문제 하결을 위해 불필요한 양보를 많이 하였다는 주장 도있으나, 이는 균형된 시각이 아니며, 다른 한편 핵문제는 제로.섬 게임으로 볼것이 아니라 VARIABLE-SUM게임으로 보아야 해결이 가능한 것임.

라. WILLIAM ARKIN

(동인은 GREEN PEACE 의 핵담당과장으로서 LEONARD SPECTER 와 함께 NON-PROLIFERATION 의 권위로 알려져 있는 바, SPECTER 에 비해 훨씬 LIBERAL 한 입장을 취하고있 는 인물임)

. 냉전의 종식으로 핵문제의 중요성은 사실상 많이 감퇴되었으나 아직도 핵문제가 중심 유슈로부상 (LONG NUCLEAR SHODOW) 되고 있는 이유는 부쉬행정부가 가장 다루기 쉬운 이슈로서 핵문제를 부각시키기 때문임.

. 핵문제에 대한 지나친 집착은 균형감각의 상실을 초래할 수도 있는 바, 가령 카 작스탄공화국의 나쟈르바에프 대통령이 최근 BUSH대통령 면담시 면담의 90 퍼센트가 핵문제에 할애되었다는 것은 NON-SENSE 임.

. 북한이 핵무기를 개발하더라도 미사일에 적재할수 있기 위해서는 많은 기술적문제 (G GRAVITY,DETONATION TIMING 등)를 해결해야 하는 바, 북한이 이러한 기술을 보유하고 있는지는 의문임.

. 북한이 핵무기를 보유하고 있는지는 미지수이나, 북한 핵문제를 강조한 나머지 북한은 핵무기 보유국가가 누리는 영향력 (NUCLEAR POWER STATUS) 을갖고 있는 듯이 행세하는 것으로도 관찰됨.

3. 관찰 및 평가

. 금일 세미나에서 SPECTER 가 발표한 IAEA 사찰 (특히 SPECIAL INSPECTION) 의한계성 및 이와비교한 남.북한 상호사찰의 중요성에 대한 강조는 종합적이고 균형감각을 갖춘 것으로서, 금후 IAEA사찰의 진행에 따라 상호사찰의 필요성에 대한 의문이 제기될시 참고가 될 수 있을 것임.

. 금일 세미나에서는 (1) 북한 핵문제가 남.북대화에 미치는 정치적 비요, (2)핵문제의 집착으로 북한이 누리게 되는 정치적 영향력, (3)남.북한 재처리 시설포기의 적절성, (3) 미국의 영향력 (WHO CALLS THE SHOT) 등에 대한 질문이 많이 제기된 바, 안서기관은 이러한 회의적 시각시정을 위해 노력하였고, SPECTER 연구원도 여러차례의 INTERVENTION 을 통해 북한 핵문제 해결의 필요성을 역설하였음.

(대사 대리 - 국장)

PAGE 3

0238

외 무 부

관리
번호 92
-6P1

종 별 :

번 호 : USW-2718

일 시 : 92 0528 1759

수 신 : 장 관 (미이 이호진 과장)

발 신 : 주 미 대사 (임성준 참사관)

제 목 : 엄연

1. 금 5.28. 연합통신은 이동복 대변인을 인용, 우리측 정보에 의하면 북한이 130-180 본 정도의 핵폐기물을 보유하고 있고, 재처리시 15KG 이상의 플루토니움 생산이 가능하다고 발언한 것으로 보도하였음.

2. 이와관련, 발언의 진위및 그 배경등을 회시하여 주시기 바람. 끝.

예고: 독후파기

미주국

No. 250

   The Embassy of the United States of America presents
its compliments to the Ministry of Foreign Affairs of
the Republic of Korea and has the honor to inform the
Ministry of the arrival of Ambassador Ronald Lehman,
Director for Arms Control and Disarmament Agency and
Richard D. Kauzlarich, Deputy Assistant Secretary.

They will arrive at Kimpo airport on May 31, 1992 via
NW-29 at 17:05 hrs. Ambassador Lehman will depart on
June 3, 1992 via NW-30 at 14:00 hours and Mr. Kauzlarich
will depart on June 2, 1992 via NW-60 at 17:45 hours.

   The Embassy will appreciate the assistance of the
Ministry in arranging for the use of the VIP lounge at
Kimpo airport and permitting the Embassy Expeditor to
handle customs, immigration and baggage formalities upon
arrival and departure.

   The Embassy avails itself of this opportunity to
renew to the Ministry the assurances of its highest
consideration.

0240

Embassy of the United States of America,
   Seoul, May 28, 1992

관리	92
번호	-292

외 무 부

종 별 :

번 호 : USW-2729   일 시 : 92 0528 2010

수 신 : 장 관 (미이)미일,국기,정특,기정)

발 신 : 주 미 대사

제 목 : 죠지.워싱톤대 학술회의   검토필(1992. 6. 30.) 印

1. 죠지.워싱톤대와 요미우리 신문이 공동주관하는 동북아 관계 학술회의가당지 죠지.워싱톤대에서 5.28-30 간 개최되고 있음.

2. 국무부 동아. 태국 SOLOMON 차관보는 동 회의 참석자를 위한 5.28. 리셉션에 참석, 기조연설을 행한바, 그 요지를 하기 보고함.(동 회의에 참가중인 최광수, 이봉서 전장관및 정종욱 교수이외에 당관에서는 임성준 참사관 참석)

    - 냉전 종식후 아시아에 긍정적인 상황(인도지나, 필리핀등)이 전개되고 있어 미국은 이를 고무적으로 받아들이고 있음.

    - 이러한 전반적인 역내환경의 개선에도 불구하고 미국은 북한의 핵개발 가능성을 깊이 우려하고 있음.

    - 작년까지만 해도 핵문제 해결의 가능성에 대한 회의가 있었던 것이 사실이나, 91.9 부쉬 대통령의 전술핵 철수 선언, 노대통령의 비핵화선언, 이어서 91.12. 남. 북한간에 이루어진 기본합의서 및 비핵화 공동선언등의 중요한 과정을거쳐 핵문제 해결의 실마리가 마련되었음.

    - 이에따라 북한은 IAEA 핵안전 협정에 서명하였고, 남. 북한간에 JNCC 가 구성 되었으며, 최근에는 BLIX 총장이 방북, 핵시설을 시찰하였음.

    - 이제 마지막 남은 절차 (ONE LAST LEG)는 상호사찰에 대한 합의인바, 이는 IAEA 를 보완할 뿐더러 남. 북한간의 CMB 과 화해증진을 위해서도 매우 중요 하다고 보며 단기간내에 (IN A FEW WEEKS) 매듭되기를 기대함.

    - 이렇게 되면 북한 핵개발에 대한 국제사회의 의혹이 해소되고, 남. 북 관계의 폭넓은 진전과 무기통제 및 군축을 통한 긴장해소가 가능할 것임.

    - 미국의 입장은 지난 1 월 KANTER 차관이 김용순에게 분명히 전달한바 있는바, IAEA 와 상호사찰이 다같이 이루어져야 미.북한 관계개선이 가능하다는 것임.

미주국 안기부	장관	차관	1차보	미주국	국기국	외정실	분석관	청와대
								0241

PAGE 1   대고문대 의거 재분류(19   )   92.05.29   10:49.
                                                                외신 2과 통제관 BZ

- 냉전체제 종식의 마지막 장애물인 핵문제가 해결되어 남.북한 관계가 진일보
되기를 기대함. 끝.
  (대사 현홍주-국장)
  예고: 92.12.31. 까지

<table>
<tr><td>관리
번호</td><td>92
-706</td></tr>
</table>

외 무 부

종 별 : 지 급

번 호 : USW-2751

일 시 : 92 0529 2007

수 신 : 장 관 (미일(미이)국기,정특,기정)

발 신 : 주 미 대사

제 목 : GW 대-요미우리 주최 학술회의

연: USW-2636, 2729

검토필(19 ʔ2. 6. 30.) 영

금 5.29. 오후에 개최된 표제회의 한반도 문제 토의 결과를 아래 보고함. (아측은 최광수 전 외무장관, 정종욱 서울대교수, 북한측은 김병홍 평화군축연구소부소장, 이근 연구원, 일측에서 하지메 이주미 하바드대 객원교수가 주제 발표)

1. 주제발표 요지(텍스트 파편 송부 예정)

가. 최광수 전외무장관 (탈냉전시대의 한국)

- 지역 균형자로서의 미국의 지속적 역할 중요

. 중국, 러시아는 국내문제로 지역문제에 적극적 역할 수행이 어려운 입장

. 일본의 영향력 및 역할증대 모색

. 미.일 협력관계가 아. 태지역 장래를 위해 긴요

- 최근의 남북한 관계 진전에도 불구, 한반도의 대결구조 상존

. 남북한 합의사항 이행, 특히 북한의 핵개발 포기가 관건

. IAEA 사찰 및 남북한 상호사찰 실시만이 북한의 핵개발 의혹 해소 가능

. 북한 핵문제 해결시 군축문제에 대한 진지한 협의 가능

- 한반도 냉전구조 종식은 동북아 신질서 수립에 긴요

. 한국은 남북한 합의의 조기 이행및 북한 핵문제 해결을 위해 대북한 설득노력 지속 예정

. 미.일과의 협력관계 강화및 중.러와의 관계 증진을 통해 동북아 신질서 수립과정에 적극적 역할 수행 용의

나. 정종욱 서울대 교수(냉전후기의 남북한 관계)

- 남북한 합의서 채택등 최근 북한의 변화는 미.일과의 관계개선이 주요 목적

. 심각한 국내경제문제 해결을 위해서는 한반도 긴장완화 및 미.일과의 관계개선이

미주국	장관	차관	1차보	미주국	국기국	외연원	외정실	분석관
청와대	안기부							

0243

PAGE 1

92.05.30 10:36
외신 2과 통제관 BX

긴요하다는 인식

　- 남북간 각종 합의에도 불구, 관계진전에 장애요소 상존

　. 가장 큰 장애요인은 북한의 핵문제이며 이의 해결을 위해서는 남북한 상호사찰 합의를 통한 불시사찰 허용이 긴요

　- 화해의 모멘텀에도 불구, 향후 남북한 관계는 잘못 관리할 경우 냉전적 대립 격화 초래 위험

　. 상호 체재인정을 통한 평화공존 및 지배전략 (STRATEGY OF DOMINANCE) 포기 필요 (북한은 통일전선 전략을, 남한은 흡수통일 전략을 포기해야함)

　. 단계적 신뢰구축 조치를 통해 점진적 군축합의 이행 필요

　. 중요한 정치적 전환기에 있는 남북한이 국내정치적 목적을 위해 상대방의 국내문제에 간섭하거나 비방하는 행위를 자제할 필요

　- 남북한 통일 실현을 위해서는 당분간은 단순한 상부 구조 (MERE SUPERSTRUCTURE) 로서의 연방체제 (FEDERAL FRAMEWORK)하에서 완전한 자치권을 행사하는 2개의 상이한 정치체제가 양존하는 과도체제가 불가피

　. 여사한 상부구조는 점진적으로 중앙구조 (CENTRAL STRUCTURE)로 대체되어야 할 것임.

　다. 김병홍 북한 평화군축연구소 부소장(남북대화와 고려연방제 통일 방안)

　- 7.4. 남북 공동성명의 3대 원칙에 기초하지 않는한 남북관계 진전및 통일은 실현 불가

　. 남북한 합의서도 외세간섭 없이 자주성의 원칙에 입각, 이행되어야함.

　. 통일실현을 위해서는 군축및 한반도의 비핵지대화 필요

　- 민족 대단결이 이루어질때 고려연방제 통일실현 가능

　. 1민족, 1국가 아래 2체제, 2정부가 양존하는 연방제 통일이 합리적 방안

　. 지방자치 정부에 권한을 대폭 부여하되 동 권한을 점차 중앙정부에 이양함으로써 연방제통일 완료 가능

　. 흡수통일은 민족 대단결을 해치는 결과 초래

　라. 이근 평화군축연구소 연구원 (동북아 경제협력 전망)

　- 냉전 종식에도 불구, 미국은 계속 아. 태 지역에서의 주도권 불포기

　. 일본도 영향력 확대기도

　. 북방도서 문제 해결후 일.러 평화조약이 체결될 경우 미군의 한. 일 주둔정당화

명분 상실
　- 북한의 대미.일 관계 개선은 한반도와 동북아지역 안정에 긴요
　. 미국은 남. 북한을 동등하게 취급해야함.
　. 일본은 일.북한 관계정상화와 무관한 문제를 가지고 수교교섭에 장애를 초래하는
행위를 자제해야함.
　- 북한의 대미.일 경제교류는 동북아의 평화안보 환경조성에 기여
　. 정치적 환경개선을 통해 경제교류 확대 가능
　. 대북한 금수조치 해제 필요
　. 나진, 선봉, 청진지역의 경제특수에 외국기업의 투자진출 기대
　마. 하지메 이주미 일본 시즈오카대학 교수(한반도 통일과 지역안보 전망)
　- 남. 북한 통일은 느슨한 연합체 (LOOSE CONFEDERATION) 형태에 의해서만 가능시
　. 남한은 과다한 통일 비용을 고려해야 하며 북한은 사회주의 체제 유지 필요성
절실
　- 한반도 통일 촉진을 위한 다자지원 체제 (INTERNATIONAL CONSUORTIUM) 형성
분위기 성숙
　. 남북한의 주변 4 강과의 관계정상화 여건 성숙
　(미.일과의 수교를 시도하고 있는 북한이 한. 중 수교를 반대할 명분은 없으므로
남한이 대만과의 관계를 단절할 경우 한. 중 수교 조기실현 전망)
　- 북한의 핵문제가 통일의 장애요인
　. 북한의 방사능 화학연구소 존재와 소량의 플루토늄 추출 사실 시인으로 북한의
핵개발 잠재력에 대한 의혹 증폭
　. 북한의 핵 의혹 해소를 위해서는 IAEA 사찰 뿐 아니라 남북한 동시사찰 수용
필요
　- 남북한의 핵무기 보유방지를 위한 주변 4 강의 개입 필요
　. 남북한이 핵개발 능력을 일본에 대한 지렛대로 사용하고자 할 경우 일본의
안보에 미치는 심각한 영향에 대한 남북한의 인식이 부족하다는 인상
　. 한반도 핵문제를 남북한에만 맡겨둘 수 없음.
　- 한, 일간 상호 군사 위협에 대한 우려 증대가 양국관계 악화로 발전되지
못하도록 미국의 중재 (HONEST BROKER) 역할 필요
　. 일본의 군사위협에 대한 한국의 우려와 주한 미군이 대북한 억지력 뿐아니라

장래 일본의 군사위협을 견제하기 위한 것이라는 한국내 일부 시각의 부당성 지적

. 남북한 통일이 반드시 지역안보 환경개선에 기여할 것으로 기대할 수 없음.(단, 여사한 견해가 일본이 한반도 통일을 원하지 않는다는 의미로 해석되어서는 안된다고 부언)

2. 질의 응답 요지(동 세미나에 참석한 국무부 한국과 HASTINGS 담당관이 당관 박흥신 서기관에게 설명한 내용)

가. 한.미.일 3 자 협의.

- HASTINGS 담당관은 정종욱 교수가 북한의 핵문제 해결을 위한 일본의 역할을 문의한데 대한 답변을 통해 일본이 북한 핵문제의 해결에 있어 핵심적인 역할을 하고 있음을 설명하고 한국 언론에도 보도된 바와 같이 금주말 서울에서 한.미.일 3 자 실무협의가 개최 예정임을 밝힘.

- 3 자 실무협의 개최 사실 언급은 북한에 대한 압력수단의 일환으로 3 자 협의 사실을 공개하는 것이 바람직하다는 아측 입장을 감안한 것인바, 북한측 참석자들 및 요미우리 신문기자들을 통해 큰 홍보 효과가 예상됨.

나. 북한측 참석자 답변내용

- 북한측 참석자들에 대해 세부적인 답변을 요하는 구체적 질문 (POINTED QUESTIONS)은 없었으며, 김병홍이 5 분 내외, 이근 및 장일훈이 각각 2-3 분 내외의 발언을 통해 이미 알려진 북한측 공식 입장을 밝히는 기회로 이용하였음.

3. 세미나에 대한 평가 (HASTINGS 담당관)

- 이미 예상된 바와 같이 북한측 참석자들은 동 세미나를 핵문제에 대한 북한측의 공식 입장을 설명하고 북한과 미.일과의 관계개선 희망을 전달하는 기회로 삼았으며, 전혀 새로운 내용이 없었음.

- 김병홍은 주제발표및 개별 접촉시에도 전혀 융통성 없이 노동신문을 읽을수 있는 것과 같은 틀에 박힌 공식입장을 표시하였으며, 이에비해 이근은 사석에서 비교적 독자적인 발언을 하는등 상당히 개방된 인물이라는 인상을 주었는바, 이근은 앞으로 워싱톤에 북한대사관이 설치되면 자신이 초대 외교관으로 부임하고 싶다는 희망을 피력하고, 반농담조로 이번 방문기회에 워싱톤 주변에 적절한 주택관련 정보를 입수하기를 희망했다함. 끝.

(대사 현홍주-국장)

예고: 92.12.31. 일반

NK가 對美 관계개선을 얼마만큼 희구하고있는가 간접적인 시사.

공   란

공   란

외교문서 비밀해제: 북한 핵 문제 1
북한 핵 문제 총괄 1

초판인쇄 2024년 03월 15일
초판발행 2024년 03월 15일

지은이 한국학술정보(주)
펴낸이 채종준
펴낸곳 한국학술정보(주)
주 소 경기도 파주시 회동길 230(문발동)
전 화 031-908-3181(대표)
팩 스 031-908-3189
홈페이지 http://ebook.kstudy.com
E-mail 출판사업부 publish@kstudy.com
등 록 제일산-115호(2000. 6. 19)

ISBN 979-11-7217-074-5 94340
      979-11-7217-073-8 94340 (set)